The Republic and the Civil War in Spain

Each volume in this series is designed to make available to students important new work on key historical problems and periods that they encounter in their courses. Every volume is devoted to a central topic or theme, and the most important aspects of this are dealt with by specially commissioned essays from specialists in the period. The editorial Introduction reviews the problem or period as a whole, and each essay provides a balanced assessment of the particular aspect, pointing out the areas of development and controversy and indicating where conclusions can be drawn or where further work is necessary. An annotated bibliography serves as an up-to-date guide to further reading.

PROBLEMS IN FOCUS SERIES

The Republic and the Civil War in Spain

EDITED BY
RAYMOND CARR

Macmillan
St Martin's Press

© *Raymond Carr, Edward Malefakis, Richard Robinson, Stanley Payne, Burnett Bolloten, Ramón Salas Larrazábal, Ricardo de la Cierva y de Hoces, Robert H. Whealey, Hugh Thomas 1971*

First published 1971 by
MACMILLAN AND CO LTD
London and Basingstoke
Associated companies in New York Toronto
Dublin Melbourne Johannesburg and Madras

Library of Congress catalog card no. 79–148464

SBN 333 00632 1 (hard cover)

Printed in Great Britain by
RICHARD CLAY (THE CHAUCER PRESS) LTD
Bungay Suffolk

Contents

Preface

THE history of the Second Republic and the Civil War is still a highly controversial topic. Not everyone will agree with all the conclusions of these essays; the editor does not, nor has he suppressed the contradictions between them.

The next stage in the historiography of this period must be a series of local studies which examine what the years 1931–9 meant to those who lived through them in the cities, towns and villages of Spain. Only thus, for instance, can the workings of the twin war economies be evaluated. It nevertheless seemed, in the meantime, useful to gather together the general conclusions of the researches of the experts in the field.

It is impossible to examine this period in any depth without a knowledge of Spanish. Thus the bibliographies inevitably include Spanish works since these are necessary for any further study.

R. C.

Glossary of Political Terms

C.E.D.A.   *Confederación Española de Derechas Autónomas.* A confederation of rightist parties whose main programme was the revision of the anti-clerical legislation of the constituent Cortes. Leader Gil Robles, who came from a Carlist background but was a supporter of 'accidentalism' (i.e. *forms* of government were irrelevant to Catholics provided the interests of the church were protected).

C.N.T.   *Confederación Nacional de Trabajo.* The anarcho-syndicalist union; main strength in Catalan industrial region and parts of Andalusia. It abstained from 'bourgeois' politics in favour of 'direct action'; individually, nevertheless, some C.N.T. members voted for the Popular Front in February 1936.

Carlists   Or traditionalists. Historically had supported the claims of pretenders who rejected liberal parliamentarianism. The most militant of the right-wing parties, with a strong activist tradition in Navarre. Unified April 1937 with the Falange.

Esquerra   The Catalan left: the main supporter of the autonomous government of Catalonia (the *Generalitat*). Leader Luis Companys; collaborated with Azaña. The conservative Catalan party was the *Lliga Regionalista*.

F.A.I.   *Federación Anarquista Española.* An activist revolutionary group which operated within the C.N.T.

Falange   A small nationalist, anti-Marxist party, the nearest approach to a fascist party in Spain; outlawed in March 1936. Its leader José Antonio Primo de Rivera, son of the 'dictator': executed by the republicans 20 November 1936. The party grew rapidly in the early months of the Civil War and was amalgamated with the Carlists, forming the F.E.T. de la J.O.N.S., the sole political movement of nationalist Spain.

Izquierda The republican left, a grouping of republican parties
Republicana created and led by Azaña in 1934.

Popular An electoral coalition, from republican left to socialists,
Front formed to avenge the Asturian repression and to fight
the elections of February 1936.

P.O.U.M. *Partido Obrero de Unificación Marxista*. An anti-
Stalinist revolutionary Marxist party, with its main
strength in Catalonia.

P.S.U.C. *Partido Socialista Unificado de Cataluña:* a fusion of
the socialist and communist parties in Catalonia engineered and dominated by the communists.

Renovación An Alfonsine monarchist party whose main leader was
Española Calvo Sotelo; latterly influenced by French right-wing
parties in an increasingly militant direction.

U.G.T. *Unión General de Trabajadores*. The trade union federation of the socialist party; its most prestigious leader
Francisco Largo Caballero.

U.M.E. *Unión Militar Española*. An organisation of officers opposed to the policies of the Popular Front.

U.M.R.A. *Unión Militar Republicana Antifascista*. An organisation similar to U.M.E. but supporting republican
governments.

Part One

The Second Republic

1. Chronological Table

13 September 1923 General Primo de Rivera stages a *pronuncia-miento* against the constitutional government.

28 January 1930 King dismisses Primo de Rivera. Interim royal governments until 14 April 1931.

17 August 1930 Republican leaders agree at San Sebastian on overthrow of monarchy and Provisional Government; socialists join conspiracy in October.

12 December 1930 Abortive military rising at Jaca.

12 April 1931 Municipal elections: republican victories in large towns.

14 April 1931 King leaves. Provisional Government of Republic (agreed on at San Sebastian) takes over.

10–11 May 1931 'Burning of the convents' in Madrid and the south.

28 June 1931 Election for constituent Cortes; shift of power to left.

14 July 1931 Constituent Cortes opened. The debate on the religious issue (9–14 October) causes resignation of the prime minister, Alcalá Zamora, and of the minister of the interior, Miguel Maura.

Azaña becomes prime minister with the support of the socialists.

January 1932 Extensive C.N.T. strikes, including a rising in the Llobregat valley in Catalonia.

Dissolution of the Jesuits and further anti-clerical legislation.

10 August 1932 General Sanjurjo's rising in Seville fails. The general reaction enables the government to pass the Catalan Statute and a mild agrarian reform act.

May 1933 Law limiting drastically the activities of the regular orders.

October 1933 Azaña resigns: 'caretaker' government to supervise elections.

19 November	1933	Defeat of the 'Azaña coalition' in the elections and emergence of the C.E.D.A. as a political force. Lerroux (radical) becomes prime minister.
13 July	1934	Foundation of *Claridad*, organ of maximalist socialists and Largo Caballero.
6 October	1934	Rising in Catalonia and Asturias. Preceded by formation of Workers' Alliances.
April	1935	Azaña begins the formation of the Popular Front from the republican parties; this extended to socialists in December 1935, with Largo Caballero in disagreement.
16 February	1936	Popular Front wins majority of seats in Cortes. Azaña prime minister of pure republican cabinet. Prieto for co-operation; Largo Caballero increasingly hostile. Franco proposes military action against any illegal assumption of power, forced by street agitation.
15 March	1936	Falange outlawed.
7 April	1936	Alcalá Zamora deposed as president: Azaña becomes president and Casares Quiroga prime minister (12 May).
May	1936	Largo Caballero blocks the formation of a ministry including the 'parliamentary' socialist, Indalecio Prieto.
May–June	1936	Increasing sporadic disorder and increasing attacks on government by right for failure to maintain public order.
13 July	1936	Assassination of Calvo Sotelo.
17–20 July	1936	Military rising, first in Morocco, then in metropolitan Spain.

2. Editor's Introduction

REGIMES are usually overthrown because those who man the system have lost confidence in themselves and consequently lack political nerve and staying power. Alfonso XIII, on the whole a well-intentioned monarch, had backed the unconstitutional dictatorship of General Primo de Rivera (1923–30). His own position as a constitutional king was thus fatally undermined; the political classes who had manned the constitutional monarchy deserted it in adversity. Even aristocrats, whose *raison d'être* had been the court, observed the fall of the monarchy, as one of them remarked, as they might have watched a bad film.

Capable of resisting an ill-planned military coup in December 1930, the monarchy could not resist this erosion of monarchical sentiment. A lack of grip on public opinion, rather than the strength of the political groups who had plotted together in San Sebastian in the summer of 1930, proved fatal. In April 1931 the great cities of Spain voted republican. Only one minister counselled resistance. The memoirs of General Mola, later to become one of the conspirators against the Popular Front in 1936, reveal a police force ill-equipped to deal with sedition – it had to use taxi-cabs to get to student riots; the commander of the Civil Guard, General Sanjurjo, another conspirator, would not guarantee the loyalty of his men. Without a reliable police force and army, the street demonstrations in the cities would have toppled the monarchy by force. The king, without formally abdicating, left the country. 'Even the navy,' he complained to Lord Londonderry, 'deserted me.'

The Republic was welcomed with apparent enthusiasm throughout most of urban Spain. But what did it stand for, apart from a government without a king? The debate of the next five years was over the 'content', in the language of the time, not the form of republican government.

The Provisional Government which took over with remarkable smoothness and respect for form on 14 April had been 'composed' by the group of republican conspirators who had met in San Sebastian in the summer of 1930. Composition gave little real indication of future policy. The prime minister, a former liberal monarchist, Niceto Alcalá Zamora, envisaged a moderate government, respectful of Catholic

sentiment and not vastly different from a progressive liberal government under the monarchy; but his cabinet also included committed
republican anti-clericals and socialists who wanted real changes in
society.

Optimism for a time hid the fissures. There was no *a priori* reason
why democratic government should not work in Spain or why different
parties might not represent different sectors of opinion. In April 1931,
apart from a few disconsolate and isolated right-wing monarchists,
only two significant groups did not accept the premises of bourgeois
parliamentarianism: the anarcho-syndicalist trade union the C.N.T.
(especially when it was dominated by the activist anarchists of the
F.A.I.) and, far less important in 1931, the Carlists of the Basque
provinces and Navarre, whose inherited creed condemned anything but
a 'traditional' Catholic, anti-parliamentary monarchy.

The first two essays explain how the general consensus of April
broke down and violence took over. With hindsight and faith in historical determinism, one can argue this breakdown was inevitable. The
social conflicts of a semi-industrialised 'backward' country were too
violent – landless labourers against large landowners in the south and
west, militant labour against obstinate employers in the industrial
sectors – to be contained within a parliamentary framework. Others
maintain that the political tradition of Spain inhibited compromise and
acceptance of electoral defeat, without which parliamentary democracy
cannot function; that the 'politics of civility', in Edward Shils's phrase,
lay outside the Iberian tradition.

Once these two arguments are combined and it is argued that only
radical social change backed by a disciplined revolutionary party could
have created a viable republic, then there is little point examining the
history of the years 1931–6 to find out 'what went wrong' with the
Republic. It is clear that, given the social structure of Spain and the
strength of conservatism in the broadest sense of the term, a civil war
would have been the result of such a radical policy unless it was
accompanied by fierce political repression. When it came in 1936, civil
war was less a response to a threatened social revolution than a response
to a collapse of political and social structures. That, on social matters,
the Republic between 1931 and 1933 pursued the worst of all possible
courses is probably true. Agrarian reform was ineffective as a bid for
peasant support yet frightened conservatives; income tax and banking
laws were farcically inadequate. Like Blum in France, Azaña frightened
capital without satisfying labour. Nevertheless it must be stressed that

organised labour did get its reward in the years 1931–2 and Largo Caballero, the U.G.T. leader, as minister of labour pushed through an advanced labour code. Farm labourers' wages, for instance, doubled in 1931–3. The trouble was that the machinery of arbitration and the patronage of the new system went to socialists; the C.N.T. saw no reason to be grateful, and repeatedly staged revolutionary strikes and 'risings' (January 1932; December 1933).

The question the historian must ask is *when* and *how* a democratic Republic that could be accepted by the majority of Spaniards became an impossibility. The reply is not clear, but at least the framework of an answer is contained in the political chronology. The weakness of such a fault-finding approach is that it will underestimate the achievements of the Republic in its constructive phase. One of these achievements, unacceptable to the right, was nevertheless remarkable. Catalans had since the latter nineteenth century demanded regional self-government, since they considered their language, their culture and their economic interests (Catalonia was the most important industrial area in Spain) neglected by the central government. In April Macìa, the leader of the Catalan left, had declared for an independent Catalonia within an 'Iberian Federation'. In the end the Statute of Autonomy which created the Catalan *Generalitat* gave Catalans enough self-government to satisfy their aspirations and yet kept them 'within Spain'.

Yet it was this political success that began a process of alienation that was to gather momentum. It did not matter much that intellectuals such as Ortega y Gasset announced their disillusionment; more important, sectors of the army, always centralist in tradition, grew restive. Together with a handful of monarchical conservatives, the discontented tried military sedition in August 1932, when General Sanjurjo 'pronounced' in Seville; one of their demands was the preservation of the historical unity of Spain. 'Spain One and Indivisible' was the cry of the army again in 1936.

The wide political spectrum of the Provisional Government from liberal Catholics (Alcalá Zamora and Maura) through Jacobin anti-clericals to socialists could not last. It would be wrong to argue (as many do) that the breakdown of the San Sebastian coalition marks the beginning of the end of democracy in Spain. Nevertheless this breakdown took place in an unfortunate manner and over an issue that in retrospect seems irrelevant to the important social and political problems facing Spain: the position of the church in Spain.

Socialists and most republicans were dogmatic anti-clericals and they too readily assumed that most Spaniards were indifferent to the church. The passivity of left republicans and socialists when churches were burnt by urban mobs in May 1931, and the anti-clerical legislation of the constituent Cortes forced moderate Catholic republicans like Miguel Maura, minister of the interior, and the prime minister, Alcalá Zamora, out of the government (14 October 1931); but the break was not absolute. Alcalá Zamora became president of the Republic and Maura never ceased to be a republican. Some republicans now argue that historically conditioned, dogmatic anti-clericalism was a mistake – particularly as the Vatican wished to avoid an open clash by negotiation. This repentance neglects the enormous symbolic significance of the church *at the time*; at the local level, above all, the tensions and divisions of Spanish society were expressed in terms of loyalty to or hatred of the church.

It can be argued that, since approximately half of Spain might be called 'conservative', the church issue forced the emergence of a right-wing party. That party ultimately became the C.E.D.A., described in Chapter 4. Why could not Spanish politics revolve round a conservative Catholic party and a socialist–republican left? The answer lies, as we shall see, in the reaction of the left to the electoral victory of the right in December 1933, and of the right to that of the left in February 1936.

The elections to the constituent Cortes (June 1931) had altered the political balance of the Republic and had made a frontal attack on the church inevitable (p. 28). The new prime minister, Manuel Azaña, had only two courses open: either to veer to the right via an alliance with Lerroux's radical republicans – historically an anti-establishment party but now fundamentally a petit-bourgeois anti-socialist party – or to steer resolutely to the left via a coalition with the socialists. Why he chose the latter course is explained on pp. 26–7.

The Azaña coalition committed, as all governments do, political blunders which had electoral consequences. Azaña could not behave exactly like an English prime minister when confronted with a military revolt of the right (10 August 1932) or revolutionary strikes set off by the C.N.T. His use of the Law for the Defence of the Republic and his police repressions enabled the right to caricature his democratic pretensions. It looked to them as if any party, such as Gil Robles's Popular Action, which aimed to change the laws regulating the church by electoral propaganda would be automatically branded by Azaña as 'anti-republican' and therefore denied legal existence (p. 54). The excuse was that Azaña suspected the democratic bona fides of Popular

Action. Did it not include professed monarchists? Even if elected, would it not destroy the 'content' of the Republic? His government 'wore out'; he lost, for example, the allegiance of intellectual prima donnas who refused to recognise that politics involve conflict on fundamentals.

The loss of the election of December 1933 was inevitable. Why did a predictable swing to the right (Azaña's coalition forces were defeated by almost two to one) mark the first real threat to democratic processes? There are two main reasons.

First, the socialists broke with the left republicans of Azaña. This not merely made electoral defeat (given an electoral system which favoured combined lists) inevitable; it imperilled the reformist strand in Spanish socialism which had been strong in 1931–2. To the distress of Marxists like Besteiro, who argued that the time was not ripe for a proletarian take-over, and of moderate parliamentary socialists like Indalecio Prieto, the 'maximalist' wing of the socialist party became increasingly 'revolutionary' and increasingly influential. Largely, it seems to me, because the maximalists argued in terms of what was happening to socialism under fascism in Europe, and because it was always confronted with a truly revolutionary party as a competitor for proletarian loyalty – the C.N.T. In the summer of 1933 Largo Caballero, to become the figurehead of the maximalists, argued that socialism could not carry out its task within a bourgeois democracy.

Secondly, the party which showed the most remarkable gains was Gil Robles's C.E.D.A. The ambiguous nature of the C.E.D.A., in the eyes of its political enemies, is a central factor in the process of republican breakdown. Even after the victory of Gil Robles's legalism within his own party, to socialists and left republicans the C.E.D.A. was a fascist party; 'accidentalism' appeared a dangerous nonsense that hid a determination to destroy the 'content' of the Republic to such a degree that it would cease to be a republic. To its leader the C.E.D.A. was a constitutional party which would accept the Republic and legal processes in order to *modify* the 'content' of the Republic – above all its anti-clerical legislation. His moderate language, after the elections, cut him off from the men of the right without gaining him any credence on the left (p. 60).

Thus when Lerroux, an ageing ex-radical whose ambition was to dominate a 'centrist' Republic, was forced in October 1934 by his parliamentary position to ask the C.E.D.A. to join the government, the socialists argued that they were confronted with a 'fascist' threat and the left republicans saw in prospect a criminal 'distortion' of the Republic as designed in the legislation of 1931–3. The socialists therefore considered revolution justified as an inevitable measure of self-defence. It is clear that their attention, understandably, was focused on Europe: German socialism had not resisted at all and Austrian socialism had resisted too late. Quite simply 'an anti-Marxist front is a fascist front'. The Workers' Alliance – an attempt to bring together the U.G.T., the C.N.T. and the communists, was conceived by the socialist left in August 1934 as 'the insurrectional preparation for the conquest of power . . . the tool of insurrection'. They could count on the Catalan left, irritated at the attitude of Madrid governments to autonomy and fearful of their own extremist nationalist wing. The revolt was a failure in Catalonia, where the C.N.T. remained inactive and indifferent to an alliance either with socialists or Catalan nationalist extremists. In Asturias there was a wide working-class alliance which turned the miners' revolution into a fortnight's proletarian epic, the most dramatic and destructive proletarian revolution in the West since the Paris Commune.

It is, therefore, of the utmost importance to attempt to analyse the nature of the C.E.D.A. and to see if there is any justification for believing in the reality of a 'fascist' threat. That a Lerroux–C.E.D.A. government would, and did, dismantle many of the 'conquests' of the left in 1931–3 is true; most conservative governments do attempt such a process, especially when resistance to wage demands seemed the orthodox answer to the growing depression. That the government was as ruthless against socialists as the socialists had been against the C.E.D.A. is true. But surely a fascist government would have used the October revolution to destroy its opponents. As it was, its repression, severe enough indeed, created a myth of enormous power which was the emotional motor of the Popular Front, whose creators (Azaña above all) could conduct a propaganda campaign and organise meetings in such a way as to build up a formidable electoral power. If this was fascism, it was, as the Falange was to maintain, a very milk-and-water edition of the true faith. Socialists might have reflected that they, like the C.E.D.A., had their own form of accidentalism. They were a party in theory committed to major social changes which must destroy bourgeois society, but they had been willing to co-operate in a bourgeois parliamentary government.

The revolution of October is the immediate origin of the Civil War. The left, above all the socialists, had rejected legal processes of government; the government against which they revolted was electorally justified. The left was later to make great play of the 'legality' argument to condemn the generals' revolt in July 1936 against an elected government.

The breaking point had come. Socialists could not live in a Republic whose 'content' might be determined by the C.E.D.A.; the C.E.D.A. would not inhabit a society built by socialists. There were groups to the left of the socialists (the communists and the C.N.T.) who were willing to draw them to the left; there were violent men on the right of the C.E.D.A. who would swamp the 'tepid' legalism of Gil Robles and drive him, ultimately, to desert it.

The Popular Front which won the elections of February 1936 was a revival of the Azaña coalition (Azaña, indeed, was its driving force and symbol) but with a significant difference: the socialists did not enter the government.

As a purely republican party concern, the governments of the Popular Front lacked authority; the real force on the left, it was increasingly apparent, lay in the proletarian parties. Thus the right could discount the moderation of the government and criticise its feebleness in dealing with strikes and social disorders as a morbid symptom of its hidden dependence on 'revolutionary' parties. The most prominent leader of the right was not now Gil Robles but Calvo Sotelo, who openly spoke of the necessity of a counter-revolution in order to save Spain from Marxism. The proletarian parties, equally, could argue that the government was incapable of resisting the mounting threat from the right or of satisfying the workers' demands.

The result was a descent into violence which was to justify, in the eyes of the rebel generals, an army take-over. The factors in this equation are complex. The economist Marshall once likened historical causation to billiard balls lying at the bottom of a wash-basin: if one moves, all move. The problem of this descent into violence is nearly always conceived in terms of detecting the first billiard ball that moved, whether it was moved by the left or the right; this is a difficult quest. Both the extreme left and the extreme right were using the language of violence. Thus an English observer, well-informed of the intentions of the left, wrote in May 1936: 'All the militants, both Anarchists and Socialists, believe that only an armed insurrection can give decisive victory to the workers.'

Let us summarise the tensions during the period of the Popular Front government.

1. The 'legal' party of the right, Gil Robles's C.E.D.A., had failed to

win the election; this failure weakened Gil Robles in the face of those on the right who had never believed that 'legalism' could stave off a 'Marxist' revolution that would destroy the Spain which was the mirror of their own interests. The language of the right became increasingly violent, and increasingly contemptuous of republican institutions. Calvo Sotelo openly declared that, after October 1934, 'the possibility of parliamentary dialogue in Spain has disappeared'; only the army could save the true Spain. It was this obvious threat which justified the 'defensive' violence of the extreme left.

2. The C.N.T. had always believed that revolution was a duty; so had the growing communist party, and even after it had accepted the policy of a Popular Front with the bourgeois republicans it could not change its rhetoric. More important is the growing revolutionary militancy of the socialists and trade unionists who followed the lead of Largo Caballero. Largo Caballero, influenced by advisers close to the communist leadership who had cast him in the role of the Spanish Lenin as early as August 1933, was alarmed that the revolutionary zeal of the C.N.T. might draw off his own left wing. He believed that the socialists must take power for themselves when the bourgeois parties were 'exhausted'; and that the sooner these parties were discredited the better. His supporters were obsessed by the belief that Spain was, somehow or other, in a prerevolutionary situation comparable with that of Russia in 1917, and in consequence talked of 'Bolshevisation'.[1] Besteiro warned, in vain, that the parallel was hopelessly inexact in a country where conservative forces were strong and increasingly militant.

Largo's rival for control of the socialist movement, Indalecio Prieto, disagreed profoundly with Largo's talk of proletarian government. It would merely narrow the political basis of the Republic and 'socialise misery'. He wished to continue the co-operation of 1931–3; but a ministry of concentration with Prieto as prime minister was blocked by the unrelenting opposition of Largo Caballero – an action for which Prieto took his revenge in May 1937. Prieto would have probably lost any control over the party in October 1936. Meanwhile the socialist split increased political confusion, as did the bitter local struggles between the socialist U.G.T. and the C.N.T.

3. A striking characteristic of the 'tragic spring' was the increasing influence of youth movements and paramilitary organisations. Thus the Socialist Youth (captured by the communist party) and the C.E.D.A. Youth Movement became increasingly important. On the right the

influence of young militants increased; the Falange had always been a
student–youth movement and its efforts to win working-class support
for a nationalist, anti-capitalist, anti-Marxist state had been unsuccessful. Street clashes between paramilitary youth organisations
became one of the most notorious symptoms of violence to those who
wished to prove the Republic was failing to maintain public order. Even
in the army, it was the young officers who were the most serious conspirators.

4. The voting figures (disputed as they are in detail) of February
1936 suggest that about half Spain would welcome a right-wing coup
brought off by the army if such a course were the only alternative to
what the right called 'Marxism'; the other half would have no alternative but to support a left-wing revolution. A right-wing coup would
thus set off a left-wing counter-revolution.

5. What did the generals and those who supported them mean by a
'revolution', to prevent which they must revolt before it destroyed
Spain? For propaganda purposes the generals or their agents published
a *communist* plot to seize power. Perhaps nationalists believed their own
propaganda; but we cannot now believe in a *specific* communist plot
although the communists never ceased to talk of revolution. What the
'right' (i.e. those not committed to the proletarian parties or the left
republican parties) sensed was the *threat* of revolutionary change, which
they detected in the language of the Caballerista socialists, in the actions
of the C.N.T. and in the growth of the communist party; and, what was
scarcely distinguishable from it, a complete collapse of the political and
social order which would leave them defenceless. Gil Robles gave a
famous catalogue of church burnings, assassinations and revolutionary
strikes in the Cortes. On 13 July the most powerful right-wing politician
of the time, Calvo Sotelo, was murdered with the connivance of government police. This collapse of order is impossible to measure quantitative-
ly and testimonies differ; but it seemed to army officers real enough,
and the signal for them to resume their traditional role: to save society
from the anarchy created by the ineptitude of politicians. One of the
gravest miscalculations of the government was that, relying on the
loyalty of the senior commanders and its knowledge of the general
staff of the army (p. 97), it underestimated the effect of a relatively
well-organised conspiracy which 'simply swept aside' the loyal but
elderly commanders.

The attribution of 'guilt' for the Civil War has so occupied historians that an important question has gone by default. What did the

republican experience mean to Spaniards?

The simple answer is that the Republic represented a wholesale process of politicisation: for five years it incorporated, for good or evil, the mass of Spaniards into political life.

We can best study the phenomenon of mass politicisation at the local level. Carmelo Lisón-Tolosano, in his study of a small Aragonese town, has shown how violent, sudden and apparently thorough this process was.[2] The town had been a relatively stable society of smallish proprietors and labourers, historically dominated by the *pudientes* ('the powerful ones') who possessed enough land to enable them to set the tone of town life. Suddenly the tensions between rich and less rich were dramatised and publicised; and they corresponded with the division between Catholic and anti-Catholic. Party organisers came from the city; there were mass meetings. The local council became the focal point for the new political rivalries. Personal relations, in the old style, became impossible. Catholics turned religious fiestas into political demonstrations; the left soaped the church steps so that the devout would slip up. Socialist control of labour exchanges destroyed old relationships in agriculture. Even women, excluded from public life in traditional Spain, began to take part in politics.

This politicised and divided town is an example of the schisms that came to the surface in Spanish society during the Republic. The republican experience, it is important to stress, did little to diminish the economic gap between rich and poor, the *pudientes* and the rest. The left, at the local level, wanted simply to *replace* the right in the name of Liberty, to invert the inherited social structure; the right wished to cling to its predominant position in the name of Order. Half the population had come to the conclusion it could not live with the other half.

The lessons to be drawn from politicisation were not lost on General Franco. Spaniards must never again be made politically conscious by political parties; they were the particular furies which would destroy the nation. The conclusion of the victors of the Civil War was, therefore, that Spain must not be allowed the luxury of politics.

Finally there is the question of political style. Almost all politicians were ready to indulge in extreme statements which went far beyond their commitment to political action. The falangist rhetoric of nationalist revolution is one example; Largo Caballero's maximalist outbursts another. Azaña was, in essence, a moderate politician; yet he consistently spoke in a way that could only provoke anger. Miguel Maura once asked

him why he chose to wound and rub salt into the wounds he had inflicted
on his political enemies. 'I do it,' he replied, 'because it amuses me.'
Politicians of the right were equally irresponsible in their abuse of the
Azaña government.
Verbal excess brings its own reward. But so does false analogy.
Luis Araquistain, one of 'Largo Caballero's intellectual props, argued
that backward societies like Russia (in 1917) and Spain (in 1936) are
open to revolution. 'History, like biology, is full of leaps.' In fact the
conservative tissue of Spanish society was living and strong – a point
constantly stressed by Besteiro, who saw that 'Bolshevisation' would
entail a dictatorship either of the left or of the right, the latter supported
by the army. It was this conservative Spain which was to call a halt to
the process by which the majority of Spaniards were being drawn into
political life.

NOTES

1. The policies of the maximalist socialists and the process of Bolshevisation
have recently been studied by Stanley G. Payne in *The Spanish Revolution*
(New York, 1970), which appeared after this essay was written. The process
is examined from a different standpoint by Ricardo de la Cierva in the two
works cited on p. 211.
2. Carmelo Lisón-Tolosana, *Belmonte de los Caballeros* (Oxford, 1966).

3. The Parties of the Left and the Second Republic

EDWARD MALEFAKIS

THE most pronounced characteristic of the Spanish left prior to 1931 had almost always been its weakness. It had periodically come to power but less through its own efforts than through the incapacity of its opponents to resolve the terrible strains to which nineteenth-century Spain was subjected. Once in power, it easily split over the fundamental dilemma as to whether to risk acting upon its most radical aspirations, or recognise its debility and compromise with the moderates, on whose acquiescence it ultimately relied. Partly because of its ineffectuality, it could not win the active allegiance of large masses of the population. Consequently, each temporary triumph left behind some new legislation, but none was capable of creating a radically different society such as had sprung, for example, out of the French Revolution.

This pattern is evident from the War of Independence, during which the Spanish left was born. The Constitution of 1812 could be written only because the king was in exile and the nation overrun by Napoleon's armies; its defenders were easily dispersed in 1814 when Ferdinand VII returned to restore royal absolutism. The leftist triennium of 1820–3 originated in an army revolt, was quickly rendered ineffective by factional conflicts, and gained so little popular support that it could be swept away with scarcely a shot by the French armies sent to intervene. The profound crisis produced by the first Carlist Wars gave the left another opportunity, but it governed intermittently (1840–3 and 1854–6) only at the cost of subjecting itself to a military leader who suffocated its most idealistic impulses. The widespread revolt of 1868 against the Bourbon dynasty brought a newly purified and invigorated left to the portals of power once more, though it would not win office until 1873, when the alternative of a democratic constitutional monarchy failed. The First Republic, founded by default and faced with revolution in the Carlist north and in Cuba, could have survived only through iron discipline. Instead, the latent conflicts within the left immediately erupted as the extreme wing of the federal republicans launched the Cantonalist revolt. This split their party, further alienated the unitary republicans and provided the justification for the military *coups* of 1874 by which the Bourbon monarchy would be restored.

The Restoration period (1875–1902) was a time of deep eclipse for the Spanish left. The trauma of the Cantonalist revolt handicapped the various republican groupings for decades, whereas the two dynastic parties – the conservatives and the liberals – brought unaccustomed political stability to the monarchy by their agreement to alternate in office. Since the army, earlier so often the catalyst of revolution, was also gradually domesticated, the left seemed threatened with permanent exclusion from power.

Nevertheless, as so often occurs with historical movements, the period of greatest decline also laid the bases for the future growth of the left. The overwhelmingly rural and localistic economy of nineteenth-century Spain was gradually transformed by industrialisation. The working classes – who could give the left the mass support it had previously lacked – began to be organised under anarchist and, somewhat later, socialist auspices. The growth of regional sentiment in Catalonia and the Basque provinces, even though primarily conservative-inspired, threatened the stability of the established order by raising the spectre of regional separatism. A new ethical basis for the left was laid as the European-wide redefinition of liberalism in the late nineteenth century was supplemented in Spain by the teachings of Giner de los Ríos, who decried the concept of the neutral state and saw government as a moral instrument to be used for the betterment of the people.

These changes were to produce a resurgence of the left after 1902 and especially during the First World War, when the Renovation movement of 1917 threatened for a moment to upset the political structure inherited from the Restoration period at the same time as the social edifice was imperilled by an unprecedented wave of strikes. Although the Renovationist alliance – which stretched from Catalan conservative regionalists to socialists – proved impermanent, and although the strike wave receded after 1920, the left had once more obviously emerged as a major political force.

Given its new vigour and Spain's more highly developed social and economic structure, could the left have escaped after 1920 the pattern of the past and come to power by its own efforts? The answer is by no means certain. With the old army alliance now outdated and the proletariat neither firmly allied to the radical bourgeoisie nor organised to the point of being able to carry out a successful revolution, the left was rendered primarily dependent on legal means – that is, elections. Yet despite universal suffrage and several decades of urbanisation and proselytisation, it had never gained as many as 10 per cent of the seats in the parliament, even in the relatively honest balloting of the 1910s and early 1920s.[1] This in part reflected the extremely fragmented nature of the Spanish electorate. In contrast to other European nations, the most industrialised regions of Spain constituted an uncertain source of support for the left because of their preoccupation with regional autonomy rather than with national politics as such. This was especially true so long as the conservative forces which had, after the federal republican failure of 1873, organised regional sentiments remained dominant. The bourgeois left was excluded from Biscay and Guipúzcoa by the strongly Catholic Basque nationalist party; in Catalonia it was reduced for a long period to a bogeyman used by the conservative *Lliga* to frighten the national government into granting its demands. Consequently, it had to rely primarily upon the secondary urban centres and Madrid for its vote.

Economic and social cleavages in the electorate also prevented the left from adopting a successful electoral platform. This was especially true in agriculture, which still employed more than half the population. Rural society in the southern third of Spain was composed mostly of landless labourers whose chief interests were an increase in wages and a radical land reform to break up the large estates on which they worked. In northern and central Spain, by contrast, small peasant proprietors predominated who, like their counterparts in northern Europe, distrusted any attack upon property, objected to any rise in labour costs, and demanded only adequate credit and secure markets.

Religious cleavages were also important. Anti-clericalism was a psychological necessity to the bourgeois left, which tended to make the church the principal scapegoat for the many defects of a society which had remained 'invertebrate' for nearly three centuries. It also acted as a magnet for the embittered working classes, who felt that they had been abandoned by the church in the nineteenth century. It was a great obstacle, however, to the recruitment of followers in those regions and among those groups whose intellectual and economic indignation was not so great. The small peasant proprietors of northern and central Spain, for example, in many ways natural adherents of a moderate republicanism, remained alienated from the left because of its anti-clerical bias.

The cleavages within the left itself also handicapped it. Because of the economic backwardness of the nation, the middle classes, even had they not been divided by the regional and religious issues, were too small to give power to a strictly bourgeois movement. More than in the rest of Europe, the left depended as well upon purely working-class groups. This was not an insurmountable obstacle when dealing with the socialists, who, despite their rhetoric, resembled their sister parties in northern Europe in their *de facto* acceptance of gradual change. Relations with the anarcho-syndicalists, far more numerous than the socialists until 1931, were quite another matter. Chiliastic in its outlook, anarcho-syndicalism refused collaboration of any sort with the other leftist groups. For example, it deprived the bourgeois left and the socialists of potential electoral support by urging its followers to abstain from voting. It also kept alive the fear of violent social revolution by rejecting the legitimacy of a transitional democratic regime and insisting upon the immediate abolition of all forms of property and government.

The bourgeois left was also divided. Two traditions struggled within it: one idealistic and intellectual, the other a survival of the nineteenth-century spoils system. The personalistic nature of Spanish politics likewise contributed to bourgeois disunity (the strength of their ideologies rescued the working-class movements from a similar fate). Rather than institutionalised parties in the English, German or even French sense, the Spanish republican groups were primarily factions clustered around outstanding leaders.

These factors, together with the difficulty of penetrating the normally apathetic Spanish electorate, suggest that the outcome of the crisis of the first two decades of the twentieth century might well have been the long-postponed transformation of the two dynastic parties into more active democratisers of the monarchical regime, rather than a sudden overthrow of the Restoration system of politics by the left. This was the meaning of the reformist currents which swept both the liberal and conservative parties from 1918 to 1923 and led, along with the king's growing involvement with the unpopular military campaigns in Morocco, to a loosening of their ties with the monarchy. It may also help to explain the surprisingly high tolerance the Madrid governments of the period displayed towards the post-1917 social upheavals.

This possible outcome was forestalled by the impatience of the court, army and much of the public, with the momentary paralysis of government that accompanied the confused search for new values within the old parties, as well as by the fear of the king and army that the disastrous defeats suffered in Morocco would be used to discredit them. Not the left but General Miguel Primo de Rivera (with the tacit approval of the crown) swept away the Restoration system of politics in 1923. His *coup* was unopposed at the start, and many aspects of his administration were successful. Nevertheless, Primo's seven-year dictatorship served in the end only to shift the political spectrum far to the left of what it had been in 1923.

How can this ironic outcome be explained? Primo's overhauling of municipal governments destroyed the political machines on which the conservative and liberal parties had been based. His attempt to crush Catalanism only strengthened regional feeling. His persecution of the anarcho-syndicalist C.N.T. accelerated the radicalisation of that labour union, while his attempt to buy the co-operation of the socialists enabled their union, the U.G.T., to extend its power. He alienated the students and intellectuals by petty vendettas and by permitting the Catholics entry into the hitherto secular sphere of university education. At the same time, Primo failed to build new bases of support. He offended much of the army, which he had never really dominated, by personal affronts to leading figures and by crassly conducted efforts at military reform. He lost the industrialists and landowners by schemes for labour legislation which were nevertheless insufficient to bring him the active support of the workers and peasants.

Yet beyond these specific reasons lay a more subtle cause. Beneath the surface, a strong concept of legality had been developing in Restoration Spain. The crisis of 1917-23 had sufficed to bring momentary doubts about, but not a profound rejection of, the parliamentary tradition. Had Primo been motivated by ideology, he might yet have seized the moment to implant a new legal basis for his rule. As it was, his vacillations between a corporative vocabulary borrowed from Mussolini and statements that his was only a transitory regime intended to restore constitutional government convinced no one. When he was eased from power in January 1930, Primo left behind him a legal void.

The king's attempt to revive constitutional rule during the year after Primo's fall also proved futile. Some of Alfonso XIII's former supporters, both in the army and among the dynastic parties, sought to avenge the tribulations that Primo's rule had caused them by placing conditions on a renewal of their aid and by flirting with anti-monarchical movements. More important, Alfonso's violation of the very constitutional tradition in which he now sought refuge caused even his strongest supporters, and perhaps the king himself, to lose confidence in his legitimacy. The royal governments that followed Primo were confused, half-hearted and totally lacking in nerve. The freedom of agitation they allowed their enemies and the mildness of their repressive measures are incredible in retrospect. It was a bankrupt, timorous regime against which the left had to fight between January 1930 and April 1931. The identification of the monarchy with Primo's dictatorship had given to the left a popularity and legitimacy far greater than it could have acquired solely on the basis of the changes that had occurred in the social and economic structure of Spain during the preceding decades. Although the extent of the transformation in opinion was not to be apparent until the municipal elections of 12 April 1931 (called as part of Alfonso's attempt to return to legality) had been concluded, a former conservative minister captured the new mood when he said in early 1930: 'In my house, everyone down to the cat has gone republican.'[2]

II

A coalition of party chiefs formed at San Sebastian on 17 August 1930 to organise the revolution that, up to the very end, everyone assumed would be necessary to overthrow the monarchy, took office as the Provisional Government of the Second Republic on 14 April 1931. It possessed two advantages never before enjoyed by a leftist regime in Spain. First, because the planned revolt had failed and the Republic had unexpectedly come into being instead in the aftermath of elections, it enjoyed an aura of greater legality and was less bound than any of its predecessors by promises made to military chiefs. Second, the elections had given it more specific and more widespread support. The left had never been able to capture as many as 10 per cent of the parliamentary seats under the Restoration monarchy. In the elections of 12 April 1931 the San Sebastian parties won 61·5 per cent of the municipal posts in the provincial capitals and at least 47·9 per cent of those in the smaller towns and villages in which the elections were contested. The balloting for the constituent Cortes, held on 28 June 1931, substantially increased this majority, giving to the San Sebastian parties and their associates approximately 85 per cent of the parliamentary seats. Even areas which the left had never before been able to penetrate returned sizeable votes for the San Sebastian candidates. In

the traditionally Catholic region of Old Castile, for example, they won
41·9 per cent of the contested municipal posts in the April elections, and
approximately 60 per cent of the parliamentary seats in June.[3]

Nevertheless, the problems of the past had not been completely
overcome. First of all, the left had not received so overwhelming a
mandate as the elections suggested. The vote reflected more a withdrawal of support from the monarchy among large sectors of the population than a specific endorsement of radical change. Those members
of the established classes who had acquiesced to the proclamation of the
Republic in particular expected that it would be a moderate regime
which would not depart too sharply from the predominant patterns of
legislation of the past fifty years. This expectation was shared by the
two most prominent leaders of the San Sebastian coalition during the
transitional period. Niceto Alcalá Zamora, a liberal party minister prior
to 1923, and Miguel Maura, son of a great conservative party chief, had
lent their prestige to the republican cause on the assumption that there
was a moderate majority in Spain which would assert itself and hold the
Republic to a safe course.[4] The oldest and largest of the Republican
groups, the radical party of Alejandro Lerroux, also played an ambiguous role, since it was isolated from the rest of the left by its reputation for opportunism, as well as by its tradition of opposition to regional
autonomy. Many of the millions of votes it received in the April and
June balloting (it was by far the most successful of the bourgeois
republican parties in both elections) were cast in favour of limited
change, not drastic reforms.[5] Thus, both within the San Sebastian
coalition itself and in the electorate at large, the old dependence of the
left on the acquiescence of the moderates had not truly been broken,
despite the appearances of the moment.

The groups which were unquestionably leftist in their outlook also
had not been so successful in overcoming the handicaps of the past as
at first seemed. The regional question continued to have mixed effects,
though to a lesser degree than before. In Catalonia, where a leftist
coalition known as the *Esquerra* had managed to break the monopoly
of the conservative *Lliga* in the late 1920s, the recapturing of leadership
of the regional cause gave to the bourgeois left a stronger position than it
was to acquire in any other region of Spain. In Galicia, the rise of a new
regional party, the O.R.G.A., also contributed to the lesser republican
success there. But these triumphs remained ambiguous in their effect,
because they did not assist the growth of left republican parties of
national scope. Moreover, the continued leadership of the regional cause

by the conservative Basque nationalist party in Biscay and Guipúzcoa prevented the left from taking root among what were in many ways the most progressive middle classes of Spain.

On the national level, then, if the radical party is left aside, the bourgeois left was reduced to two relatively small groups – Republican Action and the radical socialists – whose basis of support was restricted primarily to Madrid and the secondary provincial capitals. Both were new creations, dating from the late 1920s. Republican Action, much the smaller of the two, was a semi-elite group which reflected the idealistic, intellectual side of the republican tradition. The radical socialist party relied chiefly on the lesser intellectuals and on the provincial professional classes, but was more unstable and demagogic because it tried to be all things to all men. Its lack of a firm ideology also made it peculiarly subject to the fissures and personalistic politics that had been the bane of republican groups under the Restoration monarchy.

The relative weakness of the unquestionably leftist bourgeois parties meant that they could not easily reduce their traditional need for working-class support, particularly since the proclamation of the Republic was followed by a sudden rise in specifically working-class consciousness (the U.G.T., for example, quadrupled its membership in a year, and socialist candidates, who had won less than 10 per cent of the municipal posts in the April 1931 election, won 24·9 per cent of the parliamentary seats in June). This dependence presented fewer problems than in the past because the socialists began to surpass the anarchosyndicalists in strength and adopted a more openly collaborationist policy than before. Nevertheless, many socialists continued to doubt the ideological legitimacy of co-operation with a bourgeois regime, and the extraordinary increase in socialist membership made it more difficult for the national leadership to control the ranks. As to the anarcho-syndicalists, the persecution they had suffered under Primo de Rivera, their exaggerated hope that they could turn against its authors the revolutionary process which the middle classes had inaugurated in overthrowing the king, and their hatred for their increasingly successful socialist rivals, caused them to become even more intransigent against the Republic than they had been against the monarchy. The terrible source of weakness that had handicapped the left since the 1870s, the opposition it had to endure from its most militant working-class members, was in no sense overcome.

Finally, although the right had indeed suffered a severe setback, it had not been routed quite so completely as the June elections in particular

B

suggested. Taken by surprise by the fall of the monarchy (which also discredited the few rightist leaders who had survived the political experimentation of Primo de Rivera) and unable to agree on what policies to follow, the right groped blindly towards new forms of organisation. It failed miserably in the atmosphere of republican euphoria engendered by the birth of the new regime. Even had the Provisional Government not further handicapped it by the electoral decree of May, which assigned a disproportionate number of deputies to parties able to form broad electoral coalitions (and thus – as the left was to discover to its sorrow in 1933 – penalised those parties which were undergoing periods of crisis), it is doubtful that it could have gained as many as a quarter of the parliamentary seats in the June elections. Nevertheless, a rightist presence was maintained in the Cortes; from it, new leaders and new programmes would eventually spring.

For all these reasons, the sweeping victories of mid-1931 greatly exaggerated the strength of the left. The honeymoon period of April and May, whose passing the republican leaders were later so plaintively to lament, was a time of illusion. The left had not miraculously, without bloodshed, won permanent victory. It had only gained the opportunity to transform the vague, negative consensus that had arisen against the monarchy into a positive, republican consensus.

The ease with which the overthrow of the monarchy had been accomplished, as well as the presence of avowed moderates in the cabinet, meant that the Provisional Government would not rule in a Jacobin mood. The first six months of the Republic were characterised by an attempt to avoid any actions that would destroy the aura of legality which surrounded the new regime, and by an urge to maintain the unity that had been established at San Sebastian. Thus, when Maciá, the *Esquerra* leader, tried during the change-over of regimes to declare the independence of Catalonia within an 'Iberian Federation', the Provisional Government prevented a repetition of the disastrous experience of 1873 by forcing him to await a resolution of the regional question by the Cortes. The extremist faction in the radical socialist party was defeated when it sought a clear break between the moderates and radicals in the Provisional Government prior to the June elections.[6] Few major changes were inaugurated by decree: as it had done with the Catalan question, the Provisional Government insisted that all fundamental legislation must await parliamentary debate and approval. The single seemingly Jacobin act, the failure to stop immediately the church burnings of 10–12 May 1931, was caused partly because the religious issue was the blind spot of many republican leaders, but its main source was the inexperience of the new government. The real attitude of the Provisional Government towards public disorder was to be manifested in July, against the first serious strikes of the anarcho-syndicalist C.N.T. These were put down with such ferocity as to further undermine the influence of the reformist groups within the union and cement the power of the intransigently revolutionary F.A.I. faction, thus ending whatever small chance may have remained of a *modus vivendi* between the Republic and the extreme working-class left.

Yet dissensions within the San Sebastian coalition could not for ever be bridged, nor the solution of fundamental problems indefinitely postponed. The failure of the progressive party of Alcalá Zamora and Maura to expand itself into a large 'right republican' party during the June elections meant that power within the coalition was divided fairly evenly among three groups: the radicals of Lerroux, the two regional and two national left republican parties which increasingly acted in tandem, and the socialists.[7] The orientation of the Republic could be clarified in one of two ways: either by a movement towards the right in which the bourgeois parties from the progressives to the radical socialists would unite, excluding the socialists, or by a movement towards the left, in which the left republicans would collaborate with the socialists in preference to the more moderate bourgeois groups. The balance of power in either case was held by the left republicans. The alternatives differed in that the natural leader of a moderate Republic would be the head of the largest bourgeois party, Lerroux, whereas in an alliance with the socialists the left republicans would dominate the cabinet, since the socialists had no other possible allies, and were in any case prevented by ideology from accepting full responsibility in a capitalist regime. This consideration alone might not have sufficed to bring about the left republican socialist solution which actually resulted, had not all of his associates in the San Sebastian coalition so intensely distrusted Lerroux because of his reputation for corruption and opportunism. The masses might vote for the radical chief in overwhelming numbers, back-benchers in other parties might find him attractive, but the leaders of the new regime, who were so concerned with the purity and honesty of their creation, would have accepted him as their head only in the absence of any alternative. This possibility ceased to exist when the rise of Manuel Azaña, leader of Republican Action, gave to the Republic another figure of prominence.

The chief stages in the redefinition of the Republic can be quickly recounted. The June elections seriously undermined the position of Alcalá Zamora. Since the four left republican parties were not yet firmly tied either to each other or to the socialists, however, and since Lerroux was the only clear alternative for prime minister, the original allocation of posts in the Provisional Government was not altered. In August and September, these obstacles were removed. The star of Azaña rose, the left republican parties came closer together because of radical socialist and Republican Action support for regional rights in the Constitution, and the socialists abandoned their objections to Catalan autonomy in return for constitutional recognition in principle of a possible socialisation of property. Anti-clericalism was another important factor in welding together the new coalition. It served, on 14 October 1931 (exactly six months after the Republic had been proclaimed), as the specific issue on which Alcalá Zamora and Maura would escape from their increasingly untenable position by resigning from the cabinet.

The departure of the progressives was not in itself of great immediate importance because of the small size of the party. Since it signified, however, a still closer rapprochement between the left republicans and socialists, and a further isolation of the radicals, it was soon followed by a more consequential break. The specific issues over which the new cleavage developed (aside from Lerroux's resentment that Azaña and not he had replaced Alcalá Zamora as prime minister) were the scope of the proposed agrarian reform and the controversy as to whether the constituent Cortes should continue in being as the first regular parliament of the Republic or whether new elections should be held. After Lerroux was defeated on both issues, he directly posed the underlying question by demanding in December 1931 that Azaña eliminate or reduce socialist representation in the government as the price for continued radical collaboration. Forced to choose, Azaña sided with the socialists and the broad coalition created at San Sebastian came to an end.

The fact that a clearly leftist government had now been established did not bring a dramatic change in the tenor of the Republic. The Azaña coalition was not much more Jacobin than the San Sebastian coalition as a whole had been. The socialist leaders in particular were careful to establish their respectability: the intemperate statements they had occasionally uttered while they still feared exclusion from the cabinet were not repeated. Alcalá Zamora, though dropped as prime minister, was sponsored by the Azaña forces for the office of president of the Republic. The left republican–socialist coalition did not use its new-found power to push through a radical land reform; in fact, the drastic bills that had emerged from parliamentary committee during the autumn of 1931 were made more palatable to the opposition. An income tax was introduced, but its term were preposterously mild (persons who earned less than the equivalent of 93 times the average *per capita* income were exempted, while the top tax rate of 7·7 per cent applied only after approximately 1000 times this income had been earned). Only in connection with the clerical issue did the new government show strong determination as it hastened to apply some of the measures that had been agreed upon during the constitutional debates.

The reasons for this continued moderation have already been touched upon. They have to do with the predominance within the cabinet of the left republicans rather than the socialists (who in any case were still strongly reformist), and with the differing priorities of the regional, national, bourgeois, and working-class parties which had been loosely united by Azaña. More interesting is the question as to why, despite its basic legislative moderation, the coalition failed to establish a solid consensus in its favour either among the masses or among the established classes. Several reasons can be cited; they range from the idiosyncratic to the structural.

First, rhetorical excesses and a profound sense of self-righteousness often concealed the coalition's essential malleability in practice. Azaña's equitable plan to reduce the size of the officer corps, for example, was made to appear vindictive by his boasts that he had 'pulverised' the army. The reputation of the government also suffered because of its frequent violations of basic civil liberties. A fundamental contradiction existed in this regard within the coalition. Although it was so legalistic in its legislative programme and general administrative policies as to give the impression that it did not seriously fear its enemies, its reaction to specific instances of opposition resembled those of a regime that felt itself to be in desperate straits. Not only were anarcho-syndicalist strikes frequently suppressed without legal cause, but the Catholic and conservative press was repeatedly suspended for statements that would have been tolerated in most democracies. As time went on, the adamant refusal of the government to dissolve the Cortes (which after all had been intended to serve only constituent, not regular legislative, functions) and allow new elections also was used to mock its claim that it was democratic.

Second, inability to satisfy the impossibly high hopes that many persons had held for the Republic weakened the coalition. Azaña's great achievement of providing, at long last, an acceptable solution to the regional problem was blemished because the anti-Catalan pronouncements of such distinguished figures as Unamuno and Ortega y Gasset gave intellectual respectability to the wave of Castilian nationalism which arose in opposition to the Statute of Autonomy. Enthusiasm for the agrarian reform was diminished because the elite 'Group at the Service of the Republic' spoke out against any attack on the property of non-absentee bourgeois owners, without which the reform would have been an empty gesture. To the degree that the moderates and intellectuals counselled harmony and tried to temper the excessive anti-clericalism of the Republic, their position was laudable. But because they refused to recognise the inevitability of conflict and created a false opposition between what Ortega once called the 'joyous' days of April 1931 and the 'sad and disagreeable Republic' which had since arisen, they diverted attention from the real problems of Spain and weakened confidence in the government.

Third, because Spain had not in fact 'ceased to be Catholic', as Azaña once asserted, the issue on which the coalition was most united and could therefore act most decisively gave to its opponents a means by which they could recapture a mass following. Azaña did not aim at total elimination of Catholicism, in fact, his church reforms were no more drastic than those to which France had learnt to adjust since the Combes legislation of 1905. The church was disestablished; restrictions on the worship of other faiths were removed; the Jesuit Order was dissolved; the property rights of religious establishments were restricted; divorce was permitted; civil marriages and burial were required; and – perhaps most important of all – the vast Catholic educational network was threatened with destruction as religious personnel were prohibited from teaching. Nevertheless, because the Spanish church was incomparably stronger than the French, and because Spain had not passed through as much of the intermittent official anti-clericalism and preparatory legislation that France had experienced since 1789, the shock produced by the new measures was far greater. The Azaña government made matters still worse by its openly anti-Catholic attitudes, manifested in such demagogic utterances as Alvaro de Albornoz's cry for 'A slave church in a free state'. Some anti-clerical legislation was both inevitable and desirable, particularly in view of the increase in Catholic influence under Primo de Rivera and the opposition of much of the church hierarchy to the Republic. To refuse to distinguish between liberal and conservative Catholicism, however, and to concentrate so much energy on the achievement of what were in the final analysis merely symbolic victories,[8] constituted a tragic flaw in the political imagination of the Azaña coalition.

Nevertheless, by far the most important reason for the failure of the coalition to take deeper root in the nation was its inability to solve the social problem. The fate of the Republic, which had come into being primarily because of political disputes among various sectors of the middle and upper classes, was to be decided chiefly on the basis of social conflicts. In comparison to these, even the clerical and regional issues, decisive though they may have been at certain moments, were of secondary import.

As we have seen, the Provisional Government was confronted almost immediately with the hostility of the anarcho-syndicalists. To counterbalance this, as well as to satisfy its humanitarian idealism, it displayed a willingness to institute social reforms and a predisposition towards granting the demands of the socialists even while the progressives and radicals remained in the cabinet. The limits of bourgeois republican toleration were expanded (and the danger that the socialists might gradually be driven into opposition avoided) by the emergence of the Azaña coalition in the autumn of 1931. As a result, several major improvements were realised. Wages rose, particularly in agriculture, where they had been abysmally low under the monarchy; institutional means of settling labour disputes were expanded by the creation of rural arbitration boards similar to those introduced by Primo de Rivera in industry; all the socialist labour unions were strengthened by the greater favour they now enjoyed with the government, and the rural unions were specifically assisted by the Municipal Labour Act, which prevented landowners from breaking strikes or undercutting wages by hiring migrant workers; the long-disputed Agrarian Reform Law was finally approved in September 1932; an anticipatory step towards the actual redistribution of land was taken in the winter of 1932-3, when 40,000 peasants were temporarily settled on some of the large estates of Estremadura.

Yet in the end, Azaña's attempt to incorporate the working classes into the Republic failed. One reason was the continued intransigence of the anarcho-syndicalists, who fought for the overthrow of the reformist regime. On three separate occasions – in January 1932, January 1933 and December 1933 – the C.N.T. launched insurrectionary movements of national scope. In innumerable other instances, local revolts and violent strikes threatened public order. The vicious circle – provocation by the anarcho-syndicalists, brutal repression by the government, heightened militancy among the anarcho-syndicalists – which had first been established even before the victory of the F.A.I. faction in the C.N.T. in the autumn of 1931, caught Spain in a death-grip because neither side could as yet win total victory.

Another reason was the underlying ambivalence of the left republicans. Committed by their political position to rapid social reform, they nevertheless did not feel enough enthusiasm for it to push on despite all obstacles. The regional parties rarely rendered effective support because of their preoccupation with the issue of autonomy and because the two principal social initiatives of the Republic – the Municipal Labour Act and the Agrarian Reform Law – had been drafted in response to conditions in the large landholding provinces of Andalusia and Estremadura, and were therefore either irrelevant or actually prejudicial to the smallholding rural society of Catalonia and Galicia.[9] Republican Action and the radical socialists were much more active. Nevertheless, they too were more concerned with other issues, were confused by the conflict which existed between their respect for private property and the need to expropriate land, and were unable to decide whether they wished primarily to serve the interests of the landless day-labourers or the frequently contradictory needs of the modest tenant farmers and peasant proprietors. The result was an increasingly half-hearted fulfilment of promises, which finally served to disillusion the left republicans' socialist allies.

Perhaps the greatest obstacle to the solution of the social problem, however, stemmed from the weakness of the Spanish economy, particularly as it reeled under the impact of the world Depression of the 1930s. Backwardness placed limits on the capacity of the economy to absorb change without injuring excessively the interests of the labour-employing entrepreneurs who, because of the failure of giant economic conglomerates to develop in Spain, constituted a not unsubstantial proportion of the population.[10] The crisis in agriculture (where as late as 1962 26 per cent of even the small entrepreneurs still used some hired help) is easily understandable since wages approximately doubled between 1931 and 1933, while the price of farm produce was falling, thus leaving many farm operators with scarcely any profit. But similar crises also occurred in industry and commerce, despite lesser worker gains.

Still more important was the inability of the economy to provide jobs for all those who sought them. Because of the social permissiveness introduced by the Republic as well as because of the Depression and the attempt of employers to cut back labour costs, the hundreds of thousands of underemployed workers that lie hidden within the folds of all backward economies now swelled into an army of highly visible unemployed.[11] The state did not possess the resources to pay unemployment insurance to so many persons, nor could its ambitious public works employ more than a minority of them. Since the Azaña reforms mentioned earlier primarily benefited workers who could find jobs, not those without them, the problem of massive unemployment was never solved. And while it continued, all working-class organisations, whether anarcho-syndicalist or socialist, were subjected to almost intolerable pressures for greater militancy.

The efforts of the left republicans on behalf of the workers consequently gave the worst of all possible results. The expectations of the proletariat were stimulated but not satisfied, and social disorder increased apace.[12] Significant portions of the middle and upper bourgeoisie – particularly in agriculture, where the disaffection also spread to many tens of thousands of modest peasant proprietors – were alienated by the economic losses they endured as well as by the fear that the new assertiveness of the labour organisations engendered in them. Since many of these same persons had already been antagonised on religious grounds, a massive source of opposition appeared which had not existed in 1931.

On several levels, then, support for the Azaña coalition began to dissipate almost from the start. The decline first became noticeable during the summer of 1932, when the coalition encountered enormous difficulties in the Cortes debates on the Catalan Statute and the Agrarian Reform Law, and when a bumper crop led to a sharp fall in wheat prices. The rapid defeat of the absurdly ill-prepared military revolt headed by General Sanjurjo on 10 August reversed the trend, revived some of the initial enthusiasm for the Republic and permitted the government to secure quick approval of its agrarian and Catalan legislation. The rediscovered sense of unity and vigour once again began to diminish during the winter of 1932, but the beneficial effects of the Sanjurjo windfall were not entirely lost until January 1933, when another accident occurred. A score of hapless peasants who were seconding a nation-wide anarcho-syndicalist insurrection were brutally massacred at Casas Viejas by a detachment of Assault Guards (the specifically republican and highly favoured police force created in 1931 to supplement the *Guardia Civil*). Lerroux's radicals and the rightists seized upon the incident to launch a highly effective campaign of calumny against

Azaña, whom they charged with personal responsibility for the disaster; although the left republicans and socialists held firm, many of them sensed a loss in the moral legitimacy of their rule.

The situation might possibly have been salvaged had Azaña braved the dangers and contradictions that existed and frankly turned to a socially radical course capable of attracting the workers and landless peasants, as well as the youth and portions of the middle classes. But it was precisely now that the ambiguity of the left republicans manifested itself most strongly. The Agrarian Reform Law, already seriously weakened by the lethargic support the left republicans had given it in the Cortes debates, was made a mockery by the bumbling legalism with which it was administered and by the decision to allocate only 1 per cent of the governmental budget to its implementation. The demands of the socialists for unemployment insurance or, alternatively, for laws that would prevent employers from discriminating against their union members in hiring were disregarded. The submission to the Cortes of the Rural Lease and Agricultural Credit legislation that might have helped win over the hitherto neglected tenant farmers and peasant proprietors was repeatedly postponed. Instead, Azaña kept to the previously agreed schedule and sought to rekindle enthusiasm by presenting to the Cortes further anti-clerical legislation. Under the new circumstances that had arisen since 1931, this legislation was insufficient to serve as a rallying point for more than a narrow group of ideologists. Rightists and radicals delayed its approval for more than three months; relations with the president, Alcalá Zamora, who had broken with the San Sebastian coalition precisely over such legislation, were embittered; and in the nation as a whole, social disorders rose to their greatest peak since the proclamation of the Republic.

The signs of deterioration began to multiply rapidly in the spring and summer of 1933. Municipal by-elections held in April in 2478 rural townships containing some 10 per cent of the population gave a two-thirds majority to the radicals and to various rightist groups. In June, at the fourth congress of the radical socialist party (the largest and ideologically least well defined of the left republican groups), a group of dissidents headed by Gordón Ordás proposed abandonment of the socialist alliance and a rapprochement with the radicals as a means of recovering popular support. In July and August, the leading liberal periodicals turned against Azaña, the dissension within the radical socialist party widened, and the socialists were frightened by the increasing insecurity of their position into rash warnings of the consequences that would follow their exclusion from power. Meanwhile, the rightists won victory after victory in the long-postponed Cortes debates on the Rural Lease Law because the left republicans were in such disarray that they would not even attend the sessions. The final blow came in early September, when elections held among some 35,000 municipal officials to select judges for the newly established Supreme Court gave another two-to-one majority to candidates not affiliated with the Azaña coalition. Alcalá Zamora quite logically concluded that the government no longer represented the nation and asked Lerroux to form an alternative ministry. Since the new ministry could not win a vote of confidence in the Cortes, it was soon replaced by a caretaker government under Lerroux's lieutenant, Martínez Barrio, who was charged with the preparation of national elections to be held in November.

During the two months between the ouster of Azaña and the elections, the left republican–socialist coalition completed its disintegration into its working-class and bourgeois components. The process had been initiated in June by Gordón Ordás, but by his own efforts this muddle-headed man could only have accomplished the splitting apart of the radical socialist party into supporters and opponents of continued collaboration with the socialists, an event which actually occurred in late September. The larger split required the assent of the socialists, who, displaying for the first time the hubris that would become their tragic flaw, concluded that the alliance with the bourgeoisie was of no benefit to them and rejected further collaboration even with those left republicans who had stood by them. Disaster followed under the terms of the electoral law which the left republicans and socialists had them-selves created. The actual vote received by the two groups probably did not decline quite so drastically from the 1931 total as is sometimes assumed, but because they forfeited the premium granted to coalitions by the electoral law, they ended up with only some 20 per cent of the Cortes seats.[13] The catastrophe was greatest for what remained of the national left republican parties, who showed their lack of real roots in any important sector of the population by dropping from approximately 85 to less than 10 seats. The two regional parties, with a more solid base in their restricted fiefs, gained 23 seats, about half their former number. The socialists, who also benefited from a ready-made clientele, ex-perienced approximately the same fate as the regional parties as they declined from 117 to 59 deputies. On every front, the left had been routed.

Nevertheless, as in 1931, appearances were deceptive. The old Azaña leftist coalition had, after all, won almost 40 per cent of the vote in November, despite the unusually severe electoral boycott that the anarcho-syndicalists maintained against their now much-hated rivals. Moreover, the possible basis for an eventual rapprochement with the C.N.T. began to appear almost immediately after the elections, when the F.A.I.'s attempt in December 1933 at yet another national insurrection taught it that the Azaña government had held no monopoly of repression. The outlines of an even more exotic understanding with the Basque nationalist party also began to become vaguely discernible as this reactionary group found in the summer of 1934 that its long-standing alliance with the Catholics and conservatives had not brought their agreement to the satisfaction of its single overriding passion, regional autonomy for the Basque provinces.[14] Of greater immediate importance was the refusal of part of the radical party to accept Lerroux's decision to co-operate with the right, without whose support he could not control parliament. Slightly more than one-fifth of the party followed Martínez Barrio in May 1934 when he established the cautiously leftist (once again Spanish political nomenclature is misleading) 'radical democratic' faction. Finally, given the fact that officially leftist parties were almost twice as strong in the new Cortes as officially rightist parties had been in the 1931–3 parliament, and that their opponents were never nearly so united as the Azaña coalition (or even the San Sebastian coalition) had been for most of its existence,[15] there was scant possibility that the reversal in political fortunes would be followed by a wholesale annulment of past republican legislation.

The tragedy of the Spanish left, and ultimately of Spain itself, was that in 1934 it lacked the patience and self-confidence to ride out the crisis through which it was passing as the right had ridden out its own crisis in 1931–3. The reasons are several. On the one hand, while the right had passed through a long period of self-questioning and dis-organisation prior to 1931, the left had been ousted from power immediately upon its greatest victories, just as the political constellation appeared to have shifted permanently in its favour. What had been acceptable to the right in its state of enervation was not equally so to the left in its recently triumphant mood. In consequence, the left almost immediately began to draw dangerous distinctions between 'true' republicans and 'false'. It also employed against the new Catholic C.E.D.A. party the technique that the rightists had earlier used against the socialists – that of attacking the legitimacy of the entire government on the grounds that it had become the tool of the largest and most extreme party, whose alleged purpose was to overthrow the existing regime and establish a dictatorship. The difference was that while the right had for the most part not believed its own rhetoric, portions of the left apparently did, and so embarked on policies that would belatedly give truth first to the rightist argument and then to the leftist. This is not to say that the left lacked psychological justification. Given its history of repeated defeats through *coups*, its strained relations with most of the military and police forces and the unfavourable international political configuration with which it was confronted in the 1930s, the left probably operated from even greater feelings of insecurity than had the right during its time of troubles.

The new mood of militancy penetrated practically every stratum of the leftist spectrum, yet its consequences might have been quite different had Azaña and his immediate circle retained the influence within the left that they had enjoyed from 1931 to 1933. Because of their crushing defeat in the November elections, however, the two chief remaining power bases of the left were the autonomous government of Catalonia, the *Generalitat*, which the *Esquerra* still controlled, and the enormous socialist trade union organisation that had been built up since 1931. Both were subject to special pressures that did not affect the national left republican groups. In Catalonia, the sudden appearance of an unsympathetic central government and the conflict which raged during the spring and summer of 1934 as to whether the Constitution granted the *Generalitat* the right to determine its own agrarian legislation or reserved this right to Madrid, undermined Catalan confidence in the Statute of Autonomy and revived the extremist factions which cried for full independence. As to the socialists, whose faith in gradualism had already been undermined by the failure of the Azaña coalition, they now found themselves the principal victims of a new regime which could agree on little else than the removal of the most controversial of the special privileges they had enjoyed since 1931.

Since the radicalisation of the socialists was the principal cause of the catastrophe that followed, a few words must be said on it. Control of the movement had long been disputed between a rigidly doctrinaire group headed by Julián Besteiro, whose insistence upon the long historical view that Marx had taken when writing as a scholar made him peculiarly contemptuous of tactical flexibility (though not of democratic values), and a philosophically less well-grounded group headed by the long-time trade union leader Francisco Largo Caballero, which was greatly concerned with immediate gains and losses. Wavering between the two groups was the eminently practical Indalecio Prieto. The early triumphs and subsequent disillusionments of the Azaña experiment left unaffected the *Besteiristas*, who combined with the consolation that their faith in the ultimate self-destruction of capitalism offered them a keen awareness of the disasters that might follow any socialist attempt at immediate revolution. Among the more volatile *Caballeristas*, such cautious, long-term considerations were held in contempt. Given the acquiescence of Prieto, the highly vocal support of the socialist youth movement and of some of the newer intellectuals, and the unwillingness of the leading *Besteiristas* to resort to dilatory tactics like those Prieto was to use in the not dissimilar situation which was to arise in the spring of 1936, it is difficult to see how the sudden coups that the *Caballeristas* scored on the national committees of all the socialist organisations in January 1934 could have been prevented.

Stoicism *à la* Besteiro was clearly impossible as a policy at a time when peasants and workers, already embittered by the frustrated expectations of the Azaña period, were suffering retaliations from employers whose security they had so lately endangered. Nevertheless, since there were limits to what employers could do so long as the socialist trade unions remained in being,[16] an intensification of revolutionary rhetoric might have sufficed to satisfy socialist honour until the political pendulum again returned the left to power. This indeed seemed to be the tactic adopted by the new leadership at the start. It was successful to the extent that socialist threats helped prevent the radicals and rightists from undoing any of the Azaña social legislation, except for the universally detested Municipal Labour Act, on which even the left republicans would no longer support the socialists. Increasingly, however, the *Caballeristas* and their allies began to move towards more drastic remedies. Having convinced themselves that the C.E.D.A. was a fascist group which would follow Dollfuss's recent example in Austria and destroy them if it were to accede to power, a justification for preventative revolution lay at hand.[17] Undeterred by the destruction of their peasant unions after a rash attempt at a nation-wide harvest strike in June 1934, by the lack of enthusiasm for the new policies within some of their industrial unions (whose locals were often still controlled by *Besteiristas*), as well as by their failure to create effective Workers' Alliances with other proletarian groups, the socialists stumbled towards their revolution with a carelessness comparable only to that displayed by General Sanjurjo in his revolt of 10 August 1932.

Having been prepared with so slight a sense of responsibility, the revolution which broke out on 4 October 1934 in response to Alcalá Zamora's and Lerroux's acceptance of three C.E.D.A. ministers in the thirteen-man cabinet was rapidly defeated in every part of Spain except Asturias. In that region full-scale civil war developed as the miners, who had gained the alliance of the local anarcho-syndicalist and communist unions, fought off the advancing military forces for almost two weeks. The other power base of the left was also destroyed after the *Generalitat* hastily declared Catalan independence only to discover that the socialist rising was not succeeding, the C.N.T. would not act, and even its bourgeois followers would not effectively support it.

A long period of eclipse followed for the left, which might well have proved permanent had its opponents indeed been fascists. As it was, the excesses of the military forces which carried out the pacification of Asturias, the subsequent brutality of prison officials in that region, Lerroux's unprincipled attempt to establish Azaña's complicity in the Catalan rising, and the government's refusal to go to the point of amnestying most of the many thousands of militants who had been arrested, obscured the fact that – once order had been restored, at least – the suppression of the revolt was not disproportionate to the event itself.[18] The basis for a mythology that would ultimately revitalise the left had been laid. Its success was ensured by the fact that the revolt swung the balance of power to the more reactionary forces within the centre–right coalition, thus permitting them to defeat, in March 1935, the attempt by the liberal C.E.D.A. faction led by Giménez Fernández to ease class conflicts. Once this had occurred, they were able to proceed to the long-postponed emasculation of Azaña's social legislation, which gave employers even greater freedom to persecute the workers and peasants than they had already acquired after the self-destruction of the socialist unions during the previous year.

The short-sightedness of most radicals and rightists caused them to accumulate enemies by the wagon-load in the last nine months of 1935. Wages (particularly in agriculture) fell to their pre-republican levels; tens of thousands of tenant farmers were expelled; the peasants settled in Estremadura by Azaña in 1932 were evicted; the Catalan Statute of Autonomy remained suspended; and many of the civil servants were alienated by bumbling efforts at government economy. Lacking any positive programme, the centre-right cabinets which rapidly succeeded each other after March 1935 were unable to develop any countervailing sources of support (one of the most striking characteristics of the 1936 elections was to be the sharp rise in electoral abstention in such old rightist strongholds as Old Castile and León).[19] Their moral bankruptcy was dramatically confirmed in the autumn of 1935 by financial scandals that wrecked Lerroux's radical party. Faced with the prospect of being forced to grant power to a purely rightist cabinet headed by Gil Robles, the C.E.D.A. leader, Alcalá Zamora decided instead to call new parliamentary elections for 16 February 1936.

The prospects for the left were more favourable than in 1933. Having recovered a mythology because of the events of Asturias, a leader because of Azaña's renewed popularity after the legal persecution he had endured, and a myriad of causes to defend because of the unenlightened policies instituted by the centre-right, the left lacked only organisation. The traditional obstacle to its unity had been removed in that the anarcho-syndicalists were willing to tolerate (though not to join formally) their former rivals as the lesser of two evils. Smaller working-class organisations, such as the syndicalist party of Angel Pestaña, the 'Trotskyite' P.O.U.M. and the communist party,[20] were also driven by the course of events to accept an alliance with the progressive bourgeoisie. Only the unrepentant Largo Caballero fought against union, but since Prieto and other leaders who had acquiesced to the maximalist line followed in 1934 had been shocked back into their senses by the disastrous outcome of the October revolution, the socialists also agreed to sign the manifesto by which the Popular Front coalition between working-class and left republican forces was cemented in January 1936. In the elections, the accumulated grievances of the previous two years, the transfer of some formerly centre votes to the left because of the disappearance of Lerroux's radical party, and the premium which the electoral law granted to coalitions, gave the Popular Front a clear victory.

Although Azaña once again assumed the premiership, the new leftist government found itself in an entirely different position from that of 1931–3. The left republicans, who were now organised into three parties (the Catalan *Esquerra*, Azaña's *Izquierda Republicana*, and Martínez Barrio's Republican Union), were themselves in a more militant mood, in which they refused to be bound by legal formalities as much as in the past. Infinitely more important, however, was the pressure to which they were subjected from the proletariat. 14 April 1931 had been a political victory which the urban masses had celebrated with jubilation; 16 February 1936 was a social victory from which both they and the now fully aroused peasantry sought vengeance. Yet the differences between the two dates might somehow have been bridged had not the communists gained through the elections an effective platform from which to voice their propaganda and – far more important because they were numerically so much larger – had not the *Caballeristas* fought against the *Priestistas'* attempt to restore the socialist movement to its former moderating role. With the incitements of these two groups now added to those of the anarcho-syndicalists, and with the Azaña government not daring because of its political position to invoke the type of determined repression it had employed against the C.N.T. in 1931–3, Spain quickly moved into an era of unprecedented social chaos.

The spring of 1936 was consumed by a struggle for dominance within the Popular Front. On one side were the *Prietistas*, resorting to every possible stratagem to keep the *Caballeristas* from forcing them out of the leadership posts they held in the socialist hierarchy, and the left republicans, accepting every worker initiative and sponsoring radical social reform of their own in the hope that the intoxication of the proletariat would pass and it would allow itself to be reincorporated into a progressive bourgeois Republic. The other side was less united. It included the *Caballeristas*, who urged the workers to take the law into their own hands and sought alliances with the non-socialist proletarian groups and the anarcho-syndicalists, who rejected the advances of the *Caballeristas* and kept their own counsel, but at the same time asserted their greater militancy by especially active participation in the strikes that shook Spain. Somewhere in the middle was the rapidly growing communist party, attempting to maintain amicable relations with all leftist factions while stealing some of their following and reserving its thunder for the momentarily unassailable task of driving the centrists and rightists permanently from political life. In balance, the *Prietistas–Azañistas* controlled the cabinet and retained influence in the Cortes; the *Caballeristas*–anarcho-syndicalists controlled the streets.

What would have been the outcome of the struggle if it had been allowed to play out its course? One can only guess, since so many contradictory signs existed. At least three scenarios seem possible. In the first, the *Caballeristas*, increasingly aware that, rather than establishing themselves as the leaders of a grand alliance of workers, they were being stymied by the enmity of the anarcho-syndicalists and by the duplicity of the communists, would resume their ties with the *Prietistas* and the bourgeois republicans, whose good faith was meanwhile being proved by their willingness to accept radical social reform. The occasion for this reversal of policy might be a new attempt at insurrection by the anarcho-syndicalists (despite the C.N.T.–F.A.I.'s silence on this issue in 1936, one can scarcely believe, in view of both its past history and future attitudes, that it had rejected the possibility), which the *Caballeristas* – always more ready with rhetoric than with action – would not find it in their hearts to support. Signs that point in this direction include the bitter street clashes between C.N.T. and socialist militants in the Malaga strike of June, and Largo Caballero's decision during the same month to accept a state-sponsored settlement of the important construction strike in Madrid despite the C.N.T.'s insistence that the strike continue.

In the second possible scenario, the increasing collapse of the economy under the pressure of worker demands would undo the formal gains granted to the proletariat and spur it on to still greater militancy. The government would try to check this by mild localised repression, which would only have the effect of driving the *Caballeristas* and anarcho-syndicalists closer together, perhaps even to the point of a joint revolt which might or might not be successful. Signs that point in this direction include the near-certainty of a major attempt by the peasantry to seize land in the autumn of 1936, which the government would have been forced to resist more than it did the land seizures that had occurred in Badajoz shortly after the Popular Front had come to office, but which it might not have used to institute a general repression.

In the third possible scenario, the *Prietistas*, having been driven from the posts they retained in the socialist hierarchy at the party congress scheduled for October, and deeply disturbed by the increasing social anarchy,[21] would have formally split with the *Caballeristas* to form an independent democratic socialist party. This, together with the growing economic collapse and rising proletarian militancy, would have given the left republicans the courage to risk a union of all moderate forces from the progressive wing of the C.E.D.A. to the *Prietistas*, whose purpose would be the repression of open worker violence without, however, complete abandonment of social reform. Signs that point in this direction include the left republican government's attempt to exclude from the legislation it presented to the Cortes some of the shibboleths it had relied upon in 1931–3, the respect many of its leaders felt for the liberal Catholic Giménez Fernández, and the open for a 'Republican dictatorship' of such figures as Miguel Maura and Felipe Sánchez Román.

None of these scenarios were played out, either in their entirety or in their many possible variations,[22] because to large portions of the population the overriding reality seemed the imminent collapse of Spanish society. Political institutions to which they might turn for defence were steadily being destroyed. In February and March, under the pressure of mob action, hundreds of municipal councils were unseated and replaced by leftist 'executive committees'; in April, legal chicanery had been employed to oust the moderate president, Alcalá Zamora; in early July, the communist party introduced legislation to the Cortes for the proscription of the C.E.D.A. and other parties not allied to the Popular Front on the grounds that they were 'fascist'; in mid-July, the leading rightist spokesman, Calvo Sotelo, was murdered by leftist extremists.[23] Social order was also increasingly threatened. The number of industrial strikes in the six months that followed the February elections was far greater than in the whole of any previous year; in agriculture, conditions of latent civil war existed; street clashes between gangs of falangist and working-class gunmen terrorised the cities. It was not the wealthy or the middle classes alone that were alarmed. Large numbers of peasant proprietors, clerks, and all the other millions of unorganised, religiously oriented, socially fatalistic poor for whom the English language unfortunately lacks an adequate term, also could not be reassured by the intermittent signs of moderation in the left republican government or the disunity that existed among the working-class movements. Nor could they be concerned, in their growing panic, with the fact that the centre-right governments of 1933–6 bore heavy responsibility for what was happening because of their insensitivity to the plight of the landless peasants and workers.

Had the left been less preoccupied with its own internal divisions and acted more vigorously against what was ultimately the most important political institution in Spain, the army, those who feared the Popular Front would nevertheless have been forced to endure it. As it was, the increasing chaos served to accomplish the difficult feat of overcoming the loss of self-confidence the army had suffered as a result of the failure of Primo de Rivera's experiment, as well as its fear that a new revolt might produce the same disastrous results as had Sanjurjo's insurrection of 1932.[24] The preparations of a group of generals who had been planning a rising since April became complete in late June when Franco ended his long procrastination and decided to join them. The assassination of Calvo Sotelo on 13 July provided an emotionally charged issue under whose cover they could act. Garrisons in Morocco revolted on the seventeenth, and were supported by risings in Spain on the eighteenth.

The left republicans attempted to stave off defeat or civil war with a variation of the third scenario described above. On the evening of 18 July they formed a cabinet, headed by the most moderate elements in the Popular Front (e.g. Martínez Barrio and Sánchez Román), whose purpose was to seek a government of national concentration in which the rebels would be represented. An initiative that might have succeeded prior to the rising now failed because the insurgent generals refused co-operation and the urban masses began to demonstrate against the 'treason' of the bourgeoisie. Left with no other alternative, Azaña turned over power on the nineteenth to a new cabinet which authorised the arming of the people. Since the defence of the Republic now depended primarily on the masses, the long struggle for predominance within the Popular Front was finally settled. The *Caballeristas* and anarcho-syndicalists were the heroes of the day; the bourgeois parties and the *Prietistas* were reduced to impotence as social revolution filled the political vacuum that had been created by the military insurrection.

Although a new political constellation would arise as military defeats discredited the extreme militants and as the supremely realistic communists increased their strength, the basic position of the Spanish left had been permanently altered. If it had finally overcome its central weakness of the past by rooting itself among a large proportion – probably the majority – of the population, dominance within it had passed from the bourgeoisie to the proletariat. In part this resulted from the divisions that the bourgeoisie had created in their ranks over the religious and regional issues. Fundamentally, however, it only illustrated the evolution that almost inevitably must occur in all nations whose economies are so poor and whose ruling classes have been so unresponsive to human needs as to deprive large numbers of their inhabitants of most of the benefits of society.

SUGGESTIONS FOR FURTHER READING

To understand the background of republican politics, the following are especially important: Raymond Carr, *Spain 1808–1939* (Oxford, 1966); Juan Linz, ' The Party System of Spain: Past and Future', in Seymour M. Lipset and Stein Rokkan (eds), *Party Systems and Voter Alignments: Cross-National Perspectives* (New York, 1967); Miguel Martínez Cuadrado, *Elecciones y partidos políticos en España 1868–1931* (Madrid, 1969).
As to general histories of the republican era itself, two outstanding studies from the rightist point of view, both entitled *Historia de la Segunda República Española*

and both in four volumes, have been written by José Plá (Barcelona, 1940) and by Joaquín Arrarás (Madrid, 1964–8). Gabriel Jackson, *The Spanish Republic and the Civil War* (Princeton, 1965) is the best presentation from the left republican viewpoint; Antonio Ramos Oliveira, *Politics, Economics and Men of Modern Spain* (London, 1946), is an extremely useful socialist account; Carlos Rama, *La crisis española del siglo XX* (Mexico, 1960), is a provocative synthesis sympathetic to the anarcho-syndicalists.

Important monographs on two of the major problems that confronted the Republic are Stanley G. Payne, *Politics and the Military in Modern Spain* (Stanford and Oxford, 1967), and Edward Malefakis, *Agrarian Reform and Peasant Revolution in Spain: Origins of the Civil War* (New Haven, Conn., 1970). Gerald Brenan's classic *The Spanish Labyrinth* (Cambridge, 1940) has many sensitive insights into the working-class movements. José Peirats, *La CNT en la revolución española*, 3 vols (Toulouse, 1951–3), is indispensable for the anarcho-syndicalists. Burnett Bolloten, *The Grand Camouflage* (London, 1961), and Franz Borkenau, *The Spanish Cockpit* (London, 1937), are the best accounts of the social revolution that occurred in the first days of the Civil War. The pivotal figure of the republic, Azaña, is best studied in his *Obras completas*, edited in four volumes by Juan Marichal (Mexico, 1966–8). For the elections held between 1931 and 1936, we must rely on Jean Becarud, *La Segunda República Española* (Madrid, 1967).

NOTES

1. Juan J. Linz, 'The Party System of Spain: Past and Future', in Seymour M. Lipset and Stein Rokkan (eds), *Party Systems and Voter Alignments: Cross-National Perspectives* (New York, 1967), p. 210. Manipulation of voting results in rural areas and the habitual abstention of anarcho-syndicalists help explain this startling fact.

2. Angel Ossorio y Gallardo, as quoted, in José Antonio Balbontín, *La España de mi experiencia* (Mexico, 1952), p. 207. On the complex transition from monarchy to Republic, see Raymond Carr, *Spain 1808–1939* (Oxford, 1966), pp. 591–602, and Stanley G. Payne, *Politics and the Military in Modern Spain* (Stanford, California, 1967), pp. 224–65.

3. Electoral statistics are taken from Linz, op. cit. p. 235, and Jean Bécarud, *La Segunda República Española* (Madrid, 1967).

4. Maura's memoirs – *Así cayó Alfonso XIII* (Barcelona, 1966) – are silent on this complete misreading of the *immediate* state of opinion (in the long run his assumption was not necessarily inaccurate, as was to be proved by the elections of 1933).

5. A study of the rhetoric used by radical candidates in the June elections would help settle the dispute over the extent to which they were elected by conservative voters who had no other place to turn, rather than as leftists. In fact, a detailed history of the radical party is one of the major needs of twentieth-century Spanish historiography.

6. Balbontín, op. cit. pp. 227–8.

7. Party strength from 1931 to 1933 was approximately as follows: left republicans 133 (radical socialists 59, Republican Action 26; *Esquerra* 32; O.R.G.A. 16); socialists 117; radicals 93. Various centrists or centre-leftists held about 70 seats, and various rightists or centre-rightists 60.

8. I consider the anti-clerical struggle largely symbolic because the secularisation of the Spanish mentality at which it aimed could have been accomplished only over the course of several generations, and its success or failure would depend on many factors other than the legislation that could be introduced in 1931–3.

9. The restrictive hiring practices imposed by the Municipal Labour Act, while strengthening the unions, caused serious economic disruption in areas like Galicia and Catalonia, where municipalities were small in size and contained insufficient reserves of manpower to draw on. As to the Agrarian Reform Law, certain technical errors that resulted from excessive socialist zeal produced the ironic effect that perhaps three times as many small owners as large were threatened with expropriation. The technical incompetence of the left was not the least of the reasons for its ultimate failure.

10. The notoriety of the large estates in southern Spain, and the excessive financial power concentrated in the hands of a few bankers and industrialists frequently obscure the fact that Spain was (and remains) to a considerable extent a country of small shops, factories and farms whose owners were engaged in their own private class struggle with their handful of increasingly militant employees.

11. Average unemployment rose from 446,000 to 796,000 between 1932 and 1936. Agricultural unemployment usually accounted for slightly less than two-thirds of the total.

12. The official agricultural strike statistics, for example, report 85 strikes in 1931, 198 in 1932 and 448 in 1933. The level of violence also increased. A superficial count in the Madrid press of rural conflicts in which deaths occurred found 9 such incidents in 1931, 15 in 1932 and 26 in 1933.

13. The 1933 elections are the least well studied of the republican elections. Scattered sources suggest that the former Azaña parties won 39 per cent of the vote, not a particularly great drop from their 1931 totals, given the fact that radical votes made up a large proportion of the ballots which had gone to San Sebastian candidates in that year.

14. On the growing split between the Basques and the rest of the right, see Gabriel Jackson, *The Spanish Republic and the Civil War* (Princeton, 1965), pp. 141–2.

15. There were between 60 and 65 rightist deputies in the constituent Cortes, depending on how some of the independents are classified. In the Cortes of 1933–6, the officially leftist parties had 88 deputies at the start and 110 after Martínez Barrio joined them in May 1934. As to the greater unity of the Azaña coalition, one need only contrast its protracted stability with the frequent cabinet changes that plagued the centre–right coalition of 1933–6.

16. Even in agriculture, where employer retaliation was harshest, pay scales did not generally fall to anything approaching their pre-republican levels until well *after* the Socialist unions had precipitated their own destruction by their adventurous policies of June and October 1934. In some cases, as among railway workers, wages actually increased in 1934.

17. To what extent did the socialists really believe that the C.E.D.A. would so act? It is impossible to doubt that their endlessly repeated rhetoric and the course of events in other countries convinced many (though perhaps not most, if the lukewarmness of numerous industrial locals is any indication) of their followers and a majority of their new leaders of the immediacy of danger. Nevertheless, much evidence, including a remarkable article by Luís de Araquistáin in *Foreign Affairs* of April 1934, suggests that when the rhetoric was first unleashed, at least, an offensive rather than defensive spirit predominated.

18. Although a handful of leaders were condemned to death, all but two sentences were commuted (despite C.E.D.A. protests) by Alcalá Zamora and Lerroux. There was nothing like the white terror unleashed against unsuccessful worker revolts in post-First World War Europe, or against the Parisian workers in 1848 or 1871.

19. Seven of the ten provinces in Old Castile and León had abstention rates of more than 30 per cent in 1936, as opposed to only one province in 1931 and two in 1933.

20. The communist party, despite a promising start in 1921, remained relatively unimportant until 1934–5 when the polarisation of society after Asturias offered it a second chance. Since Comintern policy finally began to correspond to Spanish realities, this second opportunity was used more effectively than the first, though the party was still small on the eve of the civil war.

21. Prieto's editorials in *El Liberal* of Bilbao during the spring of 1936 are perhaps the most eloquent testimony we have of the increasing desperation felt by men of reason before the rising tide of violence.

22. Gerald Brenan, *The Spanish Labyrinth* (Cambridge, 1960), p. 305, suggests that Largo Caballero may have been deliberately trying to provoke a military rising in the expectation that it would follow the course of Sanjurjo's 1932 revolt – i.e. its failure would lead to a shift to the left which would bring his faction power.

23. These actions unquestionably constituted a far greater break with political continuity and democratic practice than had occurred after the centre-right took power in November 1933.

24. Only the profound radicalisation of the Republic could have reunited the long-divided right. Given Franco's hesitations in 1936, for example, it is doubtful that this decisive figure would have thrown his weight behind an insurrection against a progressive but legalistic government like that of Azaña in 1931–3.

4. The Parties of the Right and the Republic

RICHARD ROBINSON

THE purpose of this essay is to explain and assess the role played by the parties of the right in the political history of Spain during the Second Republic (April 1931–July 1936), and to weigh the responsibility of the right for the outbreak of the Civil War. As will be seen, the essay seeks to explode the popular myth, still quite common even in historical circles outside Spain, that the burden of blame for the causation of the Civil War lies primarily with the right. The evidence demonstrates that the right was not simply, as many used to think, a monolithic bloc of more or less fascist reactionaries who were bent on destroying a progressive democratic Republic and on thwarting the desires of the vast majority of the Spanish people. On the contrary it appears that the socialist movement was primarily responsible for undermining the democratic system and leaving the right the stark choice between extinction and violent resistance. To say this does not of course imply that democracy was, is and always will be unworkable in Spain, nor that the Civil War was engineered by some sinister foreign conspiracy.

The history of the Republic presents a bewildering kaleidoscope of events to the reader. The period from April 1931 to July 1936 has therefore here been somewhat arbitrarily divided into six phases in the hope of providing a clear understanding of the stages in the development of the parties of the right and their responses to events. The analysis of the right's part in the Republic is prefaced by a brief account of the right as it existed before 1931. This part of the essay, taken in conjunction with the section following the main survey, which explains the sources of ideological inspiration for the right-wing parties and gives some idea of their social bases, is intended to deepen the reader's knowledge of the various groups, as well as to provide useful background information for the study of the politics of nationalist Spain. The essay ends with a final assessment of the right's share of responsibility for the advent of civil war.

In any study of a modern historical subject the definition of political terms presents problems. In this essay 'the right' is taken to mean those parties and individuals who saw the defence of religious interests as their fundamental political task – the definition generally used by right-wing Spaniards themselves in the 1930s. Though the attitude to religious issues was the principal dividing line in the politics of the time, the definition becomes a little blurred on occasion, particularly when it is necessary to deal with Catholic parties which had non-Spanish nationalist aspirations or with ultra-nationalist groups which subordinated religion to Spanish nationalism. Nevertheless the basic definition of a party of the right as one which stoutly defended the church as well as other causes is the most convenient one, and, in terms of the Spain of the 1930s, the most correct.

When King Alfonso XIII left Madrid for exile on 14 April 1931 and the Provisional Government of the Republic found itself unexpectedly in power, it would hardly be an exaggeration to say that no properly organised political party of the right existed in Spain. The strength – or rather weakness – of the right was dissipated among several different groups. For the sake of convenience, brevity and clarity, these right-wing groups may be categorised as follows: 'traditionalists', 'social Catholics', 'authoritarian Alfonsine monarchists' and 'liberal Catholics'. Who were these people and what did they represent?

The 'traditionalists' were the heirs and perpetuators of nineteenth-century Carlism, a movement of die-hard Catholic reaction in the provinces of northern and eastern Spain against the 'anti-Spanish' ideas of enlightenment, religious tolerance and centralised bureaucratic rule which had entered the country from France in the later part of the eighteenth century. The movement had come into existence in the 1830s to uphold the claims of Don Carlos, younger brother of King Ferdinand VII, and unsuccessfully to oppose changes made in the laws of succession by this monarch which permitted the 'usurpation' of the throne by his infant daughter Isabella. From the 1830s the Isabelline monarchy represented for Carlists rule by the supporters of the politico-religious sin of liberalism: thus the schism within the ruling Bourbon family and the clash of ideologies became intertwined. After defeat in the Second Carlist War in the 1870s the movement went into sharp decline. Essential support in Catalonia and then in the Basque provinces drifted away with the rise of regional nationalism in these areas, while the remaining Carlists fell out among themselves. Some remained loyal to their pretender before all else, some thought Carlist or 'traditionalist' principles of prime importance, and as the years passed other deviationist factions arose, so that by 1931 Carlism seemed a thing of the past, even if 'traditionalist principles' still held a certain fascination for some intellectuals.

Social Catholicism in its modern form may be said to have emerged in Spain in the first decade of the twentieth century, but for the most part the seed of social regeneration through the Catholic conception of social justice fell upon stony ground. Attempts to form Catholic trade unions to redeem the lower classes from the injustices of the oligarchic liberal system and to prevent their apostasy to the atheistic creeds of socialism and anarchism met with little success except in the regions of Castile and León. An attempt to start a social Catholic political movement in 1922 was still-born, if only because within months the parliamentary system was overthrown by a military *coup*. Nevertheless social Catholic ideas had by 1931 begun to take a hold among young Catholic intellectuals owing to the efforts of an energetic layman, Ángel Herrera, editor of the influential daily *El Debate*. Loyal to Alfonso XIII, social Catholic forces were, however, unlikely to make spectacular progress so long as the church remained tied to the extreme social conservatism of the ruling oligarchy upon whose support the monarchy depended.[1]

A third group of rightists active before the Republic may loosely be called the 'authoritarians'. Such people had been civilian supporters of the dictatorship of General Primo de Rivera, a pragmatic (if at times unpredictable) soldier who had believed it his duty in 1923 to close parliament in order to rescue Spain from the clutches of selfish professional politicians. Many of the 'men of goodwill' who served under him were, like his young and able finance minister, José Calvo Sotelo, former followers of the old conservative leader Antonio Maura. From Maura such people had learnt that Spain was in urgent need of 'regeneration' by a 'revolution from above' which would purge the liberal parliamentary monarchy of corruption. Unlike the aged Maura himself, these younger men were willing to give the general's methods a try. They were interested in getting things done in an efficient technocratic way, but they were not dogmatic anti-parliamentarians. When the dictator fell from power in January 1930, such people found themselves politically isolated because the king was trying to find a path back to constitutional parliamentary government. The former ministers of the dictatorship hoped for a solution which would combine parliamentary institutions with a strong executive power: to use a contemporary term, they were 'Gaullists' rather than 'fascists'. By the spring of 1931, however, their ideas were out of fashion and they were not helped by the foundation of the first 'fascist' group in Spain in April 1930, the rowdy but insignificant blue-shirted Legionaries of Spain, led by the paranoid neurologist Dr Albiñana.

Liberal Catholics who were active in politics between the end of Primo de Rivera's dictatorship and the departure of the king were a motley crew. From the fall of Primo de Rivera in January 1930 the king was desperately trying to win back the allegiance of the political establishment which had ruled Spain before 1923 and which had been mortally offended by the monarch's acceptance of military rule. Some of these old political notables were willing to take part in Alfonso's two transitional governments, headed in turn by General Berenguer and Admiral Aznar; others preferred to show their displeasure by boycotting these governments. That these old politicians can be labelled 'liberal Catholics' in 1930–1 when many of them twenty years earlier had favoured limiting the number of religious orders in Spain may seem surprising, yet the label can be justified when the views of the republican opposition to the monarchy are considered.

None of the old politicians wanted radically to alter the position of the church in Spanish society, whereas many of those who subscribed to the 'Pact of San Sebastian' in August 1930, which created the republican–socialist alliance, were bitterly anti-clerical. Anti-clericalism, if not anti-Catholicism, was by tradition an important tenet of belief – usually the most important – for a Spanish republican. By comparison, therefore, the old politicians who vacillated in their attitude towards Alfonso can be termed 'liberal Catholics'. Two representatives of the old oligarchy feared rather more for the future of their class and beliefs than did the rest. They were Niceto Alcalá Zamora, a former liberal minister, and Miguel Maura, a son of the former conservative leader; as the leaders of the new liberal republican right, they emerged as the figureheads of the anti-monarchist coalition. Having joined the republicans and socialists with the intention of putting the brakes on extremism in social and religious matters by leading the anti-monarchist movement, they made soothing pronouncements about the gradual separation of church and state by negotiation and envisaged the primate sitting in the upper house of their parliamentary Republic. Such pronouncements had their effect, for much of the electorally vital Catholic urban middle class voted republican in the municipal elections of 12

April 1931, thus precipitating the downfall of the Alfonsine monarchy. The first phase in the history of the Second Republic may be defined as the period between 14 April and 14 October 1931, that is to say from the time that the Provisional Government of the Republic assumed power until the day on which the two leading members of this government, Alcalá Zamora and Maura, resigned. As will be seen, by 14 October hopes of creating a moderate 'liberal Catholic' Republic had been irrevocably dashed. To show why the liberal Catholic experiment failed necessitates some account of the work of Alcalá Zamora as head of the Provisional Government and of Maura as minister of the interior. In this context it is essential to examine their relations with their ministerial colleagues and to study relations between the Provisional Government and the church, which was of course a very powerful institution in Spain.

The first government of the Republic was composed of representatives of an uneasy amalgam of forces which had come together in opposition to Alfonso. Of the twelve ministers, eight were decidedly left-wing and anti-clerical: three socialists and five members of bourgeois republican groups whose primary objective was the elimination of the influence of the church from Spanish society. The two liberal republican rightists, Alcalá Zamora and Maura, who advocated gradual and moderate changes, might have hoped to count on some support only from their two radical colleagues. Alejandro Lerroux, leader of the radical republican party, had by 1931 evolved from the position of chief anti-Catholic and social revolutionary demagogue which he had enjoyed in Spanish politics some twenty years before to a position in the centre of the political spectrum. The aged politician had been a convinced republican far longer than anyone else in the government and now that the Republic had at last arrived he was determined that it should take root in the country. Like the liberal rightists he and his radicals wanted to win over conservatives to the new regime by standing firm against revolutionary social change and measures which might unnecessarily inflame the feelings of good Catholics. Lerroux's laicist convictions, however, divided him somewhat from his liberal rightist colleagues.

The Republic had come to Spain as a consequence of the municipal elections held on 12 April which had resulted in victory for anti-monarchist candidates in the vast majority of provincial capitals. This shock for the king's ministers, together with demonstrations in Madrid and the unwillingness of the police and armed forces to act positively to uphold the monarchy, prompted the king's departure, even though the victory of monarchist candidates was assured in rural areas.[2] Because the republican–socialist coalition had won only a psychological and not a numerical victory the liberal rightists were able to make their cautious views prevail in the first days of the new regime. The Juridical Statute of 15 April was moderate and vague, though it specifically proclaimed complete freedom of religion, which had been prohibited by the Concordat and the former Constitution. The Statute was not so much an attack on the church as a statement of tolerant laicism. It was accepted as such by the liberal-minded papal nuncio, Mgr Tedeschini, who discreetly opened negotiations with a view to revising the legal position of the church now that its age-old protector and master, the monarchy, had disappeared.[3]

The ascendancy of the liberal rightists within the government did not however last long. On 11 May the burning of churches and other religious buildings by irresponsible revolutionary elements took place in Madrid after minor incidents had occurred following the inauguration of a monarchist club; the next day similar outbreaks took place in parts of southern and eastern Spain. Within the cabinet Maura, as minister of the interior, fought hard to persuade his colleagues to call out the police so that Catholic and conservative opinion should not be alienated, but to no avail. Alcalá Zamora vacillated while the anti-clericals refused to take action.[4] The episode shattered illusions. In the country Catholic opinion in general lost what confidence it had in the ability of the liberal rightists to defend religion; conservative laicists who feared disorder pinned their hopes on Lerroux, who as minister for foreign affairs had been fortuitously absent at the time.

Despite the church-burnings, the ending of compulsory religious instruction in the schools and other infringements of the Concordat, the nuncio and the Vatican did not turn against the Republic. Indeed, the expulsion of a bishop and then of the primate himself, the fiery Cardinal-Archbishop Segura of Toledo, were virtually condoned by the Vatican. Bishops declared their 'obedience to the constituted power' (i.e. to the Provisional Government) in accordance with Catholic doctrine and expressed their 'sincere desire not to create difficulties for the Republic'.[5] Laymen who went to Rome to advocate opposition to the Republic and its works were informed that such ideas were erroneous.[6] In short, the policy of the church was to do everything possible to maintain amicable relations with the new regime.

The next blow to the hopes of the liberal right for a negotiated revision of the position of the church was struck by the electorate in June when the deputies for the constituent assembly were chosen. The performance of the liberal right was very poor: well over 350 deputies were elected to the constituent Cortes for the other parties supporting the government, but the liberal right found itself with only two dozen seats. Alcalá Zamora and Maura were therefore the prisoners of their anticlerical ministerial colleagues. They could hope for little support from outside the government bloc, where only two equally small heterogeneous parliamentary groups existed: the twenty-four 'Agrarians' and the fifteen members of the 'Basque–Navarrese Coalition'.[7] The trend of events soon became apparent when the left-wing partners in the coalition government rejected a draft constitution which proclaimed freedom of religion. In mid-August a new draft, with much more stringent religious clauses, was drawn up by a parliamentary committee on which determined anti-Catholics were in a majority.

Breaking point came for the Catholic deputies early in October when the religious clauses were debated. The most notorious of these was Article 26, which said that the ecclesiastical budget must end within two years and stated, in effect, that the Society of Jesus would be dissolved in Spain and its property confiscated. Other religious orders were to be subject to a special law forbidding them to engage in trade, industry or education. Furthermore, Article 48 stated that laicist primary education would be compulsory. The day of reckoning dawned on 14 October: after an all-night session of heated argument Article 26 was passed by the Cortes, but among those voting against it were Alcalá Zamora and Maura (now respectively leaders of the progressive and conservative republican parties). They resigned and the second government of the Republic was formed by Azaña, the passionate anti-clerical who had declared that Spain had ceased to be Catholic. Alcalá Zamora and Maura stayed on in the Cortes, but any chance of a harmonious negotiated solution to the all-important religious question was now dead – as indeed was the cause of liberal Catholicism.

The second phase in the history of the Republic may be said to have begun on 14 October 1931 with the formation of Azaña's republican-socialist coalition government and the withdrawal from the constitutional debates in the Cortes of the two right-wing groups, the 'agrarians' and the 'Basque–Navarrese', who took the initiative in opposing what they saw as an anti-religious constitution. The right-wing opposition to the government was henceforth to be led by men who had never been party to the anti-monarchist coalition of April 1931, the most prominent among whom was the young social Catholic José María

Gil Robles. This second phase of republican history may be said to have ended on 10 August 1932 with the failure of a military *coup*.

Who were the 'agrarians' and the 'Basque–Navarrese', and what political forces did they represent? The 'agrarian' group was a parliamentary amalgam improvised from disparate political forces. Half the deputies in the group were ex-monarchist liberal Catholics who joined together to defend the church, the rights of property and the interests of Castilian wheat-growers. Two were traditionalists, while the rest adhered to a new organisation started by the social Catholic Herrera in April 1931 with the name of National Action. It was 'not a new political party' but rather 'an electoral organisation to bring together the elements of order'. Although people still loyal to Alfonso XIII, who were advised by the exiled monarch to accept the new republican government, could and did join, National Action was 'not a monarchist organisation'; it existed to defend religion and Catholic social ideals and made 'the consolidation of the *de facto* regime' (i.e. the Republic) 'a patriotic imperative'.[8]

The 'Basque–Navarrese' parliamentary group was the fruit of a tactical alliance made for the elections of June 1931 between the Basque nationalist party and traditionalists in the provinces of Biscay, Guipúzcoa, Álava and Navarre. The Basque nationalist party dated back to the first decade of the century and was formed from former Carlists who came to the conclusion that the Carlist movement was no longer useful for the defence of the Basques' ancient rights and customs (*fueros*) against governments in Madrid. It was now led by a young footballer, José Antonio de Aguirre, who described it as a party of 'virile and integral Catholicism'. It could therefore be classified as a party of the right, but because its ultimate aim was 'full sovereignty' for 'Euzkadi' (the Basque country)[9] it cannot properly be called a party of the *Spanish* right. Its tactical allies, the traditionalists of Navarre, saw themselves as stalwart defenders of the church, whether their allegiance was still to the pretender or simply to Christ the King. After the 'accession' of a new pretender, Alfonso Carlos, the traditionalists buried their factional differences and, faced with an 'atheistic' Republic, reorganised themselves in 1932 in the Carlist–Traditionalist Communion for the defence of God, country, king and *fueros*. The *fueros* of the traditionalists were not, however, to be confused with Basque nationalist ideas on self-determination, and the alliance could not last long. 'Basque Nationalism represented centrifugal traditionalism and the Navarrese centripetal traditionalism. The former wanted not to depend on Spain for anything; the latter wanted the whole of Spain to depend on them.'[10]

The complete text of the Constitution was not approved by the Cortes until 9 December 1931. Alcalá Zamora was then elected the first president of the Republic and Azaña formed a new republican–socialist coalition government without Lerroux's radicals. However, the forces represented by the 'agrarians' and 'Basque–Navarrese' had already begun a nation-wide campaign for the revision of the Constitution on 15 October, a campaign the motive power for which was provided by National Action under the leadership of Gil Robles. The campaign received the indirect blessing of the bishops just before Christmas when they collectively criticised republican governments for rejecting a negotiated settlement of religious issues and condemned the Constitution as an outrage against the church. Nevertheless the bishops stressed that they were not opposed to the republican form of government *as such* but only to the legislation enacted. All Catholics were asked to unite, or at least work together, to get the laws of the land changed by legal means and not by violence.[11]

The non-violent revisionist campaign, with its frequent mass meetings, was an undoubted success. Catholic right-wing opinion was mobilised and organised as never before in numerous local political groupings adhering to the organisation led by Gil Robles, which was forced by government decree to change its name in April 1932 from National Action to Popular Action. Moreover, Azaña's government unintentionally contributed to the growth of the Catholic right-wing reaction in two ways. On the one hand the government set about enforcing the anti-clerical provisions of the Constitution by secularising cemeteries, legalising divorce and civil marriage and dissolving the Society of Jesus, thus keeping religious issues to the fore. On the other hand the dictatorial Law for the Defence of the Republic of October 1931, which empowered the minister of the interior to disregard civil rights guaranteed in the Constitution whenever he wished, was applied in a partisan and haphazard manner, thus seemingly lending credence to right-wing propaganda that Spanish Catholics were the victims of persecution by freemasons in the government.

By launching an attack on the church the left-wing government had aroused powerful passions and given rise to an increasingly formidable right-wing political organisation. From the spring of 1932 opposition increased still further when debates began on a statute of autonomy for Catalonia and a law of agrarian reform. As the debates dragged on in the Cortes the government ran into greater difficulties, because many republicans were uneasy about handing over some of the powers of the central government to a region in which the dominant political figure, Maciá, was a known advocate of independence. Similarly, many republicans were wary of plans for agrarian reform which were bound to affect the rights of property-owners. Although social Catholics were not opposed to agrarian reforms, and although they and the traditionalists favoured decentralisation 'within the unity of Spain', the rightwing groups often found themselves in agreement with radical and conservative republicans in opposition to what they denounced as 'separatist' or 'socialist' measures. The parties of the centre and right were also becoming alarmed at the government's apparent inability to keep order. Therefore the Catalan and agrarian issues stiffened and broadened opposition to the government, though it must be noted that Basque nationalist support for Catalan autonomy brought the 'Basque–Navarrese Coalition' to an end and this issue also estranged the Catalan Regionalist League – a conservative liberal Catholic regional party founded in 1901 – from the Spanish right.

By July 1932 certain members of the officer corps had become convinced that Azaña's government was no longer representative of public opinion; the most prominent of these was General Sanjurjo, who as director-general of the Civil Guard had done nothing to support the monarchy in April 1931. Traditionally officers who came to such a conclusion felt it their duty to overturn the government so that the national will could have a chance to express itself, and Sanjurjo was no exception. Although Lerroux would not conspire and Gil Robles publicly stated that military action was quite unjustifiable,[12] Sanjurjo nevertheless made contact with Alfonsine monarchists (some of whom were members of Popular Action) and with officers disgruntled by Azaña's military reforms. Sanjurjo and General Barrera (the official leader of the plotters) did not intend to rise against the Republic as such, but they did want to oust the existing government to save Spain from 'dismemberment', disorder and the socialists and to save the army from humiliation by civilians. The coup on 10 August was an abysmal failure in Madrid and in Seville the garrison deserted Sanjurjo's cause before midnight. Azaña's prestige rose and for a time it looked as though the generals had undone all the careful work of legalists like Gil Robles.

The third phase in the history of the Republic began with the failure of the military coup of 10 August 1932 and may be said to have ended on 3 December 1933 with the defeat at the polls of the forces represented in Azaña's coalition government and the victory of the forces led by

C

Lerroux and Gil Robles. This period saw the decline and fall of Azaña's coalition under pressure from outside opposition and internal decomposition. It saw too a diversification and realignment among the right-wing forces which in no way sapped their strength because Azaña and his colleagues, after successfully pushing the Catalan Statute of Autonomy and the Law on Agrarian Reform through the Cortes in the wake of Sanjurjo's failure, rashly brought religious issues to the fore again in 1933. Azaña also to some extent sabotaged the Republic as a form of government by attempting to equate the form of government, not only with the Constitution of 1931, but also with the controversial complementary legislation which his coalition sponsored.

Although the aim of Barrera and Sanjurjo had been to overthrow the government but not the Republic, Azaña nevertheless stated that their aim had been to 'oust the republican regime'.[13] Armed with the Law for the Defence of the Republic, Azaña had 145 suspected conspirators deported to the Spanish Sahara, an action which prompted Mussolini to exclaim: 'He has used my own methods!'[14] Three months after the attempted *coup* 5000 people were still detained, only 137 of whom had been tried.[15] Although very few members of Popular Action had had anything to do with the conspiracy and Gil Robles had opposed it, many of its branches were closed and its members arrested. Its meetings were still being banned well into 1933. The attempt by Azaña and the left-wing republicans, backed by the socialists, to identify their own legislation with the form of government – in other words, to brand anyone seeking to change their laws as an 'anti-republican' – became clearer in June 1933 when the Court of Constitutional Guarantees was set up: appeals against the constitutional validity of laws passed by the constituent Cortes lay outside the Court's jurisdiction.

It was in the atmosphere of repression following the attempted *coup* that Gil Robles set out to turn the amorphous organisation which was Popular Action into a homogeneous political party. The fact that a number of prominent members who were known monarchists had been involved in the plot culminating in the events of 10 August gave him his opportunity. From the start the organisation for the defence of religion and Catholic social ideals had two salient characteristics: one was its insistence on working within the existing legal framework and shunning violence as a political method; the other was its adherence to the Catholic political doctrine of 'accidentalism'. 'Accidentalism' meant that members had to obey the established form of government (in this case the Republic), but forms of government were of secondary (or 'accidental') importance compared with the fundamental (or 'essential') importance to be attached to legislation. This vital distinction may best be illustrated as follows: for someone like Gil Robles it was essential that the laws of the land should not conflict with the teachings of the church, but it did not much matter whether Spain was a monarchy or a republic.

The first stage on the road to Popular Action becoming a cohesive Catholic party, neither republican nor monarchist but accepting the Republic as the established form of government, was completed with the holding of an assembly of the movement in Madrid in October 1932. The outcome of the debates was a victory for the accidentalist and legalist policies of Gil Robles; those who would not undertake to forswear violence or to campaign for the return of the monarchy had to leave. In March 1933 Gil Robles achieved his goal when Popular Action and other groups with similar policies, such as the Valencian Regional Right, formed a nation-wide political confederation known as the C.E.D.A.; with its 735,000 members it was the biggest political party in Spain.[16] The Alfonsine monarchists ousted from Popular Action formed their own party early in 1933: Spanish Renovation. Under the leadership of a former conservative minister of the monarchy, Antonio Goicoechea, they hoped to profit from the reaction against Azaña's government, propagate authoritarian monarchist doctrines and make contacts in the army and with the Italian authorities with a view to overthrowing the Republic by force.[17] The party was never to be a great success.

As previously noted, Azaña's government received an injection of vigour by its suppression of the military movement of 10 August; but from the start of 1933 it was increasingly on the defensive. The first sign of impending doom for Azaña came with the suppression of an anarchist rising in January at Casas Viejas, after which republican Assault Guards shot a number of innocent inhabitants. It was not clear whether the officer had been acting on the orders of the government, but the radical and right-wing opposition turned the affair into a national scandal. They began deliberately to obstruct legislation in the Cortes and when the radicals and the right beat candidates of the governing parties in partial municipal elections in April they claimed that public opinion supported them. The government at this time was trying to get the Cortes to pass the Law on Religious Confessions and Congregations, based on a strict interpretation of Article 26 of the Constitution. Though the radicals, being laicists, grudgingly supported the government, the right-wing groups used obstruction against what they considered a further act of persecution introduced in an effort to revivify the government. Catholics said they were prepared to resort to passive resistance if the measure became law, which it did in June. However, threats of civil disobedience were not put to the test because Azaña's exhausted coalition at last disintegrated in September 1933 before the teaching ban on the orders was due to take effect.

Azaña's republican–Socialist government was succeeded by a republican coalition under the lifelong republican Lerroux. Lerroux's aim was to consolidate the Republic by applying the laws passed by Azaña's governments in a lenient manner so as to permit the C.E.D.A. to become the right-wing party in the Republic acting as a counterweight to the socialists. The socialists and left-wing republicans like Azaña were not, however, prepared to accept the C.E.D.A. as a right-wing republican party. Azaña affected to believe that the C.E.D.A. was a monarchist group hostile to the Republic,[18] although its leader had told the exiled king face to face that he would 'serve Spain within the Republic . . . even though this may be detrimental to the restoration of the monarchy'.[19] The socialists were even more determined opponents of Lerroux's policy of appeasing Catholic feelings: in September they announced the beginning of 'a new revolutionary phase' – which was only to be expected, because as early as November 1931 Largo Caballero had said that their exclusion from government would mean a switch to revolutionary methods, while dissolution of the Cortes would oblige them 'to proceed to civil war'.[20]

President Alcalá Zamora was anxious to dissolve the constituent Cortes quickly before the reaction against Azaña's work should turn into a reaction against the Republic itself. General elections were therefore held on 19 November 1933, with second contests where necessary on 3 December. The C.E.D.A., Spanish Renovation, the Traditionalist Communion and liberal Catholic 'agrarians' formed an electoral coalition, the 'Anti-Marxist Front', for the revision of the Constitution, the defence of agricultural interests and 'an absolute amnesty for all political offences'.[21] Alliances were made in some areas with radical and conservative republicans, and on 3 December these alliances were extended, the better to trounce the socialists. Since the elections were held in an atmosphere described by a socialist leader as one of 'full-scale civil war',[22] it was to be expected that Gil Robles, as leader of the right, should vie with socialists in making qualified threats. While denying that he was a 'fascist' who wanted to use violence, he advocated a

Catholic corporative state for Spain: 'We need complete power and this is what we demand. . . . Democracy is for us not an end, but a means for proceeding to the conquest of a new state. When the time comes parliament either agrees or we make it disappear.'[23]

The results of the elections proved very satisfactory for the right. The C.E.D.A., monarchists and agrarians together received 3,085,676 votes and the radicals 1,351,100; the total for all the left-wing parties together was 2,854,325 votes. All the parties in opposition to Azaña's government together got almost twice as many votes as those which had supported it. In terms of seats in the new Cortes the C.E.D.A. had 117 and the radicals 104.[24] Given the antipathy between the radicals on the one hand and the socialists and left-wing republicans on the other, Lerroux could only hope to govern with the support of C.E.D.A.

The fourth phase in the history of the Republic may be said to have lasted from the general elections of 1933 until the attempted revolution by the socialists and their allies early in October 1934, an episode which has justly been called 'the great divide in the history of the Republic and the prelude to the Civil War'.[25] This crucial stage in the evolution of the Republic witnessed some very important developments. The period saw the foundations laid for co-operation between the conservative laicist Lerroux and the Catholic Gil Robles, a development which brought about a real division between the accidentalist and monarchist parties of the right. After the elections Gil Robles steadily beat a retreat from the authoritarian tone of speeches delivered during the campaign. This period also saw the stark revelation of the attitudes of socialists and left-wing republicans towards the republican form of government and democratic methods; in this context it will be helpful to stray briefly from the main theme of the essay in order to be able properly to assess the responsibility of the main party of the right for the breakdown of the democratic system in Spain.

Lerroux formed a coalition government based on his own radical party with the participation of liberal Catholic elements, and presented it to the Cortes on 19 December 1933. His aim was to govern in such a way as to reconcile all Spaniards after the deep political divisions which had become apparent during the election campaign; since he wanted to make the C.E.D.A. the right-wing party of the Republic, he set about appeasing Catholic and conservative feelings by promising to modify Azaña's anti-clerical and social legislation without violating the Constitution. For the time being Gil Robles was content to let the radicals govern in this spirit and emphasised that he interpreted the result of the elections as a national vote of censure on the work of the constituent Cortes, but not as a vote against the republican form of government. He solemnly promised that his party would act 'with complete and absolute loyalty to a regime which the Spanish people has willed', thus committing the C.E.D.A. to the republicans' interpretation of the events of April 1931. The C.E.D.A. had, in fact, become a republican party in all but name. While still insisting that constitutional reform would have to come in time, he explicitly rejected any dictatorial solutions to the country's problems and argued that it was not yet time for the biggest parliamentary group to participate in government because Catholic sentiments were still too inflamed after Azaña's anti-Catholic measures.[26]

The acceptance of the Republic by Gil Robles and his willingness to put the C.E.D.A.'s votes at the disposal of the laicist republican Lerroux – even though such support was conditional upon Lerroux doing nothing to offend Catholics – left the monarchist parties aghast. The leading monarchist daily immediately accused Gil Robles of 'treachery', arguing that he had broken the electoral pact and had ratted on those who had voted for the C.E.D.A. because it was not a republican party.[27] Before the elections Gil Robles had sworn 'never to accept pacts or compromises of any kind' with people who had voted for Article 26 of the Constitution; yet now he was supporting a government most of whose members had done just this.[28] Alfonsine and Carlist monarchists still thought of overthrowing the Republic and in March 1934 a joint delegation went to Rome to enlist Italian aid; a pact was signed but it turned out to have almost no significance until July 1936. Carlists continued to drill their militiamen in Navarre, while Alfonsines hoped to find their shock-troops in a recently founded fascist organisation, the Falange, led by José Antonio Primo de Rivera, the eldest son of the former dictator.[29]

Paradoxically there was one thing upon which monarchists and left-wing republicans were agreed, and that was that the Republic in Spain was not just a form of government in which the head of state was a president and not a king. For both groups 'republicanism' was an ideology based on the principles of complete laicism, popular sovereignty and anti-militarism – principles permeating the Constitution of 1931 and its complementary laws. For Azaña, therefore, any attempt to reform the Constitution or undo the work of the constituent Cortes was by definition 'anti-republican'. Hence a Republic governed by a life-long republican needing the support of Catholic votes was for left-wing republicans quite unacceptable: it was 'a Republic imbued with monarchism' because the election results had put the clock back to the time before April 1931.[30] If Gil Robles were attempting to bring about a Catholic Republic, monarchists and the left were agreed that he was attempting the impossible because a Catholic Republic was for them a contradiction in terms.

Sooner or later Gil Robles, as leader of the biggest parliamentary group, was going to ask to govern, and this neither the left-wing republicans nor the socialists were prepared to allow. What they wanted was a democratic system which would somehow always provide them with a majority; if it did not, then the will of the electorate was to be ignored. Socialists, however, went a stage further than left-wing republicans when faced with what they liked to claim was the threat of 'fascist dictatorship' by Gil Robles; there was for them 'only one solution: the revolutionary dictatorship of the socialist party'.[31] Shielding themselves from reality with such emotional and illogical thoughts as 'an anti-Marxist front is a fascist front',[32] the forces of the left prepared to deal the idea of a democratic Republic open to all Spaniards a fatal blow. Gil Robles protested in vain that he preferred government by a bad parliament to government by a good *camarilla*.[33]

The attempted revolution finally came when Lerroux formed a government with three C.E.D.A. ministers (out of fourteen) in the first week of October 1934. In Madrid the socialist revolutionary general strike was a failure, while in Barcelona the Catalan State within a federal Republic proclaimed by the left-wing regional authorities at the behest of separatists lasted only ten hours – the Catalan government shared Azaña's interpretation of republicanism and in the spring had passed a law on farming leases which it refused to withdraw although it was found to be unconstitutional. The Basque nationalists, having failed to persuade the Cortes to pass their statute of autonomy, sympathised with the Catalan left and did nothing to help the legal government in Madrid. The left-wing republicans gave moral support to the revolutionaries by withdrawing recognition from Lerroux's legal government. In the mining region of Asturias, however, socialists, communists and anarcho-syndicalists kept a state of civil war going for a fortnight; the memory of Asturias was to cast its shadow over the remainder of the history of the Republic.

The fifth stage in the evolution of the Republic lasted from the failure of the October revolution of 1934 until 14 December 1935, the day on which President Alcalá Zamora excluded the C.E.D.A. from

power by getting his old political friend Portela to form a government
of the centre. During this period Spain was ruled by a succession of
governments, nearly all of them based on a radical–C.E.D.A. coalition
and all of them dependent on the votes of the C.E.D.A. for survival.
With the left largely suppressed after the October revolution, the
C.E.D.A. and the radicals collaborated more closely than ever to keep
the Republic going, to the despair of the monarchists in opposition.
The radical–C.E.D.A. partnership lasted until the radical party disintegrated and the president of the Republic thereafter denied the
C.E.D.A. its democratic right to form a government.

Lerroux's ideal was the consolidation of a Republic open to all
Spaniards, 'neither conservative, nor revolutionary, neither right-wing,
nor left-wing, but equidistant from all extremisms. . . . A tolerant, progressive, reforming Republic without violence.'[34] After the October
revolution the radicals had to work with the C.E.D.A. because they
were the only two effective forces left 'in the camp of the Republic'.
While hoping that 'a great party of the left' might be formed as a
counterweight to the C.E.D.A., for the time being Lerroux was content
to collaborate with the Catholic right.[35] Gil Robles wanted collaboration with the radicals to ensure stability and permit reconstruction to
take place while preparing for constitutional reform. Lerroux and Gil
Robles solemnised their will to work together at a ceremony in June
1935 known as the 'Governmental Pact of Salamanca'. As a veteran
adviser to King Alfonso said, 'the republican sincerity of Gil Robles
leaves no room for doubts. . . . Gil Robles, who could have hastened
the opportunity for a restoration after the last elections, has consolidated
the Republic.'[36]

Gil Robles not only disproved the allegations of the left regarding his
'monarchism'; he also disproved their charges that he hankered after
dictatorship. The ultimate aim of the C.E.D.A. remained the creation
of a Catholic corporative state, but its leader resisted any temptation to
introduce the new regime when the left was powerless after October
1934. He remained true to his earlier pronouncements: his party believed in legality. Monarchists who wanted the imposition of an authoritarian regime were reminded that the fall of the throne had followed
General Primo de Rivera's dictatorship; 'a new dictatorship could produce, after a period of tranquillity, social revolution'. Impatient members of his own youth movement were told firmly to guard against indiscipline and 'juvenile paroxysms'. As war minister from May till
December 1935 Gil Robles set about the urgent task of re-equipping

the armed forces, but he made it quite clear that he had not taken the ministry from any ulterior motives: 'The army's purpose is not to carry out any *coups d'état* nor to intervene in politics.'[37] Had Gil Robles not believed so strongly in legal and democratic methods republican democracy could well have ceased to exist in 1935.

Such scrupulous adherence to republican legality did not, however, seem to make any sense to the monarchist opposition led by Calvo Sotelo, who had returned from exile in the spring of 1934 after a general political amnesty. Calvo Sotelo believed that parliamentary government was workable only where there existed a consensus of opinion on fundamental questions of social and political life. This consensus had been finally destroyed by the left in October 1934: 'The possibility of parliamentary dialogue in Spain has disappeared. . . . Let us have no illusions.'[38] What Spain needed was the immediate imposition of an authoritarian regime, because Calvo Sotelo did not believe that Gil Robles could succeed in quelling the revolutionary threat by democratic means. As leader of the National Bloc – a movement created in December 1934 to co-ordinate the activities of Spanish Renovation, traditionalists and Albiñana's Legionaries – he insisted that Spain was really already living in a state of civil war; therefore 'either Marxism is extirpated, or Marxism destroys Spain'. However, until it could be proved to right-wing electors that the C.E.D.A. had failed, the National Bloc would have to remain 'an army in reserve'.[39]

1935 saw a succession of coalition governments led by Lerroux and later by the independent republican Chapaprieta. These coalitions were based on a parliamentary alliance known as 'the Four': the radicals, the C.E.D.A., the agrarians and the liberal-democrat republicans. The Spanish agrarian party, led by José Martínez de Velasco and representing Castilian landowners and wheat-growers, had been formed in January 1934 from liberal Catholic members in the earlier 'agrarian' parliamentary group, while the liberal-democrats of Melquíades Álvarez were a conservative laicist party with aims similar to the radicals. Co-operation between 'the Four' was generally good and ensured a certain basic political stability until the radical party disintegrated in November–December 1935 as a result of financial scandals involving leading members of the party. The C.E.D.A. had three ministers in the government from October 1934 until March 1935, five from May till September and three in Chapaprieta's smaller governments from September to December. 'The Four' agreed on a draft for constitutional revision in July which was to modify the religious clauses and create a second chamber, but constitutional reform could not be put to the Cortes before 9 December 1935 according to Article 125 of the Constitution. On this very day the coalition broke up, ostensibly over budgetary policy, and it was generally expected that Gil Robles and the C.E.D.A. would at last be called upon to form a government. Alcalá Zamora, however, wanted to be rid of Gil Robles, of whose political success he was jealous, and he gave power to Portela, an old politician without support. Confronted with this presidential *coup* Gil Robles stuck to legality: neither he nor the chief of staff, General Franco, would attempt the *coup d'état* which monarchists and some military men desired.[40]

Thus ended two years of rule by the parties of the centre supported by the C.E.D.A. which were – and are – known in left-wing circles as 'the black biennium'; yet, as has been said, 'it was a period of weak government rather than determined reaction'.[41] Politically, neither the C.E.D.A. nor the radicals violated the Constitution. Lerroux suspended parts of the Law on Religious Confessions and Congregations to avert the closure of all Catholic schools but the laicist educational system was not subverted; state schools continued to be built, if at a slower rate than under Azaña. The Catalan Statute was not repealed after the October rising but only suspended, despite monarchist pressure, and in April 1935 the government decreed the return of control over all local affairs, except public order, to Barcelona. Successive governments used the Law of Public Order – passed in 1933 by Azaña's government – to suspend civil rights in various parts of the country, but such action was certainly understandable, if not justifiable, when the legal government was faced with overt threats of revolution by strong forces on the left. Doubtless the repression of the rebellion in Asturias was not gentle, but it is an odd fact that when the left returned to power in 1936 no judicial action was taken against those who were allegedly responsible for the many atrocities upon which so much propaganda was based.

In social affairs the record of the coalition governments was scarcely creditable, but there were nevertheless some positive features. The network of courts of arbitration for fixing wages and settling disputes, which had almost become an adjunct of the socialist movement by 1933, largely disappeared in 1934–5; wages were cut and workers dismissed. However, efforts to resuscitate the system by Federico Salmón (C.E.D.A. minister of labour, May–December 1935) were sabotaged by the refusal of the socialist trade union to co-operate with him.[42] Salmón was also responsible for the first law to combat unemployment in June 1935, but the need for retrenchment largely nullified its effects, except in the building industry. As C.E.D.A. minister for agriculture (October 1934–March 1935) Manuel Giménez Fernández was responsible for legislation to protect the interests of smallholders and tenant-farmers, while he and his progressive republican predecessor not only continued to expropriate land under the law of 1932 but actually distributed more land to the landless than Azaña's governments.[43] However, Giménez Fernández's single-minded pursuit of social Catholic ideals incurred the wrath of the conservative wing of the C.E.D.A. led by Cándido Casanueva, which represented landowners' interests. When the agrarian Nicasio Velayos became minister in May 1935 land reform came to a halt and existing laws were not enforced. Though the need for retrenchment and frequent changes of ministers undoubtedly contributed to the failure of social reforms, the fundamental truth was that social Catholics were outnumbered by conservatives on the right.

The sixth and last phase in the history of the Republic lasted from the formation of Portela's government on 14 December 1935 until the outbreak of the Civil War (17–20 July 1936). After the sudden collapse of the radical party there was no effective force in the centre of the political spectrum: the Catholic and right-wing masses confronted the socialist masses. The efforts of Portela and President Alcalá Zamora artificially to create a political buffer between them was a failure and the elections of February 1936 gave victory to the left. Left-wing republicans then governed in the name of the Popular Front but were unable to control their revolutionary socialist allies and therefore quite failed to keep order. In this situation of growing anarchy the initiative on the right passed out of the hands of the legalist Gil Robles, and in mid-July the left-wing republican government found itself faced with a military rising which it could not subdue. Thereafter Spain was divided into two armed camps: the Republic of the republicans came effectively to an end when the revolutionary organisations took control in the 'republican' zone.

The campaign preceding the elections on 16 February was waged in a pre-revolutionary atmosphere. Despite the serious threat posed by the left, the 'anti-revolutionary' parties were unable to agree on a common electoral programme and failed to form a truly united front; the political composition of the 'anti-revolutionary' lists of candidates varied from one constituency to another. The C.E.D.A., by far the biggest party, was the mainstay of the various coalitions, allying in some places with monarchists and in others with agrarians, conservative and radical republicans and Portela's Centre, which was desperate for votes.

In the event of victory Gil Robles promised strong and energetic government, but not dictatorship.[44] Monarchists of the National Bloc, who campaigned on their own against democracy and the Republic, demanded dictatorship. In the event of defeat for the right, Calvo Sotelo announced that the army – 'the nation in arms' – would be justified in rising against an anti-patriotic government.[45] The leader of the Falange, which did not join the 'anti-revolutionary' coalitions, declared that his group would disregard a result 'dangerously contrary to the eternal destinies of Spain'.[46] Such views were matched on the other side by Largo Caballero's statement that, if the right won, the socialists would have to 'proceed to declared civil war'.[47]

Seventy per cent of the electorate voted on 16 February in a tense atmosphere. According to the figures of the provincial electoral committees the 'anti-revolutionary' candidates obtained 4,570,744 votes to the 4,356,559 cast for the candidates of the Popular Front. Candidates of Portela's Centre got a further 340,073 and the Basque nationalists, who had refused to ally with anyone else, 141,137. In terms of seats in the Cortes, however, the workings of the electoral system gave victory to the left, with 264 deputies, compared with 144 for the parties of the right, 96 of whom were deputies of the C.E.D.A. The parties of the centre – including the Basque nationalists as well as candidates who had fought in alliance with the right, such as the radicals and the Catalan League – had 64 deputies in all.[48] Thus, although the left-wing coalition won, more votes were cast for the parties of the right even though the anarchists did not abstain to the same degree as they had in 1933.

After the polls closed on 16 February rioting broke out in many parts of the country. This prompted Gil Robles, Franco and Calvo Sotelo to press Portela to declare martial law so as to guarantee public order and ensure that the votes cast were fairly scrutinised, but Portela was overcome by defeatism and resigned as soon as he could. Azaña returned to power on 19 February to find, as he put it, 'a country abandoned by the authorities'.[49] When the new Cortes met the left proceeded to unseat some right-wing deputies on very questionable evidence of electoral malpractice; the elections in two provinces were declared null and void, but when new elections were held in May violence from the extreme left assured left-wing candidates of victory. The left ended up with 277 deputies to the right's 131. President Alcalá Zamora, whose dissolution of the Cortes in January had given the left its victory, was nevertheless dismissed from office in April by the votes of the left on the grounds that the dissolution had not been justified, even though the left had been pressing him to dissolve the Cortes for the previous two years! In May Azaña was elected president of the Republic and government was entrusted to the incompetent hands of Casares Quiroga. From 16 February lawlessness increased in Spain. Rioting, political assassinations, church-burning, seizures of property and revolutionary strikes became commonplace and the left-wing republican government seemed incapable of doing anything about the illegal activities of the extreme left. Up to 15 June 269 people were killed and a further 1287 injured in the disorder; 160 churches were totally destroyed and partial or attempted destruction of another 251 had taken place. There had been 113 general strikes, offices of political parties and newspapers had been wrecked or stormed and many bombs had exploded. The government had taken emergency powers but had used these in partisan fashion against the right and not against the extreme left. Gil Robles told the government: 'You have exercised power arbitrarily, but, moreover, with absolute, with total inefficacy.'[50] In this situation a 'fascist' reaction set in, for which Gil Robles blamed governmental inaction in the face of a revolutionary threat coupled with persecution of rightists.[51] The explanation for the growth of 'fascism' since the elections given by the socialist Prieto, it may be noted, put the blame squarely on the doings of revolutionary socialists and the prevalence of anarchy.[52]

After Azaña's return to power in February the policy of Gil Robles had been to stiffen the government's will to resist disorder and to cooperate with it for this purpose; in other respects he wanted the C.E.D.A. to play the part of a normal constitutional opposition in the Cortes. He hoped Azaña would break off relations with the extreme left and 'turn the government towards the centre'. It was necessary 'to reinforce Azaña's authority' so that he could restore order: 'The resources of government are very great, and when they are well used there is nothing to fear.'[53] The alternative, he warned, was civil war, because one half of Spain would not allow itself to be trampled on by revolutionaries. If order were not restored rightists would desert legalist parties like his own, because such parties would be powerless to protect their rights as citizens.[54] Gil Robles therefore wanted 'a very extensive concentration of non-Marxist forces to oppose the revolution in relentless fashion within the regime'; in short, 'a government of national understanding, strong and authoritarian'.[55] In April and May talks went on behind the scenes to try to bring about such a solution. The proposed leader was the parliamentary socialist Prieto, but he did not have the support of the socialist masses and members of the C.E.D.A.

were hostile to collaboration with a leader of the 1934 rebellion. With Largo Caballero leading the socialist masses and still talking of revolution, Gil Robles gave up hope of a peaceful outcome to the situation and in July authorised the transfer of part of the C.E.D.A.'s funds to the organiser of the military conspiracy.[56]

Not long after Azaña's return to power the monarchists of the National Bloc reached the conclusion that military action was the only way to save Spain from anarchy and the revolutionary threat. Primo de Rivera's Falange, which had broken with its Alfonsine monarchist patrons in 1934, also despaired of Azaña's government at the beginning of March, and its youthful gunmen began a campaign of counter-terrorism against the extreme left. Primo de Rivera and other leaders were detained on 14 March and the movement was officially banned in April, but these measures did not stop it functioning as a clandestine militia or taking part in plotting against the government. Apart from the Falange, the most active paramilitary elements of the right were the Requetés – the militiamen of the Traditionalist Communion now led by the young lawyer Manuel Fal Conde – who were longing for an opportunity to crusade against the Republic. Many members of the C.E.D.A.'s youth movement who despaired of salvation within legality after the elections left to join the Falange or the Requetés.

The organiser of the military conspiracy against the government was General Mola, who began seriously to plan for a rising in April, but the nominal leader was Sanjurjo, who had been living in Portugal since 1934 and had plotted with Carlists. Mola believed events were 'fatefully leading Spain to a chaotic situation that can only be avoided by means of violent action. Therefore the elements that love the Country must of necessity organise themselves for rebellion, with the aim of conquering power and imposing therefrom order, peace and justice.'[57] Because military conspirators sought simply to overthrow the government of the Popular Front, re-establish order and suppress the revolutionary threat, they did not want to commit themselves to overthrowing the republican form of government. Mola had great difficulty in negotiating terms for the support of the Carlists because there were convinced republicans, such as General Cabanellas, in the plot. He also had some trouble with the Falange, but these difficulties seemed to have been surmounted by the middle of July.

The psychological moment arrived for the conspirators when, early on 13 July, the leader of the National Bloc, Calvo Sotelo, was kidnapped and murdered by policemen from a barracks next to the ministry of the interior. A month earlier Calvo Sotelo, who had supplanted Gil Robles as the right's leading politician, had said in the Cortes that it was a soldier's duty to rise against the government if Spain were in a state of anarchy. To this Casares Quiroga retorted that he would hold Calvo Sotelo responsible for anything that might happen. Calvo Sotelo had lightly accepted blanket responsibility and then quoted an old saying: 'Sire, life you can take from me, but more you cannot.'[58] After the murder Gil Robles charged Casares Quiroga's government 'of shame, mud and blood' with moral responsibility for the crime and concluded his speech as follows:

> There is an abyss between the farce that parliament is performing and the profound and most grave national tragedy. We are not pre-pared to let this farce continue. . . . You can be sure – this has been the constant law of all human collectivities – that you, who are plan-ning violence, will be its first victims. Very ordinary because very well-known, but none the less true, is the proverb that revolutions are like Saturn, that they devour their own children. Now you are very calm because you see your opponent fall. Soon will come the day when the very violence you have unleashed will turn against you![59]

Two days later, on 17 July, the Army of Africa rose in Morocco and the Civil War began.

This survey of the parties of the right during the Republic would not be complete without attention being drawn to the ideological differ-ences between them. If one looks for continuity of thought and action between the right-wing parties and previous movements many links become apparent. The Traditionalist Communion obviously brought together Carlists and 'traditionalists', the C.E.D.A. was clearly rooted in social Catholicism, while the authoritarians who had served General Primo de Rivera, with some former followers of Antonio Maura, created Spanish Renovation and then the National Bloc. The amorphous 'liberal Catholicism' which had been common to most parties of the liberal monarchy found its continuation under the Republic in different small parties: conservative and progressive republican and agrarian. The traditions of regional nationalism remained embodied in the liberal Catholic autonomist Catalan League and the social Catholic Basque nationalist party, whose separatist ideals led it into alliance with the left in the Civil War. Nothing further need be said here about the regionalist or liberal Catholic groups, save that the latter defended

parliamentary institutions and in opportunistic fashion sought to defend
the social *status quo* as well as religion. The Falange was an ideological
innovation on the right though, as will be seen, it was not without
Spanish precursors.

The C.E.D.A. was really the Spanish counterpart of other European
Christian-democrat parties. Its first loyalty was to the church and the
question of the form of government was unimportant. Its social programme followed closely the teachings of the church as expounded in
the encyclicals of Popes Leo XIII and Pius XI: the rejection of class
warfare, social insurance and the family wage for workers, limited state
intervention in the economy, the right of workers to participate in the
running and profits of firms, a just distribution of wealth, a fair system
of taxation, cheap credit and agrarian reforms to create viable small-
holdings. The C.E.D.A. also wanted revision of the anti-clerical parts
of the republican Constitution, a concordat with the Holy See, defence
of the family as an institution, freedom of education (but with 'recognition of the supreme mastery of the church in educational matters'),
a measure of autonomy for municipalities and regions and a peaceful
foreign policy based on armed neutrality.[60]

There was, however, another highly controversial dimension to the
C.E.D.A.'s programme: the 'new state' of which Gil Robles spoke in
the election campaign of 1933. The inspiration for the corporative state
which he advocated came not from abroad but from the Spanish
past: 'We do not want a dictatorship that destroys the rights of the
individual; but nor do we want excess of individual liberty to destroy
collective rights. . . . We shall not resort to foreign patrons. . . . In
Tradition I find everything relating to the limitation of power, justice
and corporations.' He told his young followers: 'We are an army of
citizens, not an army that needs uniforms and martial parades. . . . We
must not have recourse to pagan Rome or to the diseased exaltation of
race. The more Catholic, the more Spanish. The more Spanish, the
more Catholic.'[61] Despite the authoritarian impatience of his youth
movement, Gil Robles was not to be deflected from legal and democratic methods. The party programme was to be put into effect gradually, as circumstances and the electorate permitted. The political transformation he desired had to be the product of evolution, and this was
'a very slow business, which sometimes takes centuries. . . . Meanwhile
we do not deceive ourselves. In Spain there is in the political sphere no
reality other than parties.'[62] For Gil Robles the 'new state' was an

ideal at which to aim; he was no more and no less of a democrat than a parliamentary socialist believing in reform, not revolution.

Gil Robles spoke of 'Tradition' as a guiding principle in his political thinking, but 'Tradition' was the very essence of the creed of the Carlists. The Carlist–traditionalist ideology was restated by Alfonso Carlos in 1934 and by the ideologue Víctor Pradera in 1935. First, Carlists believed in religious unity, in 'the close and everlasting moral union of church and state'. Secondly, they upheld the cause of legitimate traditional monarchy. Their concept of monarchy derived from theories of the Catholic monarchy of the sixteenth century: the king ruled as well as reigned and represented the sovereignty of the nation in his person. The king was not, however, an absolute dictator because his sphere of action was limited by certain 'fundamental laws' which could only be changed by representatives chosen by regions and corporations for this purpose. The person of the monarch was the connecting link between the regions, each with its own laws and customs and each ruling itself within 'the indissoluble unity of the Spanish nation'. There were to be no political parties or class warfare in the traditionalist 'new state': people would form part of a guild or corporation according to their employment and these corporations would run their own affairs with the king arbitrating between them in the national interest. The rights of the individual were to be safeguarded within the sacrosanct institution of the family and by the 'fundamental laws'.[63] Violence was considered legitimate against the Republic: 'If the laws of the state are in opposition to divine law, resistance is a duty and obedience a crime.'[64]

The programme of Goicoechea's Spanish Renovation stated: 'In the religious sphere, we are Catholics; in the political sphere, monarchists; in the judicial sphere, constitutionalists and legalists; and in the social sphere, democrats.'[65] The programme was not very precise and the speeches of Alfonsine leaders revealed that the conversion of many of them to a 'traditionalist' ideology was opportunistic. The influence of Carlist–traditionalist thought was counterbalanced in their minds by the example of Mussolini's Italy, the 'integral nationalism' of the French royalist ideologue Charles Maurras and memories of General Primo de Rivera's dictatorship. The Carlists were never fully convinced of Alfonsine sincerity and joined Calvo Sotelo's National Bloc without great enthusiasm. The ideals of the authoritarian Alfonsines were summarised in one of Calvo Sotelo's last speeches when he spoke of the pragmatic aims of his 'integrative state' which, he admitted, 'many call a fascist state':

> No more strikes, no more lock-outs, no more usurious interest, no more of abusive capitalism's financial formulas, no more starvation wages, no more political salaries gained by a happy accident, no more anarchic liberty, no more criminal loss of production, for national production is above all classes, all parties and all interests.[66]

The Alfonsines knew that they had little chance of gaining their ends without military support, and the National Bloc's manifesto therefore referred to the army in flattering terms as 'the backbone of the Country' and a 'school of citizenship'. The manifesto also spoke of the need for 'traditional historical continuity', but the intransigence of Alfonso XIII and the Carlists thwarted efforts to end the dynastic schism.[67] Calvo Sotelo did not intend the monarchy to return until some time after his 'new state' had been set up, and then there would be an 'installation' and not a 'restoration' to demonstrate that the old liberal monarchy had disappeared for good.[68]

'Tradition' was the essence of Carlism and the concept was adapted to suit the C.E.D.A. by Gil Robles; the word was often on the lips of Alfonsines, but it played little part in the ideology of the Falange. Catholicism, which was of prime importance to the C.E.D.A. and monarchists, was not so important for the Falange. Inspiration for the movement's programme came from Mussolini's Italy, but equally important was the thought of José Ortega y Gasset, one of the leading laicist intellectuals who had hoped to 'regenerate' Spain after the defeat of 1898. Ortega had hoped that the Republic would unite Spaniards for a common purpose and give Spain a new mission, but, disillusioned, he retired from politics in 1932 because the republicans had failed to create 'a new ideology and politico-social philosophy'.[69] No one followed up his pleas for a great national party with the slogan 'Nation and Labour' which would 'nationalise' the new regime.[70] However, from 1933 Primo de Rivera tried to do just this with a fascist movement for the young: the Falange proclaimed Spain, in Ortega's words, 'a unit of destiny in the universal'. The Falange wanted a totalitarian national-syndicalist state to bring about social justice after the 'national revolution'; then Spain would be 'one gigantic syndicate of producers' with a 'will to empire'. José Antonio wanted his blue-shirted youth 'to renew the revolutionary hope of 14 April' 1931.[71]

The C.E.D.A. was the right-wing party with by far the biggest following, drawing its mass support from smallholders and rural workers in the regions of León and Castile in particular, though it was also strong in Valencia, Galicia and Aragon. It also drew support from the Catholic urban middle class all over the country, except in Catalonia and the Basque country, as well as from landowners and some businessmen. The second biggest group on the right was the Traditionalist Communion, which had its real strength in the peasantry of Navarre, though it enjoyed some support in other areas of the north and east. Spanish Renovation was not a mass party and relied for support on sections of the middle class, particularly in the capital, and of the aristocracy who remained loyal to the exiled King Alfonso. The middle class and peasantry, and part of the working class, of the Basque country supported the Basque nationalist party, while the Catalan League got its votes from the Catholic middle class and the landowners of the region – its leaders were generally representatives of big business and bankers. The liberal Catholic groups had no mass support and represented landowners and part of the professional bourgeoisie. The bond which united half the Spanish electorate was religion. The Falange was predominantly a student movement, a great many of whose members were under voting age.

Now that the history of the parties of the right during the Republic has been traced it is possible to attempt some final assessment of their roles in the Republic and their responsibility for the outbreak of civil war. The main feature of the years 1931–6 was the process of increasing polarisation towards the extremes of left and right; the political forces in the centre of the political spectrum disappeared one after another. First the religious issue sabotaged the efforts of Alcalá Zamora and Maura in 1931 to create a Republic acceptable to Catholics and non-Catholics; as the former wrote: 'A constitution was put together which invited civil war. . . . The violent spirit of May [1931] acquired forms of legal expression.'[72] With the rise of Popular Action it was Lerroux's turn to try and hold the balance and make the Republic a *régimen de convivencia* – a regime in which all Spaniards could peacefully live together – but his efforts were thwarted by the revolution of 1934 and finally by the disintegration of his party in 1935. Alcalá Zamora and Portela then tried to create a new Centre, but too late: it was defeated at the polls and the president who had refused to give power to the legalist right was deposed. Attempts to form a national government in the spring of 1936 to salvage the Republic and keep the door open to a democratic future came to nothing. What responsibility can be assigned to the right in this fatal process of polarisation? Very little, because it was the revolutionary left which brought about the failure of the legalist C.E.D.A. as the party of the right-wing masses.

It must be remembered that the right as a strong organised political force only came into being as a result of the left's onslaught on the church, which was quite willing to accept the Republic. It was the left's intransigence on religious issues which was largely responsible for the swing to the right in the elections of 1933. However, the position of the legalist C.E.D.A. was made impossible, as its leader has observed. First, 'the workers' organisations, with the socialist party at their head, were not capable of seeing the new regime as the favourable opportunity for a radical and necessary transformation of Spanish society, but only as a simple instrument for dominating opponents'. Secondly, with the left-wing republicans and socialists in power, 'the period from 1931 to 1933 was characterised by the determined intention to construct a Republic only for republicans'. The left then decided to ignore the verdict of the polls and, 'as if no one else should have any influence in the republican regime, they attacked the foundations of the consti-tutional legality they themselves had created by rushing into the revolution of October 1934'.[73]

'With the rebellion of 1934, the Left lost every shred of moral authority to condemn the rebellion of 1936': such is the verdict of an independent republican, who also notes that, 'had Señor Gil Robles meant to destroy the Constitution by violent means, the defeat of the rebellion of 1934 gave him a golden opportunity to do so – and he did not take it'.[74] In retrospect it seems possible that three years of civil war might have been avoided if Gil Robles and Franco had not clung so firmly to legality in 1935. However, it was not until after February 1936, with Largo Caballero's socialists bent on revolution and the country sliding into anarchy, that leadership of the right passed from the legalist Gil Robles to the counter-revolutionary hands of mon-archists and the Falange, who looked to the army to play its traditional role by intervening to restore order and suppress revolution. The tragedy of the Republic was also the tragedy of Gil Robles. By July 1936 it was quite clear that

the law-abiding struggle of Popular Action had failed. . . . The Leftists had put an end to democracy in Spain. . . . There was now no normal outcome to the situation. We, as the Deputies of the

Rightist parties, who continued to fight on legal ground, could not succeed in restraining Spain's course towards the abyss. . . . It was no longer either right or possible to ask the Rightists to keep within the bounds of a legality which served only to crush them. . . . It was no longer a duty to obey a power which was habitually and seriously unjust. The Spanish Rightists found themselves faced by a situation uniting all the conditions which, according to the traditional doctrine of Catholic political ethics, justified resistance to oppression, not only passively, but actively, through the use of armed force.[75]

SUGGESTIONS FOR FURTHER READING

The best general history of modern Spain in any language is R. Carr, *Spain 1808-1939* (Clarendon Press, Oxford, 1966); it contains a useful chapter on the Republic. A detailed account of the period is provided by G. Jackson, *The Spanish Republic and the Civil War 1931-1939* (Princeton University Press, 1965); the author's sympathies lie just to the left of centre. S. de Madariaga, *Spain – A Modern History*, 3rd edn (Cape, 1961) is the work of a republican intellectual of the centre, well-written, informative and stimulating. The most exhaustive work on the period, written from a right-wing standpoint and containing much information on the right, is J. Arrarás, *Historia de la segunda República española*, 4 vols (Editora Nacional, Madrid, 1956-68).
On the C.E.D.A., the memoirs of its leader are indispensable: J. M. Gil Robles, *No fue posible la paz* (Ediciones Ariel, Barcelona, 1968). A lengthy history by one of the party's deputies for Seville is J. Monge Bernal, *Acción Popular* (Imp. Sáez Hermanos, Madrid, 1936); it stops in late 1935. J. Cortés Cavanillas, *Gil Robles, ¿monárquico?* (Librería San Martín, Madrid, 1935) is an illuminating polemical work by the secretary-general of Spanish Renovation.
The basic book on the monarchists is S. Galindo Herrero, *Los partidos monárquicos bajo la segunda República*, 2nd edn (Ediciones Rialp, Madrid, 1956). A standard biography of the main monarchist leader is F. Acedo Colunga, *José Calvo Sotelo* (Editorial AHR, Barcelona, 1957). A very useful work on Carlism in this period is A. Lizarza Iribarren, *Memorias de la conspiración 1931-1936*, 3rd edn (Editorial Gómez, Pamplona, 1954); the author was a regional leader of the movement in Navarre.
S. G. Payne, *Falange – A History of Spanish Fascism* (Oxford University Press, 1962) is a good standard work. The standard biography of the movement's leader is F. Ximénez de Sandoval, *José Antonio*, 3rd edn (Editorial Bullón, Madrid, 1963).
There is really nothing of value on the Catalan League during the Republic: J. M. de Nadal, *Seis años con don Francisco Cambó 1930-36* (Alpha, Barcelona, 1957), the memoirs of its leader's secretary, is not very revealing. On Basque nationalism there is J. A. de Agire Lekube, *Entre la libertad y la revolución 1930-1935* (E. Verdes Achirica, Bilbao, 1935), being the memoirs of its leader.
Of works by liberal Catholics, by far the most valuable is M. Maura, *Así cayó Alfonso XIII* (Imp. Mañez, Mexico, 1962), although it only covers the fall of the monarchy and the author's tenure of the ministry of the interior. N.

Alcalá Zamora, *Los defectos de la Constitución de 1931* (Imp. de R. Espinosa, Madrid, 1936), is rather thin as a defence of his conduct by the president. A. Lerroux, *La pequeña historia* (Editorial Cimera, Buenos Aires, 1945), the memoirs of the radical leader, though rather repetitive, gives a good insight into the politics of the years 1933–5.

A standard work on the church in this period is J. M. Sánchez, *Reform and Reaction* (University of North Carolina Press, Chapel Hill, 1964). It may be compared with a stout defence of the church by an Anglican: E. A. Peers, *Spain, the Church and the Orders* (Eyre & Spottiswoode, 1939).

It is hoped that a reasonably comprehensive study of the right during the Republic is provided by my *The Origins of Franco's Spain* (David & Charles, Newton Abbot, 1970).

NOTES

1. The church had come to terms with the liberal monarchy by the Concordat of 1851 and official recognition of Catholicism as the religion of the state had been reaffirmed in the Constitution of 1876.
2. M. Maura, *Así cayó Alfonso XIII* (1962), pp. 141, 147 and 309, openly concedes monarchist victory in the countryside where the republicans did not campaign.
3. J. M. Sánchez, *Reform and Reaction* (1964), pp. 81–4.
4. Maura, op. cit. pp. 240–64.
5. Collective Pastoral of the Spanish Metropolitans, *El Debate*, 12 June 1931.
6. J. Cortés Cavanillas, *Gil Robles, ¿monárquico?* (1935), pp. 65–7.
7. Election figures vary from one source to another; those given here are based on those of the Geographical and Statistical Institute in *El Debate*, 5 Dec 1933.
8. Quotations from *El Debate*, 29 April, 20 and 27 May 1931.
9 Speech in *Diario de sesiones de las Cortes Constituyentes* (hereafter cited as *DSCC*), 26 Aug 1931.
10. A. Ramos Oliveira, *Politics, Economics and Men of Modern Spain 1808–1946* (1946), p. 278.
11. *Declaración colectiva del Episcopado español sobre el espíritu y actuación de los católicos en las presentes circunstancias* (1932).
12. Speech reported in *El Debate*, 16 June 1932.
13. Speech in *DSCC*, 10 Aug 1932.
14. Quoted by R. Guariglia, *Ricordi 1922–1946* (1950), p. 190.
15. Figures given by Gil Robles in *DSCC*, 9 Nov 1932.
16. Figure given in *El Debate*, 2 March 1933.
17. J. Gutiérrez-Ravé, *Antonio Goicoechea* (1965), pp. 19–21.
18. Speeches of Lerroux and Azaña in *DSCC*, 2 and 3 Oct 1933.
19. J. M. Gil Robles, *No fue posible la paz* (1968), pp. 87–8.
20. *El Socialista*, 24 Nov 1931 and 14 Sept 1933.
21. Electoral pact in *ABC*, 15 Oct 1933.
22. Largo Caballero reported in *El Socialista*, 9 Nov 1933.
23. Speech reported in *El Debate*, 17 Oct 1933.
24. Figures compiled from the detailed statistics in *El Debate*, 5 Dec 1933 and 2 Feb 1936.
25. R. Carr, *Spain 1808–1939* (1966), p. 632.

26. *Diario de las sesiones de Cortes* (hereafter cited as *DSC*), 19 Dec 1933.

27. *ABC*, 16 Dec 1933.

28. Cortés Cavanillas, op. cit. p. 125.

29. *Falange Española* ('Spanish Phalanx') was founded in October 1933 and in February 1934 joined up with another fascist group dating back to 1931, the J.O.N.S. (Juntas of National-Syndicalist Offensive) of Ledesma and Redondo.

30. Speeches reported in *El Socialista*, 17 April and 3 July 1934.

31. *El Socialista*, 29 April 1934.

32. A. Ramos Oliveira, *La revolución de octubre* (1935), p. 103.

33. Reported in *ABC*, 26 Sept 1934.

34. A. Lerroux, *La pequeña historia* (1945), pp. 173–4.

35. Lerroux reported in *ABC*, 5 Jan 1935.

36. Count of Romanones, reported in *ABC*, 11 July 1935.

37. Speeches reported in *El Debate*, 23 Dec 1934 and 10 Nov 1935.

38. Speech in *DSC*, 6 Nov 1934.

39. Calvo Sotelo reported in *ABC*, 11 May and 2 June 1935.

40. Gil Robles, op. cit. pp. 314–79.

41. Carr, op. cit. pp. 635–6.

42. *El Debate*, 19 Sept 1935.

43. Report of the ministry of agriculture in *ABC*, 9 June 1935; cf. Largo Caballero's statement that agrarian reform did not exist, in *El Socialista*, 20 Oct 1933.

44. *El Debate*, 14 and 16 Feb 1936.

45. Speech of 12 Jan, in J. Pérez Madrigal, *España a dos voces* (1961), pp. 418–20.

46. J. A. Primo de Rivera, *Obras completas* (1942), p. 143.

47. *El Socialista*, 28 Jan 1936.

48. Statistics in *El Debate*, 26 Feb and 7 March 1936.

49. J. Arrarás, *Historia de la segunda República española* (1956–68), iv, 49–62; cf. Gil Robles, op. cit. pp. 491–502.

50. Speech in *DSC*, 16 June 1936.

51. Speech in *DSC*, 19 May 1936.

52. Speech reported in *El Socialista*, 2 May 1936.

53. Interview in *ABC*, 22 March 1936.

54. Speech in *DSC*, 15 April 1936.

55. Statement in *El Debate*, 24 April 1936.

56. Gil Robles, op. cit. pp. 615–27 and 798; cf. Arrarás, op. cit. iv, 273–82 and 317.

57. Quoted by I. Bernard, *Mola, mártir de España* (1938), p. 83.

58. *DSC*, 16 June 1936.

59. Speech in Cortes on 15 July, in Gil Robles, op. cit. pp. 823–32.

60. Programme summarised in Gil Robles, op. cit. pp. 821–2.

61. Speeches reported in *El Debate*, 14 Nov 1933 and 24 April 1934.

62. Interview in *ABC*, 22 Nov 1934, and speech reported in *El Debate*, 23 Dec 1934.

63. *Documentos de D. Alfonso Carlos de Borbón y de Austria-Este*, ed. M. Ferrer (1950), pp. 255–60; and V. Pradera, *The New State* (1939).

64. Pradera, quoted in *Historia de la Cruzada española*, ed. J. Arrarás (1939–43), i, 590.

65. *ABC*, 13 Jan 1933.

66. *DSC*, 16 June 1936.

67. Translation in R. A. H. Robinson, 'Calvo Sotelo's *Bloque Nacional* and its Manifesto', in *University of Birmingham Historical Journal*, x (1966), 169–73.

68. Interview in *ABC*, 14 June 1934.
69. Quoted in Arrarás, *Historia de la segunda República española*, ii, 36.
70. Speeches reported in *El Debate*, 8 Dec 1931, and *La Época*, 5 Feb 1932.
71. Primo de Rivera, op. cit. pp. 553–63 and 589–97; and *Últimos hallazgos de escritos y cartas de José Antonio*, ed. A. del Río Cisneros and E. Pavón Pereyra (1962), p. 91.
72. N. Alcalá Zamora, *Los defectos de la Constitución de 1931* (1936), pp. 50 and 91.
73. Gil Robles, op. cit. pp. 803–4.
74. S. de Madariaga, *Spain* (1961 edn), pp. 434–5.
75. J. M. Gil Robles, *Spain in Chains* (1937), pp. 7–8 and 15–16.

5. The Army, the Republic and the Outbreak of the Civil War

STANLEY PAYNE

THE army has been at or near the forefront of public problems in Spain since the beginning of liberal government. During the nineteenth century the country's political activists tried repeatedly to introduce advanced institutions while lacking the support either to install or sustain them, and the military was often called upon to play the role of a modernising elite, supplying the strength which civilian groups were unable to muster. Thus in the early and middle portions of the nineteenth century the army often served as a 'liberal' force, though the attitudes of officers became more conservative after the temporary experience of radical democracy in 1873–4.

As an institution the army was largely inefficient, ill-organised and sometimes even corrupt. During the nineteenth and early twentieth centuries, its military record, compiled almost exclusively in civil and colonial wars, was little short of disastrous. Yet civil disunity within Spain, convulsive efforts to retain remnants of the old colonial empire and the government's inability after 1908 to avoid the vortex of European imperialism in Morocco resulted in the maintenance of an expensive military establishment. Though the Spanish army was not large by comparison with that of France or even Italy, it consumed a large part of the state budget while providing little return.

Despite much publicity of the 'military problem', however, Spain and its army were little affected by the main currents of aggressive modern European militarism. There were obvious explanations for this imperviousness: relative absence of active nationalism in Spain, meagreness of new imperial ambitions, lack of involvement in the major strategic quarrels and economic rivalries of the continent, the failure of industrialisation to take hold in Spain until the twentieth century was well advanced, and the persistence of traditional values in culture.

Members of the officer corps were drawn mainly from the middle classes after the early nineteenth century. Recruitment patterns were fairly liberal, both in opportunities for entering the military academies and in promotions from the ranks. Thus the Spanish army never formed a special caste due to social background.[1]

Under the stable system of the restored constitutional monarchy after 1875, it seemed that the army officer corps had largely been removed from public affairs as a pressure group. This situation changed between 1906 and 1923, influenced by four main developments. The first of these was the institutional disarray and psychological malaise of the Spanish military themselves. Proportionate to its size, theirs was the feeblest military force in Europe. Although most of the military budget went to pay for a bloated officer corps, salaries remained low even by Spanish standards. At the same time the officers felt pressured by the politicians to maintain a status and provide an institutional backbone for the country that was beyond their means. Junior officers did not receive enough pay to support a family, yet the military was still relied upon to uphold unity at home and protect what was left of national interests abroad.

A second element was the growth of Catalan and Basque regionalism, which seemed to threaten the political and cultural unity of Spain and was also very hostile to the military. Since patriotic unity was a central peg of military values, the regionalist movements provoked a strong reaction.[2]

A third factor was the growth of the two working-class revolutionary movements during the second decade of the century. Army units were more and more frequently called into the streets to preserve order during strikes or outbursts of anarchist terrorism, occasionally even to the point of supplanting regular government under martial law.

A fourth influence was the humiliation and frustration involved in the twenty years' struggle to occupy and pacify the Spanish Protectorate in northern Morocco (1909–28). This small territory was inhabited by warlike Berber kabyles, who proved the most resolute and skilful guerrilla fighters in the Afro-Asian world during the 1920s. In 1921 approximately 9000 Spanish troops were lost in a blundering and disastrous defeat at Anual that seemed to recapitulate the defeat in Cuba of 1898.[3] The military were given the blame for these humiliations, and the government subsequently refused to support military operations on a scale sufficient to achieve victory.

It was especially because of the stress of the Moroccan nightmare that a small handful of military conspirators took the lead in overthrowing parliamentary government in 1923. The resultant regime of General Miguel Primo de Rivera (1923–30) was the first regular military dictatorship in Spanish history. Never before had an army directory assumed direct responsibility for government affairs, rather than co-operating with a civilian parliamentary regime served by individual military figures. Primo de Rivera temporarily halted domestic terrorism and brought order and unity to Spain, as well as ending the Moroccan holocaust in collaboration with the French. The Primo de Rivero regime was neither fascist nor liberal; it had no explicit creed and no fully articulated programme. Its authoritarianism alienated the country's elite, especially the intellectuals, and the dictator's manipulation of the army alienated much of the officer corps as well. By 1930 the idea of military dictatorship had become discredited even within the military.

When the Republic was inaugurated in 1931, the great majority of the officer corps had no precisely definable political convictions. They stood for patriotism, unity and the common weal, but there was little agreement as to what this meant in terms of parties and precise goals. A military conspiracy had planned the overthrow of Primo de Rivera at the beginning of 1930, and the first effort to bring in a republic had been attempted by a small motley group of plotters at the end of that year. Two officers involved, Galán and García Hernandéz, were executed and became the principal martyrs of the republican movement. The main contribution made by the leaders of the military to the inauguration of the Republic lay in the refusal of most of them to take up arms for the defence of the monarchy.

In view of the passive, almost benevolent, attitude adopted by the military towards the coming of the new regime, it may not seem easy to understand the hostility of key republican leaders towards military institutions. The forces that came to power in April 1931 were mostly the representatives of a new republican left formed during the years of the dictatorship and in reaction to military–monarchist authoritarianism. They incorporated little of the experience of the historic republican groups active prior to the 1920s, but espoused doctrinaire attitudes conditioned by the frustrations of the last years of the old parliamentary regime and civic impotence under the dictatorship. The army was seen by many of them as the source of aggression, authoritarianism, waste, incompetence and anti-civic values.

These attitudes were personified by the first minister of war under the new regime, Manuel Azaña. A fifty-year-old bureaucrat and writer, Azaña emerged as the dominant personality of the republican government. He was a middle-class radical whose goal was to install a radical democratic (not liberal democratic) constitutional system under which the two chief institutional bastions of authority and obscurantism as he defined them – the church and the army – would be reduced to impotence. As minister of war in the 1931 cabinet, Azaña quickly introduced a series of basic army reforms.[4] The most important of these was a measure of 25 April 1931 that offered all officers the option of immediate retirement at full pay for life. Within the year that followed, this arrangement prompted at least half the officer corps to resign their careers. In 1930 there had been 22,000 officers and approximately 100,000 troops; by 1932 the officer corps numbered scarcely 10,000.

The unit structure of the army was cut down by half and the organisational system streamlined. The ministry of war and command system were centralised to a greater degree than before, the old senior ranks of captain-general and lieutenant-general were abolished, and the Protectorate in Morocco placed under the direction of a civilian appointee. Educational qualifications for officer candidates were raised slightly and provisions were made for a special class of N.C.O.s (the 'Subofficers Corps'), selected and trained from the ranks. The whole system of arms purchasing and production was reorganised, special military establishments were limited and new arrangements were made with private producers and foreign firms. The functioning of military courts and the army 'honour system' were dramatically curtailed.

One thing that was not accomplished was reduction of the army budget, which actually rose in the short run under the costs of the reforms and maintaining officer and retirement salaries. It was 10 per cent higher in 1933 than in 1929. Nor was the recruitment system fully democratised. Redemption bounties were abolished, but educated recruits were let out with only token training. Most serious of all was the fact that the reforms were undertaken on the basis of abstract structural rationalisation without concern for practical measures to improve military efficiency. Combat preparation received slight attention, training facilities were not improved, and no more – perhaps less – was spent on equipment than before.

The most important thing about the Azaña reforms was not what they did but the way in which they did it. The point of these changes was not merely to reorganise the military and remove army influence from politics but to break what was understood as the old Spanish 'military spirit'. It was not merely to reform, but as Azaña himself put it, to 'pulverise' (*triturar*) the military. Azaña rarely missed an opportunity to humiliate the army as an institution or the officers as a professional group; he wanted to make it clear to them that they were no more than an unimportant sector of the state bureaucracy.

The new regime drastically reorganised portions of the command, reassigning or leaving without posts monarchist or ultra-conservative commanders, replacing them with officers considered to be more respectful of or more favourably inclined towards the new regime. The only combat elite of the officer corps were the *Africanistas*, veterans of the Moroccan campaigns. They enjoyed a reputation, probably unjustified, for professional ignorance, corruption and ferocity. The *Africanista* elite had mostly won their rank and positions through merit promotions in combat. Numbering scarcely 20 per cent of the remaining officers in the army, they represented most of the truly active elements. Azaña, however, cancelled all merit promotions won in Primo de Rivera's victorious operations and in effect demoted the combat elite of the army. This was done for two reasons: retroactive punishment or non-recognition for being involved in the achievements of the dictatorship, and downgrading of the main activist elements.[5] In Azaña's scheme of things, a combatworthy army was not necessary because Spain had no foreign policy and no foreign ambitions. The republican policy was to support the League of Nations, but to resist involvement in any sort of international activity. In 1936 the second Azaña government would not even support sanctions against fascist Italy following the invasion of Ethiopia.

The indelicacy of Azaña's policy may be better understood by comparing the Spanish experience of 1931–4 with Rómulo Bethencourt's handling of the military during Venezuela's transition to a democratic parliamentary regime after 1958. Bethencourt moved carefully in his relations with the Venezuelan army, flattered and decorated the officers and identified them with the new democratic regime rather than making them scapegoats for the past. Bethencourt was a practical politician, whereas Azaña's approach was doctrinaire.

The country as a whole had accepted the fall of the monarchy and the proclamation of the Republic, and for the most part initially supported the new regime; and so it was with the bulk of the officers. More vexing than the reforms was the attitude of the left republican government, but despite much gnashing of teeth even this was initially accepted as well. After the bitter experiences of 1917–30, very few officers were inclined to stick their necks out politically. The left republican calculation that Spain scarcely needed an army capable of waging a modern international war may or may not have been correct, but the very first weeks of the new regime made it clear that Spain still needed an army to serve as guarantor of internal security and order. The military had to be called out on frequent occasions in widely scattered parts of the peninsula and in Morocco during 1931–2 to quell disorders, particularly on the part of the anarchists. Several of these disorders were so severe as to require the use of artillery.

The provisions in the new republican Constitution of 1931 that aroused the greatest furore – the anti-clerical legislation – did not provoke serious resentment among the military, mainly because the officers as a group were not militant Catholics. The first non-military issue that seriously roused sectors of the officer corps was the preparation of the regional autonomy statute for Catalonia in the summer of 1932. By that time the wave of national euphoria under the Republic had passed. A sizeable portion of the middle classes had become restive under the disordered new regime, moderate politicians were inflamed by left republican sectarianism, clerical groups were organising for a great political *revanche* and right-wing monarchist conspirators were plotting revolt.

On the eve of the passage of the Catalan statute in August 1932, an inchoate revolt was attempted in Madrid and Seville by some 200 officers or less – about 2 per cent of the officer corps. As it turned out, this was not a serious affair, nor was the revolt greatly feared by the government. The main elements behind it were monarchist conspirators who had been organising themselves for months; but they lacked a broad base and had relied upon convincing a few military leaders to attempt a *coup*. Their figurehead, José Sanjurjo, played a paradoxical role. One of the bravest and most decorated of the *Africanista* generals and a strong supporter of Primo de Rivera, Sanjurjo had none the less had an important part in the coming of the Republic. As director of the Civil Guard in 1931, he had indicated that he would not order his troops to defend the monarchy. Only sixteen months were needed to convince him that the republican left–socialist coalition running the government was conducting sectarian government and dividing the fatherland. Suppression of the *Sanjurjada* strengthened the republican regime and brought a mild purge of the military, affecting some 300 officers. Its general consequences were to confirm the caution and aversion to political involvement already shown by most officers.[6]

In general, the 'army' or 'the officer corps' can hardly be spoken of in a corporate political sense as a monolithic entity with specific political views. The officer corps had been severely split by the political tensions of 1917–23 and by the dictatorship, while the challenges of the new regime increased divisions and uncertainties. Every political ideology in Spain was represented within the officer corps by the early 1930s. Officers who admired the extreme left were few in number, but there were several hundred in this category. Those drawn towards the extreme right or ideas of nationalist authoritarianism were more numerous, but they too were a definite minority. Most officers were either vaguely moderate pro-republican 'liberals' – using the term liberal in a loose way – or had no exact convictions at all.

Defeat of the left in the 1933 elections brought no drastic change in the relation between the military and the government, but it resulted in a relaxation of feelings. The centre-right government of 1934 tried to keep affairs on as much of an even keel as possible. Very slight increases in the military budget were intended as a token of the moderate ministry's concern for the military.

The comportment of the army in the suppression of the revolutionary insurrection of October 1934 was, as far as political responsibility was concerned, excellent. There was never either vacillation or insubordination in obeying orders. The Catalanist revolt in Barcelona was smothered by 500 troops from the local garrison, but nearly two weeks of fighting and sizeable reinforcements were required to defeat the worker insurrection in Asturias.[7]

The first major change in military policy occurred in May 1935, when cabinet reorganisation gave the war ministry to José María Gil Robles, leader of the conservative Catholic confederation, the C.E.D.A. By that time Spain was already becoming polarised between left and right, between the forces of revolution and conservatism. In this situation Gil Robles assumed the war ministry because he was convinced of the importance of reorganising, strengthening and unifying the army as a bulwark against the revolutionaries. He quickly appointed to high office a number of ultra-nationalist commanders whose political views ranged from moderate to conservative and who were also fairly efficient administrators, at least by the standards of the Spanish army.

Among these was Major-General Francisco Franco, who was made chief of the general staff. Eight years earlier he had become the youngest general in any European army:

> The officers of his generation were impressed by a series of qualities that invested him with undeniable prestige. There was his courage,

less theatrical than that of other companions in the Moroccan campaigns, but which, after being subjected to the decisive test of fire on numerous occasions, became legendary; foresight and sure instinct that enabled him to measure the strength of the enemy in order to attack coldly when the latter was weakened; the cult of discipline, which he did not hesitate to sustain with means as harsh as might be necessary, though without failing to watch over the well-being of the troops with extreme care and striving to avoid wasting lives in combat; careful preparation of operations, indispensable in a colonial campaign, where it is more important to avoid dangerous improvisations than to develop grand strategic concepts; exact knowledge of the enemy's weak points in the material and in the moral order; avoidance of any kind of dissipation that might distract him from achieving his goals, maturely conceived and implacably pursued. . . . All this contributed to surrounding Franco with a special aura that was recognised by friends and enemies, and to create a zone of isolation and reserve about him that enhanced his reputation.[8]

The main task of the Gil Robles–Franco leadership in the seven months between May and December 1935 was to strengthen and reunify the military. Political division and subversion had been on the increase since the start of the Republic and there was, if anything, even less unity than before. A new command shake-up was carried out both to raise efficiency and to strengthen anti-leftist leadership in the army. Honour tribunals were restored and a military espionage system was established to try to control subversive activities among N.C.O.s and recruits, which had become fairly widespread at Madrid and in a few other garrisons. A main goal was to raise morale and self-confidence in the military; merit promotions were restored by special decree. Special combat training manœuvres were held and the military equipment budget was expanded. Despite severe limits to what could be accomplished in so brief a period, the army reform of 1935, directed not towards organic reform but towards leadership and morale, helped refocus military identity and values. Without this, it is doubtful that the military reaction against the Popular Front in the summer of 1936 would have had the relative cohesion and support that it did.

The last regular majority-based parliamentary government in Spanish history was ended in December 1935, as a consequence of conservative selfishness and presidential manipulation. Beyond that point the chief executive, Alcalá Zamora, refused to permit the existing Cortes, with its centre-right majority, to continue, even though its constitutional mandate still had two more years to run. He proposed to bring republican politics into more 'moderate' channels through new elections in which his own centrist associates would gain increased strength and influence.

The presidential veto of the functioning of parliament in December 1935 created the first major crisis that threatened a serious military *coup*. A small right-wing clique in the army demanded military intervention to prevent the presidential intervention from providing a new opportunity for the revolutionary left. It would have been difficult for any coup to succeed without the active collaboration of the chief of the general staff. After weighing the pros and cons seriously, Franco rejected the alternative of military intervention at that time. Opinion within the army was simply too divided. Alcalá Zamora's move, though anti-parliamentary, was constitutional, for the republican Constitution gave the president the option of dissolving parliament and calling new elections up to twice during his term of office. In these circumstances, attitudes among the army were so far from uniform in their hostility to the chief executive that a *coup* seemed to have little chance of success.[9]

The subsequent elections of February 1936 – the 'Popular Front elections' – were plebiscitary in nature. Right-wing nationalist elements within the army plotted a *coup* in the event of victory by the left, but lacked the support to make preparations effective. The first, decisive round of voting occurred on 16 February. Within less than twenty-four hours the trends were clear even though not all the votes had been counted. As pressure from leftist street mobs mounted, key rightist civilian leaders and a few ultra-nationalists in the army command demanded intervention. The most insistent voice within the military was that of General Manuel Goded, chief of inspection under the war ministry. Once more a decisive role was played by Franco, who supported revolt only if properly prepared, initiated and supported. His view was that under the circumstances, martial law and military intervention to annul the leftist victory would only be successful if authorised by the legal authorities, that is, by the regular government itself. It is extremely difficult to question the accuracy of this judgement. Once the civilian authorities chose not to contest the leftist victory, Franco and other military leaders hesitated to take matters into their own hands. Even though the full electoral process was not carried out under the terms of constitutional legality, the president and the caretaker moderates in office hesitated to intervene for fear of provoking another revolutionary insurrection. Franco concluded that the army was too 'divided morally'

D

to assume responsibility itself.[10]

Under Azaña's new Popular Front regime civil–military relations quickly went from bad to worse. Another round of reassignments was immediately effected, removing appointees of 1934–5 or assigning them to less important posts, replacing them with ultra-liberal officers or scrupulously subordinate commanders. The 'military party' that had been forming in the army command during the past two years was thus broken up. Beyond this, and minor reductions in expenditures, the new Azaña government did not proceed to major changes in the army structure. Its attention was taken up almost entirely by the demands of the extreme left, and it had little desire to antagonise the military further. As the spring of 1936 wore on, the minority government of the middle-class left became increasingly paralysed by the break-up of the Spanish polity and the fatal alliance that tied it to the boa-constrictor tendencies of the revolutionary left. After the destitution of the republican president, executive leadership failed almost altogether, and the government made little effort to resist the polarisation of the extremist tendencies.

Military reaction to the break-up of Spanish politics and the collapse of constitutional government in the spring and summer of 1936 took form rather slowly, reacting to the sequences of disintegration. A series of meetings that were held by the ousted commanders at Madrid in late February and in March came to no concrete agreement, save to remain in touch, support one another and promise to revolt if the Azaña cabinet tried to dissolve the army or install a directly revolutionary regime.

If the army as an institution had no clear or unified position on political issues, the most important sector of Spanish politics in the spring of 1936 – the revolutionary left – had a clear and unified position regarding the army. They wanted to abolish it. All the revolutionary groups, from the socialists through the communists (of both the national and Russian varieties) to the anarchists, were agreed on the need to break up the existing institutionalisation of the military, purging the officer corps and replacing it with some sort of citizens' or workers' militia led by elective – and leftist – officers. Despite the confusion on other issues, there was no doubt that 90 per cent of the officer corps was opposed to the revolutionaries. On this point the lines were drawn, and as a military counterweight the tiny minority of leftist officers formed a 'Unión Militar Republicana Antifascista' (U.M.R.A.), led by a communist captain on the general staff.

Leftist anti-militarism was assisted by two important developments. One was the policy of the under-secretary of the interior in the Azaña government, Bibiano Ossorio Tafall (a Galician radical with close communist connections), to pack the national police force with leftist officers, many of whom had been purged or even convicted of crimes committed during the revolutionary insurrection of 1934. The other was the comparatively efficient military apparatus of the communists. This was composed of two sections. The first was the paramilitary formation, *Milicias Anti-fascistas Obreras y Campensinas* (M.A.O.C.), that the party had begun to organise in 1933 and which was set up apart from the 'terrorist' units that functioned in the spring of 1936. It was the only well-organised, well-led paramilitary group in the country (with the possible exception of the Carlist *Requetés*), thanks to expert assistance from the Comintern. The second aspect was the 'Anti-military Bureau' within the party, devoted to collecting information about the structure and personnel of the Spanish army, and forming subversive cells of privates and N.C.O.s. The latter had achieved a degree of importance in Madrid and a few other garrisons.[11]

In the articulation of the military conspiracy that slowly developed during the spring of 1936, there were at least five elements:

(*a*) the decision of key commanders, frequently on an individual basis;

(*b*) the agitation of a semi-secret officers' association, the *Unión Militar Española* (U.M.E.), formed in 1933–4;

(*c*) encouragement and support from right-wing conspiratorial elements, especially monarchists;

(*d*) the possibility of assistance from paramilitary organisations, primarily the Carlists and the Spanish fascist movement, *Falange Española*;

(*e*) the existence of a special combat elite – the volunteers of the Spanish Legion and Moroccan auxiliaries – in the Moroccan Protectorate, who were ultra-nationalist and anti-leftist.

No one of these elements was strong enough to attempt a serious rebellion by itself, and their combination was an exceedingly complex task, facilitated only by the steady growth of extremism and the increasingly hopeless future of the constitutional polity in Spain. The only broad association among the military that could conceivably be used as a springboard to rebellion was the U.M.E., which claimed to have enrolled about 3500 officers, or 45 per cent of those on active duty, by March 1936.[12] Yet the U.M.E. was not a tightly organised association with clear-cut goals, but an almost inchoate confederation of local garrison cliques whose members and regional sectors disagreed profoundly among themselves. When the U.M.E. had been first organised, its nominal goal had been to form a special military organisation to protect constitutional government from take-over by the revolutionaries. Some of its leading lights, however, conceived of it more specifically as an instrument to spearhead authoritarian nationalist rule. U.M.E. membership increased greatly between 1934 and 1936, but on the basis of organisational decentralization and simply as a kind of professional officers' association to protect the interests of the military. It had no national leadership worthy of the name, and local sections were virtually autonomous. It was scarcely even a 'secret' organisation because of the lack of systematisation. Some of the officers in it could scarcely be considered 'authoritarian' or 'reactionary', but were simply middle-of-the-road liberals who joined a sort of professional confraternity.

Rightist civilian conspirators were of little importance by themselves. With their contacts in the army, they had been working for a military revolt ever since 1932, but had met no success. Their only hope was that extraneous events would play into their hands, and that they might use their diplomatic contacts and financial resources to gain the ascendancy in any eventual military reaction.

The anti-leftist civilian paramilitary groups were not much better off. The Carlists had managed to send a few hundred volunteers for military training to Italian territory in 1934, and they had organised several thousand peasants for brief mountain manœuvres in Navarre, but their base of support was largely confined to that north-eastern province. Volunteers in this region were numerous and enthusiastic, but lacked equipment, leadership, training and organisation.[13]

The young followers of *Falange Española* were scarcely organised as a genuine paramilitary unit. The party began to gain membership rapidly from a base of about 10,000 followers at the time of the elections, but after the arrest of its national leadership in mid-March it was proscribed as an organisation. Reduced to semi-clandestine status, the Falange threatened to dissolve into its various provincial components. The actual identity of the membership was uncertain, and the main activist groups were simply small squads for terrorism and street-fighting, armed mostly with clubs and revolvers. Falangist leaders realised that the only hope for establishment of a nationalist authoritarian regime lay in military revolt, and made increasing efforts to interest any units. A special 'military section' of the party had been set up, but in general army officers considered Spanish fascism too sectarian, juvenile and radical. Only among the younger officers and the elite professional units of the Moroccan garrisons was there strong sympathy; there a significant proportion of the junior officers had affiliated themselves with the party by July 1936.[14]

There were only eighty-four generals on the active list in the spring of 1936. Most of these were military bureaucrats who shunned activism and held moderate – and modest – views about politics and civil–military relations. Most of the key positions had already been given to the most reliable officers, and the attitude of government leaders that there was little likelihood of a 'rebellion by the generals' was perfectly well-founded. The foci of dissidence and activism lay primarily among officers of junior and middle rank.

Only a very small minority of generals were willing to assume an active role in conspiracy. Sanjurjo, the symbol – not exactly the leader – of the 1932 revolt, had been pardoned; he lived in Portuguese exile, was rather embittered and showed little inclination to take up the cudgels again in political conspiracy, despite a visit to Berlin in early February. Several dozen ultra-conservatives who had retired in 1931 had worked in or near the monarchist plottings of the last four years, but none of these men held active commands, and almost none of them had significant influence. Several senior retired officers tried to form a 'Junta of Generals' in Madrid during April, hoping to use the new inspector-general of the army as the head of a projected revolt, but these schemes fell through completely.

The attitude of Franco well reflected the realities of the army's situation. After the elections, Franco had been removed from his post as chief of staff and relegated to the obscure command of the garrison of Tenerife in the Canary Islands. Despite his great prominence, Franco had never been a 'political' general. He had won his promotions in combat, and when the General Military Academy of which he had become director was closed by the new republican regime in 1931, he had accepted this blow with perfect discipline. Franco had avoided involvement in the events of 1932, and did not legally overstep the bounds of his appointment as chief of staff in 1935. Before leaving for the Canaries, he is said to have warned against premature and extreme moves, counselling patience and time to see whether or not Azaña could cope with the situation. Franco had never joined the U.M.E., for he was extremely wary of being compromised by slipshod association with self-appointed, loose-tongued military plotters. After arriving in

Tenerife at the end of March, he avoided alliance with any of several cliques of conspirators, but maintained contact with political forces in the peninsula through the person of his brother-in-law, Ramón Serrano Suñer, head of the J.A.P., the main political movement of Catholic youth in Spain. Franco had no illusions about the seriousness of the national crisis that was developing, but neither had he any faith in the coherence or effectiveness of a merely military reaction. He would have preferred a political post that would have provided greater influence and the security of parliamentary immunity. For this reason his name was entered on the conservative ticket for special elections to the Cortes held in Cuenca province in May. Protests from both the left and the falangists, however, led to the withdrawal of his name.

Parliamentary immunity seemed the more desirable to Franco because of the peculiar inversion of legal norms effected by the vengefulness of the Popular Front. All those revolutionaries legally convicted of crimes – from murder on down – were granted amnesty by the new government, whereas a great clamour went up for the arrest of legal authorities responsible for detaining the rebels. The liberal General López de Ochoa, who had plotted against Primo de Rivera and assisted the coming of the Republic, was thrown into jail merely because he had held nominal command of the forces pacifying Asturias in 1934. Incendiary attacks on the military by the leftist press were the order of the day. Officers were hooted at in the streets, and by late spring were occasionally being attacked by leftist mobs in some localities.

The *reductio ad absurdum* of the revenge policy of the Popular Front was the ouster of the republican president, Alcalá Zamora, in April. Despite errors and excesses in the discharge of his duties, Alcalá Zamora had endeavoured to establish the presidency as a *poder moderador* ('moderating power') above pure factionalism. His removal ended the last guarantee for impartial constitutional government and made the exercise of public power in Spain a monopoly of the left. Leaders of the U.M.E. in the Madrid garrison urged Alcalá Zamora to declare martial law and call out the troops rather than be ejected, but the outgoing president refused to oppose the nominal legal processes.

It was after this time that military conspiracy first began to take coherent form. The chief organiser was General Emilio Mola, a leading *Africanista* and the last national police chief under the monarchy. Mola had been left without assignment for three years under the Republic, made military commander in Morocco by Gil Robles in 1935, then relegated to the provincial garrison of Pamplona by the new Azaña government. Mola's political views tended to be moderate, and he had used his authority with great leniency in dealing with republican conspirators in 1930. He was naturally embittered over the treatment subsequently accorded him, but after the experiences of 1923–31, he, like Franco and other leading generals, had avoided being dragged precipitously into political action. Mola had never joined the U.M.E., but like many officers and civilians had become extremely alarmed following the Popular Front elections. An official letter of mid-April protesting at the abuse to which the army was subjected drew no reply from Madrid other than an inspection trip to check his own command. It was at this time that Mola established relations with U.M.E. leaders in north-central Spain, who agreed that he be recognised as head of planning for an anti-government move by forces in that region.[15]

It was not until more than a month later, however, that a national network for the conspiracy began to be established. This was for two reasons. The response of the military was cumulative, for only as incidents and tensions spread and became more intense was a broad reaction generated. Secondly, the vital question of authority and legitimacy was hard to resolve. Since none of the senior active generals wanted to lead, the only central figure was Sanjurjo. He had first been approached in Lisbon by the Carlists, who wanted to use his name to provoke an armed rebellion of their own. Sanjurjo was perfectly willing to transmit his personal authority as co-ordinator of a revolt to Mola, since Mola indicated in correspondence that he was planning a broad national reaction and wished to install Sanjurjo as head of an interim junta once the *coup* was effected. These arrangements were not worked out until the end of May. By that time Mola had begun to draw up detailed sketches and timetables for the convergence of rebel forces to seize power in Madrid.

As plans developed during the month of June, relations with conservative civilian groups remained vague to non-existent. Mola was disgusted with republican politics of both the conservative and leftist variety. He sketched a plan for an interim military directory that would completely replace the existing authorities, derogate the 1931 Constitution, suppress all the revolutionary groups and strengthen the armed forces as the base of the new state. The social reforms of the Republic, as well as separation of church and state, were to be maintained. The question of restoring the monarchy was scarcely considered, for monarchism had little support in Spain. There was some suggestion that power would eventually be handed over to a reformed parliamentary regime, probably organised along corporative lines with a more restricted or indirect suffrage. No commitments of that sort were actually made, however, for Mola was determined that the revolt would be basically an army movement, not obligated to any special interests. The only precise plan was for an all-military directory, even if temporary, that would seize full power over the state apparatus. There was no specific 'ideology' involved. Mola was an authoritarian but not a fascist. Like most officers, he was uninterested in political parties and political ideologies. His sketch for the new junta was based upon simple predicates of unity, authority and order.

The largest political party in Spain was the Catholic conservative C.E.D.A., committed to constitutional procedures. Gil Robles and the other key C.E.D.A. leaders would not pledge support for a military *pronunciamiento*, but in view of the impending break-up simply released their political followers from any responsibility to the party, advising them to act according to their consciences but not to compromise the party itself in illegal activities. The leading monarchist politician, José Calvo Sotelo, was vaguely informed of Mola's plans and offered full support. Financiers associated with both the monarchists and the C.E.D.A. provided economic backing for the conspirators.

The only political organisation actively connected with plans for the revolt was the Falange, whose leaders had been considering the alternative for a full year. Yet the falangists were never accepted by Mola as partners, only as auxiliaries who might provide civilian volunteers. The falangists were promised freedom of propaganda and proselytisation under the new military regime, but they were not offered any central place in the government. These negotiations led to some considerable enmity between military and falangist leaders (most of whom were in jail), and at one point near the end of June the falangists were ready to quit the conspiracy.

The real problem in organising the conspiracy was simply the army itself. The majority of the officers on active duty were not willing to commit themselves seriously and definitively to armed rebellion. The Spanish army officer corps was also a bureaucratic class, and the majority of its members were not at all eager to involve themselves in a desperate undertaking that might lead to their ruin. They had their families to think of. The republican government still existed, and the Constitution was still the nominal law of the land, even though less and less often enforced. The revolutionaries had not yet tried to take over the government; after a few months they might begin to settle down, and then the crisis would ease. Military activism in Spanish politics had compiled a disastrous record between 1917 and 1931; most officers were aware of this and all the less eager to throw themselves into the fray. Furthermore, the ferocious propaganda of the left made it clear that in any radical confrontation, defeated army dissidents would not be treated so easily as in an earlier generation.

Given these hesitations, some of the leading rebels probably entered the conspiracy only after reaching the negative conclusion that it would be more dangerous for them not to. Franco only committed himself definitively about the beginning of July, and exacted as his price command of the only fully reliable and combatworthy sector of the Spanish forces, the army of Africa in the Protectorate. During June, understandings, sometimes rather vague, had been reached with other key figures, such as the inspector-general of the Border Guards, Qucipo de Llano. Mola tried to concert his planning with that of the conspiratorial clique of retired officers in Madrid, but this was extremely difficult.

Organisation was so problematical and political backing so uncertain that by the first of July Mola was on the verge of giving up the whole enterprise and retiring from the army. Encouraging reports came in during the next few days, and the first concrete date considered for the revolt was 10 July, but this had to be given up when one of the leading falangists involved was arrested.

As the days passed, Mola grew more concerned about mustering the necessary strength, and began to doubt that the military conspirators alone would suffice. He had little faith in the amount, quality or reliability of the support that would be received from the falangists. The only other alternative source was the Carlist militia in Navarre. The Carlist leaders were stickier to deal with than were the falangists. The secretary-general of the Carlist Communion, Fal Conde, insisted upon political guarantees and at least two out of three seats in the new junta for the Carlists. Mola refused such terms; he knew that both orthodox monarchism and Carlism were weak in the country and that the *pronunciamiento* would succeed only if it could be presented as a patriotic national reaction led by the army alone without being tied to special parties. The local Carlist militia were, as it turned out, eager to strike against the leftist regime. Their leaders undercut the Carlist hierarchy by making an arrangement on 12 July promising their full assistance in return for being allowed to use the old monarchist flag and exercise control of local affairs in Navarre.[16]

Until that day the situation remained highly problematic. Most officers were willing to act only on regular orders from above, which were not likely to be forthcoming. Moreover, the action was largely generated by defensive, preventive considerations. A successful counter-revolution could be mobilised only in the face of a matured revolutionary threat, but the forces of the left kept hanging fire. The rate of economic disorder was extremely high, and the government made it clear that it was a partisan of the left and would not try to provide impartial administration *vis-à-vis* the centre and the right. But the left was extremely disunited, and there was as yet no direct revolutionary action aimed at the immediate overthrow of the republican state.

The final blow in the storm of strikes, riots, arson, street disorders and murder was struck in Madrid on the night of 12 July. Leftist police officers, recently reappointed by the left republican ministry of the interior, murdered the leader of the monarchist opposition in parliament, Calvo Sotelo. Never before in the history of a west European parliamentary regime had a key opposition leader been sequestered and murdered in cold blood by the state police. To many it seemed to indicate that revolutionary radicalism was out of control and the constitutional system at a complete end.

The military revolt was scheduled by Mola to start on 18–19–20 July, in a series of zones, spreading from Morocco to the southern part of the peninsula and then to the northern garrisons. It was precipitated in Morocco on the afternoon of 17 July by delation, and the rebels quickly gained control of the whole of the Protectorate. None the less, because of the many loose ends in the conspiracy and because of Mola's staggered timetable, there was no general peninsular revolt for thirty-six hours. Throughout 18 July and into the morning of the nineteenth the situation remained completely confused.

Since that time, historical and political comment has speculated at great length as to why the left republican government did not take more stringent measures both before and during the crisis to avert major military revolt. Criticism of the government on this issue by the revolutionary left has been overwhelming. The conspiracy was not exactly a 'secret', for though the details were not known to the government, rumours had flown back and forth for months, and most of the active plotters were indeed known by officials to be hostile to the leftist regime.

Looked at from the viewpoint of Azaña's government of the middle-class left, however, its military policy was not quite so irrational as has sometimes been made out. Azaña, by July president of the Republic, and his prime minister, Casares Quiroga, doubted the ability of military conspirators to generate an effective *pronunciamiento*. There had never been a really well-organised revolt in the entire history of the Spanish army. Successful *pronunciamientos* had won their goals in the past not because of their strength but because of the weakness or unpopularity of the governments whom they overthrew. The 1932 affair had been grotesquely arranged, and most military efforts of the twentieth century were no better than that. The government authorities calculated that they could count on the support of well over half the population, including most of the best-organised and most active political groups. In such circumstances, a confused and weakly organised revolt could be easily isolated and stamped out.

This calculation was reinforced by a negative concern of the left republican leaders. Having consummated the unbalancing of the political system to regain power, they had tied themselves to the revolutionary left and found it impossible to enforce many of the norms of the Constitution. But they were not genuine revolutionaries and did not want to establish a revolutionary government. Their ideal was the juridical *status quo* of March 1936, and they hesitated to play the all-out Kerenskyist role assigned them by the revolutionaries. Premature efforts to crack down on the army might remove the last counterbalance to the extreme left and make the republican government a helpless prisoner of the revolutionaries. Hence the only measures taken were continued reassignments of many junior and middle-rank officers who seemed most active in the conspiracy. Azaña himself seems to have been most worried about direct revolt either by the army or by the left in April and May, when he was being elevated to the presidency. The indications are that by June and July he was hoping that passions were about to subside; during those weeks the policy of the government was almost uniformly negative, a sort of holding operation to get through the summer.

The most serious miscalculation by the government leaders was their relative ignorance of the exact capacity and temper of the armed forces. Though aware of the general confusion behind the plotting, they did not appreciate the dedication and determination of the hard-core rebels, who were totally committed to the proposition that the last opportunity had arrived to save their country from revolutionary destruction and Bolshevisation. The government leaders overestimated the loyalty of the police forces to the leftist regime. Finally, the government did not fully appreciate the importance of the forces in Morocco. It relied too much on the senior pro-government generals, but did not gauge the weakness of these ageing, sometimes inept, bureaucrats in the military structure. In Morocco and a number of other key garrisons, the elderly commanders were simply swept aside.

When all is said and done, the Spanish military revolt of 17–20 July 1936 stands as an audacious *coup* by a comparatively small number of determined military conspirators. Probably no more than 1000 officers – not all of them on active duty – served as the nucleus of the revolt. Their commitment and resolution served to stiffen reluctant colleagues, overthrow reluctant senior commanders and in a minority of cases bring whole garrisons out in revolt. The rebellion was not at all the 'generals' revolt' that it has customarily been labelled, but rather a rising by the activist middle and junior strata of the officer corps. In some cases the revolt was managed by sheer bravado, courage and personal example.

Perhaps the only regions in which the revolt was simple and secure were Morocco and Navarre, at the antipodes of Spanish territory. In Morocco the military forces were powerful and fairly well united, with only a minority of officers reluctant to join the movement. In Navarre Mola encountered no difficulty because of the strong civilian support among right-wing Carlists.

But in most regions of Spain the garrison forces were neither strong nor united. The support of the civilian population was often uncertain at best, and at worst the rebels were likely to meet concerted resistance by the organised working-class groups. Owing to low budgeting and summer leaves, the available manpower of the army was only slightly more than 50 per cent of its strength on paper. Matériel was scanty and obsolescent, and supplies extremely low. As noted earlier, relations with civilian groups were distant and rather vague. Rebel leaders did not want to be tied down by civilian cliques, and save among a rightist minority, there was little enthusiasm in Spanish society for a military dictatorship. Moderate and conservative elements of the middle classes, while full of hate and fear for the left, and grave concern over the Azaña regime, were not necessarily eager for a military *coup*, and in the first two or three days of the revolt showed considerable disorientation.

The rebellion was a success in only about one-third of the peninsular garrisons, and these were located mainly in the more conservative provinces of the north and north-west, where there was sizeable civilian support for an organised anti-leftist move and the revolutionary movements were comparatively weak. Conversely, the only province that voted for the conservative list in February but was dominated by the left in the July crisis was the northen coastal district of Santander. There the leftist parties were more unified and seized the initiative themselves in a direct take-over of authority under Popular Front coalition on 18–19 July.

The keys to a quick *coup* were the large cities, for there lay the centres of authority, communication and resources, and also of organised leftist strength. The rising failed in four of the six major cities – Madrid, Barcelona, Valencia and Bilbao. It enjoyed spectacular and improbable triumph, however, in two others: Seville and Saragossa. The rebel victory in Seville was largely due to an extraordinary bravura performance by a grizzled sixty-year-old veteran, Queipo de Llano. Initially he had only a handful of officers to rely upon, and virtually no troops, but by clever bluff and manipulation he rallied nearly the entire garrison and most of the police as well. The divisions within the revolutionary movements and their uncertain tactics accomplished the rest. Saragossa was the headquarters of the anarcho-syndicalists, and supposedly a stronghold of the left, but there the garrison and the police acted rapidly in full co-operation, and dominated the city before the anarchists could react.

In the three largest towns – Madrid,[17] Barcelona[18] and Valencia[19] – the revolt never had much chance of success. The organised revolutionary groups were so large compared to the military, and the support of the police so uncertain, that only in Valencia might a positive result have been expected. In Madrid and Valencia the revolt was unco-ordinated in the extreme. Though U.M.E. elements and various cliques of retired officers had been conspiring in both garrisons for several years, recent reassignments had broken up whatever unity existed earlier. Confusion among the military was total. There was never any revolt at all in Valencia, where the main troops were confined to barracks for nearly two weeks and finally overwhelmed by the revolutionaries.

The two main demands by reluctant officers were that the order to move must come through the proper channels from senior commanders, and that the armed police must support the army. This last point was indeed important, for the forces of the Civil Guard and Assault Guard were as numerous as the army in the peninsula. They were almost as well equipped, more carefully trained and selected and in many cases more professionalised. Though many of the police were anti-leftist, they tended to follow the general trend of each individual province. In most large cities they accepted the bent of the population and stayed with the leftist authorities. In many rural provinces, however, they went over to the rebels, and the support of the police was sometimes a decisive factor.

A revolt that failed in more than half the national territory can scarcely be called a success. What it achieved was not a successful *coup* but the establishment of several alternative nuclei of armed power in the north, west and far south that could be co-ordinated into a major movement against the leftist regime, creating the conditions for full-scale civil war. This situation was grasped by the government leaders on the night of 18–19 July, bringing the resignation of Casares Quiroga's left republican cabinet and the appointment of Martínez Barrio's short-lived compromise ministry that tried vainly to make a deal with the insurgents. The only version of Martínez Barrio's proposition with any likelihood of accuracy that we have was given by one of the cabinet members, Feced, to the writer García Venero.[20] Martínez Barrio apparently offered an across-the-board compromise, bringing one of the insurgents into the cabinet, promising an abrupt about-face on internal policy, a national coalition government and the disarming of the leftist militia. This was a sound compromise in the tradition of the nineteenth-century liberal *pronunciamientos*, many of which had not been aimed at the establishment of radically new regimes but simply at fundamental alteration of government leadership or policy. It might have served as the basis of preserving representative and constitutional government in Spain, but it came too late. The position of Mola and other rebel leaders had grown too radical, and they would not settle for a reasonable compromise. Lines were too sharply drawn, and the chief conspirators had made solemn pledges which Mola refused to break at the last minute.

Within less than ten hours, the left republican government veered sharply from an across-the-board compromise in favour of the insurgent right to an almost complete capitulation to the revolutionary left. This wild careening in itself reveals the confusion and irresolution of Azaña and his colleagues of the middle-class left. The result was not so much a compromise with the revolutionary left as the transfer of effective power to them. The key decision here – the 'arming of the people' (meaning of course not the 'people' but the organised revolutionaries) – was not made officially in Madrid until the afternoon of 19 July, though some arms had already been distributed to the socialists the night before. Within a few more days the vestiges of the republican system were replaced by the Spanish revolutionary confederation of 1936–7, eventually to be superseded by Negrín's new 'Popular Republic' in 1937.

The question has many times been asked whether or not the outbreak of the Civil War could have been avoided. Of course it could have, but not by mid-July 1936. By that time the extremes of hatred, sectarianism and political polarisation were so great that some sort of blow-up was almost inevitable. The main responsibility in this situation was borne by those on whose shoulders government responsibility rested – the middle-class republican left of Azaña. This sector was in exclusive control of executive power from 19 February 1936 to the outbreak of the Civil War. No other government in recent Spanish history had such undivided dominance of the executive. It did not use that authority to carry out impartial national government on the basis of the republican Constitution but to proscribe the right and cater to the revolutionaries in almost every way, from economic legislation to police activities. This policy proved suicidal for the middle-class radicals, but Azaña was only willing to reject it when it was too late.

A fashionable explanation by apologists for the middle-class left regime was that the Azaña administration did nothing to contribute to the prevailing polarisation, but was merely the victim of it, attacked by extremes of right and left. This oft-repeated contention will not bear examination. Save for a few hours on the morning of 19 July when the belated effort was made to draw back from the precipice, the Azaña administration was not a victim of the revolutionary left, but its willing collaborator almost without exception. This was the inevitable consequence of the illiberal and anti-constitutional distinction made by the middle-class left from 1931 onwards between 'true republicans' – those of the left – and 'crypto-fascists' – the conservatives. Representative national government was never possible on those terms, and the replacement of left republican government by revolutionary dictatorship in late July 1936 was a not illogical consequence of its political theory and tactics.

The revolt was almost exclusively an army affair, for the navy and air force had little to do with it. Surprisingly the conspirators made little effort to bring their colleagues from the other armed services into the revolt, no doubt in part because they did not entirely regard them as colleagues or comrades. Most army officers had little or no contact with naval or air commanders. With the exception of the revolution of 1868, previous revolts had been almost exclusively army affairs.

Although much less is known about the attitudes of naval and air force officers, there is evidence to support the generalisation that naval officers tended to be more conservative, and air force officers more liberal or radical, than those in the army. The only sectors of the armed forces that had largely preserved exclusiveness of social origin were the navy and the artillery. Thus among the naval officers there predominated more of a conservative, almost caste, attitude. Yet this had been safe-guarded by a rigid exclusivism according to which the navy largely avoided involvement in political affairs. Though the navy would be crucial in guaranteeing transportation and communication for the vital Moroccan forces, Mola and other leading conspirators made only a few feeble efforts – and these at the eleventh hour – to arrange organised support. This was probably the greatest weakness of the entire con-spiracy. A key factor in aborting revolt by naval officers was the initiative of a junior leftist officer who at a crucial moment seized control almost single-handed of the main naval radio transmitter on the southern coast, checking rebel communications and rallying naval units for the left. Moreover, despite the strong anti-leftist attitude of the naval officers, an effective revolt was especially difficult to arrange in the navy because of the stronger caste division between ranks and poorer relations between officers and men. Sailors were more directly influenced by leftist agitation than were the troops. Communist and socialist influence was weak, but anarcho-syndicalism flourished in most of the port towns where naval units were stationed. When naval commanders tried to swing their vessels behind the revolt on 19 July, mutinies broke out and seized control of most ships, precipitating mass slaughter of officers. By contrast there was very little mutiny from the ranks in army units that attempted rebellion. Army life was more open and there were better relations between officers and men and less sense of a sort of 'class consciousness' among the lower ranks. Practically the only sectors of the navy won by the rebels were those units in the stations of the north-west where control of facilities was won not by the naval command but by successful army rebels.

The air force was, of course, the newest branch of the armed forces. Its lack of tradition, its consciousness of innovation and the require-ments of technological modernisation had made it the most 'futurist' portion of the military, and its most radical sectors had acquired a pseudo-revolutionary aura following the political acrobatics of Francisco Franco's younger brother Ramón, an air force officer, in 1930. The air force had the largest minority of pro-leftist officers of any part of the military, and the majority of the air force seemed to oppose the revolt. As a result, only about 25 per cent of its units and planes were lined up on the insurgent side, placing the latter under a distinct military handicap until this was removed by German and Italian aid.

The original revolt of 17–20 July was carried out as a nominally 'republican' rising, not a monarchist, fascist or even completely militarist rebellion. Save for the compulsory 'Viva España!' the most common slogan in the first military proclamations was 'Viva la República!' Some pronouncements went even further. Franco's first official statement on 18–19 July ended with the invocation of 'Fraternity, Liberty and Equality' [sic]. Nearly all insurgent units fought under the republican flag during the first weeks of the Civil War. Mola and other leaders had been careful throughout to hold monarchists at some distance (save in Navarre), emphasising that to tie the movement to monarchism would isolate it even within the army, and much more within the country as a whole. Thus in some ways the revolt began, or seemed to begin, in the tradition of the nineteenth-century liberal *pronunciamientos*. It does not appear that there was any clear understanding or agreement concerning exact goals in the minds of most officers supporting the revolt other than the overthrow of Azaña's administration, throttling of the revolutionaries and establishment of more moderate and nationalistic government.

Mola and most of the key leaders, however, planned from the start to replace the whole republican regime, as currently constituted, with a military directory, at least momentarily. That was why Martínez Barrio's compromise on the morning of 19 July had been rejected. The appearance of moderation or liberalism in many of the first local army announcements was due to confusion among regional commanders, and also to the fact that Mola and other main leaders preferred to let the movement appear comparatively liberal in its opening days so as to minimise opposition. Conversely, if the revolt had achieved rapid success, the military directory of 1936 would probably have retained more moderate or liberal features compared with the rigorous Franco regime that was later hammered out under conditions of revolutionary civil war.

A main theme of leftist propaganda both inside Spain and abroad during the Civil War – and for many years after – was the 'international fascist conspiracy' theory of the outbreak of the conflict, which endeavoured to explain it in terms of planned aggression engineered by Hitler and Mussolini.[21] This ploy has been thoroughly disproved by critical historiography and is no longer used even by leftist propagandists. There is no evidence of direct contacts between the leading military conspirators and the German and Italian governments prior to the end of the first week of the Civil War. Carlist leaders and Alfonsine monarchist plotters had negotiated with the Italian authorities since 1932 and had even negotiated an agreement with them in March 1934 that pledged Italian supplies and money to back an armed attempt at monarchist restoration. This plan came to nought for lack of interest or support in Spain for monarchism. Army leaders were not a party to it and the agreement was not directly applicable to the situation that developed after 17 July 1936. There were various contacts between German officials and local Nazi leaders in Spain or Morocco on the one hand and army conspirators on the other, but none of these ever reached the level of official government understanding. Some minor arms agreements were negotiated with German firms, but this was done mainly by civilian conspirators and on the private level of German business, in much the same fashion as republican arms purchases from German firms during the early months of the Civil War. The outbreak of the Spanish conflict took both the German and Italian governments by surprise. Nine days passed before the first concrete decision was reached on 26 July to aid the insurgents, and then only in response to the direct requests of emissaries from Mola and Franco, and largely on the terms suggested by the latter.[22]

Considerable stress has often been laid on the political and military miscalculations involved in the army conspiracy and revolt. There is less exaggeration here, for the miscalculations were several, and were of great significance, yet they were not perhaps so great as has often been supposed. The two points most commonly raised have to do with underestimating the degree of resistance of which the revolutionary groups were capable and not foreseeing that a mere *coup* would fail, leaving all-out civil war unavoidable. Regarding the first, it is probably correct that many of the plotters did not appreciate the leftist groups' capacity for concerted paramilitary activity on short notice, particularly in street-fighting. Some of them thought in terms of the abortive leftist rising in Madrid and Barcelona in 1934, which was easily suppressed by rather small military forces. The speed of reaction and the initial unity did come as a surprise. Yet the very reason for the revolt was fear of the strength of revolutionary groups, a power that was growing week by week. In a sense the revolt was a gamble to take over the government while the counter-revolutionary elements still had a chance.

As to the second point, it was never seriously supposed by Mola or the other main leaders that the government would fall in a seventy-two-hour *coup d'état*. The most sober calculations were based on the likelihood that the revolt in Madrid would fail, and that it would be necessary to concentrate forces from both the secure garrisons in the north and the Moroccan units in the south against the capital. Mola apparently thought that this might take up to two weeks. Hence a 'little civil war' was envisioned, though not a major one. The geographic scope and sequences of the initial struggle – through the initial phases down to about the first of November – were at least partially foreseen. What was not envisioned was the military size of the struggle or its duration, together with the success of the leftist forces initially in blockading the straits, thus preventing a rapid build-up in the south. This, along with the slowdown in the north, nearly wrecked the whole plan. But then Mola and the most perspicacious rebel leaders knew that it was a dubious, touch-and-go affair with a fifty-fifty chance of failure. That was one of the main reasons why such otherwise sympathetic officers were reluctant to be associated. As early as 31 May Mola sketched an emergency plan for retreat to a northern redoubt based on Navarre if efforts to take Madrid should fail.[23]

Rapid escalation of the conflict into total civil war greatly expanded the struggle, made it a major international issue, threatened the national sovereignty of Spain and enormously radicalised the issues on both sides of the barricades. This virtually ended the prospect of representative government in Spain for the next generation, regardless of who won, and turned the military revolt in the direction of a more radical and authoritarian military regime whose contours had been but dimly perceived by most of those engaged in the military conspiracy of 1936.

SUGGESTIONS FOR FURTHER READING

The principal introductions to the politics and structure of the Spanish Army in recent times are Stanley G. Payne, *Politics and the Military in Modern Spain* (Stanford and Oxford, 1967), and Julio Busquets Bragulat, *El militar de carrera en España* (Barcelona, 1967). Three notable sketches of the conspiracy may be found in Ricardo de la Cierva, *Historia de la guerra civil española*, i (Madrid, 1969); Joaquín Arrarás, *Historia de la segunda República española*, iv (Madrid, 1968), and José María Gil Robles, *No fue posible la paz* (Barcelona, 1968). Luis Bolín's *Spain, the Vital Years* (London, 1967) is a well-written memoir that provides a vivid account of Franco's journey to assume command in Morocco and the preparations therefor. The best biographies of Franco and Mola are Brian Crozier, *Franco, A Biographical History* (London, 1968), and General Jorge Vigón, *Mola (El Conspirador)* (Barcelona, 1957). Maximiano García Venero's *El General Fanjul* (Madrid, 1967) provides a narrative of the revolt in

Madrid and revises a somewhat distorted picture of its leader. Luis Romero's *Tres días de julio* (Barcelona, 1967) presents a superbly graphic account of the beginning of the Civil War. A great deal of partisan literature on the army, the conspiracy and the revolt appeared in Spain during the Civil War and the next two decades. The most useful of these are Mola's *Obras completas* (Valladolid, 1940); Antonio Cacho Zabalza, *La Unión Militar Española* (Alicante, 1940); Joaquín Pérez Madrigal, *Augurios, estallido y episodios de la guerra* (Avila, 1938); José del Castillo and Santiago Alvarez, *Barcelona, objetivo cubierto* (Barcelona, 1958), on the conspiracy and revolt in Barcelona; B. Félix Maíx, *Alzamiento en España* (Pamplona, 1952); Felipe Beltrán Güell, *Preparación y desarrollo del alzamiento nacional* (Valladolid, 1938); Antonio Lizarza Iribarren, *Memorias de la conspiración* (Pamplona, 1957), the best work on the Carlists in the conspiracy; and two books by Mola's personal secretary, José María Iribarren, *Con el general Mola* (Saragossa, 1937) and *Mola* (Saragossa, 1938).

NOTES

1. On the background of the Spanish officer corps in the nineteenth century, see Eric Christiansen, *The Origins of Military Power in Spain 1800–1854* (Oxford, 1967); Stanley G. Payne, *Politics and the Military in Modern Spain* (Stanford and Oxford, 1967), pp. 1–82; and Julio Busquets Bragulat, *El militar de carrera en España* (Barcelona, 1967), *passim*.
2. The only general accounts of the rise of regional nationalism in modern Spain are Maximiano Garcia Venero's *Historia del nacionalismo catalán*, 2 vols (Madrid, 1967), and *Historia del nacionalismo vasco* (Madrid, 1968).
3. The struggle in Morocco has been treated from the Spanish side in Payne, op. cit. pp. 102–22, 152–86, and from the Moroccan side in David Woolman, *Rebels in the Rif* (Stanford, 1968).
4. Azaña outlined his plans and ideas in his parliamentary speeches, which are collected in his *Obras completas* (Mexico, 1966–8), ii.
5. The reaction of the *Africanistas* was best expressed in the writings of General Emilio Mola Vidal, *Obras completas* (Valladolid, 1940).
6. The most detailed explanation by one of the conspirators is given in two books by General Emilio Esteban Infantes, *La sublevación del General Sanjurjo* (Madrid, 1933) and *General Sanjurjo* (Barcelona, 1967).
7. No full-length study of the insurrection of 1934 has yet been completed. See Ricardo de la Cierva, *Historia de la guerra civil española*, i (Madrid, 1969), 369–455, and Payne, *The Spanish Revolution* (New York and London, 1970), pp. 130–56.
8. José María Gil Robles, *No fue posible la paz* (Barcelona, 1968), p. 777.
9. Felipe Beltrán Güell, *Preparación y desarrollo del alzamiento nacional* (Valladolid, 1938), pp. 113–14; Joaquín Arrarás (ed.), *Historia de la Cruzada española*, ii (Madrid, 1940), 401.
10. Arrarás, op. cit. ii, 441; Félix Maíz, *Alzamiento en España* (Pamplona, 1956), pp. 35–7.
11. There are further details in Payne, *The Spanish Revolution*, pp. 185–214.
12. Colonel Julio Mangada Roseñorn, *El fascismo en el Ejército a la Unión de Militares Españoles* (Madrid, 1936).
13. The role of the Carlists is explained in Antonio Lizarza Iribarren, *Memorias de la conspiración* (Pamplona, 1957).

14. On the Falange, see Payne, *Falange* (Stanford, 1961), pp. 101–15.

15. Mola's role and the development of the conspiracy are treated in General Jorge Vigón, *Mola (El Conspirador)* (Barcelona, 1957) and La Cierva, op. cit. i, 735–816.

16. Melchor Ferrer, 'El general Franco y la Comunión Tradicionalista' (unpublished, n.d.).

17. The principal account of the revolt in Madrid is García Venero, *El General Fanjul* (Madrid, 1967).

18. The conspiracy and revolt in Barcelona are treated in José del Castillo and Santiago Alvarez, *Barcelona, objetivo cubierto* (Barcelona, 1958), and Francisco Lacruz, *El alzamiento, la revolución y el terror en Barcelona* (Barcelona, 1943).

19. Arrarás, op. cit. v, 463–522; Gabriel Araceli, *Valencia 1936* (Saragossa, 1939), pp. 11–31.

20. García Venero, *El General Fanjul*, pp. 287–90.

21. Propagandistic assertions dominate even a few recent scholarly books published by university presses. See, for example, Dante A. Puzzo, *Spain and the Great Powers 1936–1941* (New York and London, 1962), pp. 53–74.

22. German policy has been studied in Manfred Merkes, *Die deutsche Politik gegenüber dem spanischen Bürgerkrieg 1936–1939* (Bonn, 1961).

23. La Cierva, op. cit. i, 775–6.

Part Two

The Civil War

6. Chronological Table

17–20 July	1936	Rising in Morocco and metropolitan Spain.
28–30 July	1936	Italian and German planes arrive.
6 August	1936	Beginning of negotiations for non-intervention. The committee first meets in London on 9 September.
4 September	1936	Formation of Largo Caballero's cabinet: includes socialists, communists and left republicans.
1 October	1936	General Franco named generalissimo.
24 October	1936	Russian tanks in action.
4 November	1936	C.N.T. join Largo Caballero's cabinet.
6 November	1936	Government moves to Valencia leaving Junta for Defence to resist nationalist attack. International brigades on Madrid front.
8 November	1936	Intensive attack on Madrid.
December	1936	Formation of Condor Legion.
6–15 February	1937	Battle of Jarama.
10 February	1937	Fall of Malaga.
8–18 March	1937	Italian offensive against Madrid held at Guadalajara.
19 April	1937	Governmental crises of nationalist Spain. Formation of the new single-party state by the merging of the Falange and the Carlists in the F.E.T. de la J.O.N.S.
3–8 May	1937	P.O.U.M. and C.N.T. extremist rising in Barcelona: communist attacks on P.O.U.M. cause the resignation of Largo Caballero.
17 May	1937	Negrín's government formed, excluding C.N.T. and *Caballeristas*.
June	1937	Nationalist campaign in north: Bilbao falls (11 June); Gijón (19 October).
July–September	1937	Diversionary battles of Brunete (7–26 July) and Belchite (24 August–15 September) to relieve northern front.

10 August	1937	Dissolution of C.N.T. council of Aragon.
14 December	1937	Republican offensive against Teruel.
9 March	1938	Beginning of nationalist offensive in Aragon; reaches Mediterranean on 15 April and cuts republican zone in two.
5 April	1938	Prieto resigns under communist pressure.
24 July	1938	Ebro offensive; republican forces withdraw 15 November.
30 September	1938	Munich Agreement.
29 December	1938	Nationalist offensive in Catalonia: Barcelona falls 26 January 1939.
2–5 March	1939	Negrín's government in crisis as result of decision to continue war. Anti-Negrín Council of National Defence formed 5 March.
7–11 March	1939	Communist revolt in Madrid against Council of National Defence.
1 April	1939	End of the Civil War.

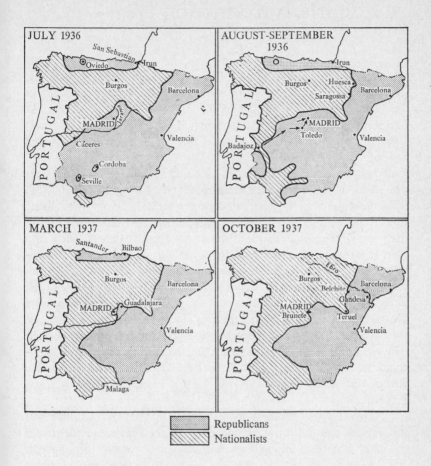

Republicans
Nationalists

7. Editor's Introduction

OF one thing we can be certain. The proletarian revolution which the generals feared was unleashed by their own rising throughout much of the territory which remained loyal to the republican government. As the F.A.I. leader, Federica Montseny observed, the generals' revolt 'hastened the revolution we all desire but which no one had expected so soon'.

Although the government, until September, remained nominally republican, real power lay in the great unions: the C.N.T. and the U.G.T. The role of the working classes in defeating military revolt in the streets of Barcelona and Madrid was certainly exaggerated in the writings of the time – André Malraux made the attack on the Montaña barracks a literary set-piece. The loyalty of the Civil Guards and Assault Guards in towns where the Republic maintained its hold was certainly as decisive as proletarian action; though at Albacete, the future base of the international brigades, the town was recaptured by workers from Civil Guards who had supported the military rising. Surprisingly enough, on the other hand, the workers' organisations in Saragossa – partly because they were unarmed and deceived by the civil and military authorities – could not retain a great C.N.T. stronghold; equally the proletarian parties did nothing to resist the risky *coup* of General Quiepo de Llano in Seville.

Nevertheless the workers' claim to have 'saved' the Republic was real enough and could not be contested by the republican parties. In the early days the working-class militia man or woman in dungarees was the symbol of resistance. Middle-of-the-road republican politicians – President Azaña, Giral the prime minister and the Catalan leader Companys – had no alternative but to allow *de facto* control to fall into the hands of the organised workers.

Thus July 1936 saw in certain areas of the republican zone the first European workers' revolution since the Great War – and that at a time when the rest of the continent seemed dominated by conservatives or fascists.

It was a 'spontaneous' revolution in the sense that it grew out of the immediate necessities of resistance and was not planned by either the

C.N.T. or U.G.T. Its key word came to be 'collectivisation' – the management of industry by syndicated workers.

It seemed to those who came from abroad to help the Republic that a workers' civilisation had at last come into existence. George Orwell's description of Barcelona, show-place of the revolution, has become classic:

> It was the first time I had ever been in a town where the working class was in the saddle.

Even in Valencia – by January 1937 a relatively ordered city – W. H. Auden wrote in admiration of workers 'doing all those things that the gentry cannot believe will be properly done unless they are there to keep an eye on them'. 'What is happening here,' wrote Ralph Fox, communist novelist killed in the olive groves on the Cordoba front, 'is the greatest thing since 1917.'

Burnett Bolloten describes the defeat of the spontaneous revolution by the communist party in alliance with 'bourgeois' republicans, the socialist party and sections of the U.G.T. Spontaneity entailed disorganisation and communists could argue that a war could not be won without centralised direction. The revolution must be postponed. 'The most revolutionary task is to win the war' ran their slogan; for defeat of the Republic meant defeat of the workers. Thus the most curious feature, in retrospect, is the alliance of the communists with the republicans and socialists against the revolution of the C.N.T. and in defence of 'bourgeois' property.

Certainly the significance of the 'spontaneous revolution' has been underestimated in retrospect by liberal historians, just as, at the time, its consequences were mainly considered as an impediment to a realistic war effort. Professor Chomsky has recently drawn attention to the unique importance, as a social experiment, of collectivisation and workers' control.[1] It is nevertheless, in my view, wrong to argue, as some do, that had the revolution not been 'suppressed' by the communists and their liberal 'stooges', then the chances of winning the Civil War by the mass enthusiasm generated by a social experiment would have been greater than those created by the success of communist discipline.

Did the workers' control exercised by the C.N.T. for instance, enhance the war potential of Catalan industry? The question is almost impossible to answer. The turn-over to war production was in itself a difficult operation: heavy metallurgical plant was more concentrated in the northern zone – hence the blow of republican defeat there in 1937. The Civil War itself created almost intractable difficulties of supply; these, perhaps, rather than deliberate restriction of credit by a central government impatient of Catalan autonomy or the 'inefficiency' of the reorganised factories, account for a decline in metallurgical production after June 1937.[2] It is certainly true that, once the C.N.T.–F.A.I. saw its political industrial strength ebbing away after May 1937, absenteeism and indifference affected production. Horacio Prieto, the C.N.T. secretary, recognised the importance of the collective factories as a social experiment and defended them against their enemies; but he admitted that their economic failure was 'notorious'. Most distressing of all, the old vices of capitalism appeared in new forms: refusal of collectivised factories to yield raw materials and manpower to others less well placed. Horacio Prieto hit out at the 'egoism of workers' and atavistic 'property mentality'. Only the centralised state, in which the C.N.T. was represented, could connect competing forces of the new economy: a strange plea for a C.N.T. leader to make in a plenum of an organisation theoretically committed to the destruction of the state.

What happened to agricultural production in the collectives? Again we know little except that, on the one hand, wheat production fell off in Catalonia (where there were few collectives) and, on the other, that the destruction of the collectives brought a sharp decline in output. As Professor Thomas points out, no lesson as to the success or otherwise of collectives can be drawn from a brief and harsh wartime experiment; certainly the 'selfishness' of the richer collectives, where living standards were higher, alarmed some enthusiasts and no effective machinery for co-ordination and the levelling out of inequalities could be improvised. In some collectives there was compulsion; in others there seems to have been an approximation to the anarchist ideal of the self-sustaining, self-governing community. What is certain, however, is that the loss of large areas of agricultural production to the nationalists caused serious shortages. Two-thirds of the wheat production, half the maize, nearly the whole national production of sugar and cotton fell early to the nationalists. Hence the food queues and shortages in the republican zone. When the nationalists entered Madrid they found a dirty, rundown and morally exhausted capital. In the nationalist zone there was plenty of food and life was 'pleasant, safe and calm'. The contrast, much publicised by the nationalists, told on republican morale.

It seems to me clear that had the 'spontaneous revolution' triumphed the war would soon have been lost. The war was kept going by Soviet supplies and the Popular Army, increasingly 'professionalised' and increasingly dominated by the communist party. Neither the Soviet Union nor the officers of the Popular Army would have supported a proletarian take-over dominated by the C.N.T. or the P.O.U.M.

Finally, were the C.N.T. (or the P.O.U.M.) in any condition to exercise power? The C.N.T. had traditionally opposed any sort of government (society would be a collection of self-governing communes or collectives exchanging products and linked by a statistical bureau) and, above all, opposed any participation in government with bourgeois parties. Their role in the early days confronted them with a cruel dilemma. In Catalonia their participation in the defence of the Republic had given them *de facto* power in the Central Militia Committee; 'formal' power was in the hands of the *Generalitat* government. How long could they 'camouflage' their real power? What would happen to their militias and collectives if a *formal* government, in the hands of their political enemies, the communists and the Catalan left, recovered *real* power? Yet, if they seized power on their own account, this could only result in a political dictatorship of the C.N.T. – the very antithesis of the whole anarchist tradition.

Most of the leaders saw that, in order to create a wide political alliance to back the war effort and in order to protect the 'revolutionary conquest' of the C.N.T., they must enter the government as they did, first in Catalonia and then in Madrid. Political participation was the only means of survival. Once the C.N.T. leaders resigned from the government in May 1937, they spent the rest of the Civil War seeking to regain their cabinet posts in order to parry the onslaughts of their communist enemies.

This acceptance of, indeed quest for, political power split the anarchist movement. Militants argued, not merely that participation was a sin in itself but that it endangered the revolutionary conquests. The C.N.T. leaders accepted the dismantling of the direct instruments of proletarian power: the militia, the police apparatus, the collectives. It was not that they had stooped to political bargaining with the enemies of the working class; they had made an appallingly bad bargain.[3]

The P.O.U.M. was at least clear about the necessity for political power. But, in its fashion, it was as unrealistic as the C.N.T. What chance was there for the victory of a Republic in the hands of the workers led by a localised vanguard? Was the issue, as the P.O.U.M. daily claimed, 'Socialism versus Fascism'? What would have followed if, acting on this analysis, the workers' parties had 'put an end to the bourgeoisie and the reformists'? Surely only defeat.

This spontaneous revolution, together with the desertion and flight of officers and civil servants, left the Republic with neither an effective centralised government nor an organised army. The republican government dissolved the army – politically an inevitable decision, but in terms of military efficiency probably a mistake. It was therefore subsequently confronted with the problem of recreating a state and an army. Power was in the hands of militia committees and other local *ad hoc* bodies; the army was a collection of improvised militia columns persuaded to act, rather than ordered to obey, by loyal republican officers. Whole areas of republican Spain were quasi-independent: Catalonia, the Basque provinces, Asturias, Santander had their separate governments or councils.

The difficulty was that the organisation of both an effective central government and an efficient army became inseparable from the struggle for power between the political components of republican Spain and between the quasi-autonomous governments and the central government. The main contenders were the C.N.T., the U.G.T., the socialist, party and the rapidly growing communist party. This struggle was bitter, and it was not solved by the formation of a government under Largo Caballero in September, or by the admission of the C.N.T. in November – formal political recognition of the strength of the two unions, the C.N.T. and U.G.T.

This struggle brought the ousting of Largo Caballero (p. 145) and his political extinction by the communists, and even internal civil war on two occasions (pp. 139–42; p. 154). The most effective agent for unified political control and efficient military discipline was the communist party; but necessary war measures were thus considered by the opponents of the party as moves in a ruthless strategy to control republican Spain in the interests of the foreign policy of the Soviet Union.

The strength of the communist party lay in its organisation, its ruthlessness and its impeccable revolutionary credentials which allowed it to 'save the bourgeoisie' without appearing as counter-revolutionary. Above all it was the home country of communism, the Soviet Union, which supplied the republican army with arms. This was a factor which Negrín, who succeeded Largo Cabellero in May 1937, could never forget or neglect. He is harshly criticised as a communist dupe (p. 150), ready to fling the socialist veteran Indalecio Prieto to the communist wolves and to allow creeping communist control of the army and police. This ruthless strategy was attacked at the time by George Orwell; but to most Western sympathisers the communists still appeared as the most energetic of the defenders of the Republic and Negrín the ablest war prime minister: George Orwell could not get his criticisms published.

What were the alternatives, Negrín's defenders ask, if, as we know, the compromise peace which Prieto and certain C.N.T. leaders favoured was not possible? Only to fight on, as Negrín argued after the shattering defeats in the north and the division of republican territory into two zones, until some change in the international situation would bring France and Britain to the aid of the Republic. After Munich (September 1938) these hopes were as illusory as Prieto's hopes of a negotiated peace. The communists alone supported Negrín's slogan 'To resist is to conquer'; he supported their political vendettas.

Indalecio Prieto had always maintained that the side with a healthy rearguard would win the war. There can be no doubt that nationalist morale stiffened with the hope of victory as republican morale disintegrated into recrimination with the prospect of defeat. C.N.T. units believed that their commanders were shot, and their wounded neglected in hospitals, by communists. Just as it is difficult to assess the economic viability in a war economy of the C.N.T. collectives, a priori it is even more difficult to judge the effects of the consistent attacks on them made by the Negrín government.

The ruthlessness of the communist party and its demoralising effects on its opponents cannot be denied; but neither can the carping dogmatism and defeatism of Negrín's enemies be excused. Negrín pulled together the Popular Front after the appalling Aragon disaster, and the communists did produce an army capable of fighting the battle of the Ebro, even if the battle was the ultimate strategical blunder.

It is unpopular to say that the policies of the F.A.I., like those of the P.O.U.M. before it, would have lost the war in a week. In extremis the F.A.I.'s remedy was guerrilla warfare – a romantic appeal to the tradition of the War of Independence. The F.A.I.'s resistance to general mobilisation which would 'leave the syndicalist movement an orphan' by conscripting committeemen was an irresponsible reaction. Communist policy was, in the jargon of the time, 'objectively correct'. There can be no certainty in such a judgement, but I believe that the policies of the F.A.I. and C.N.T. would have brought swift disaster.

In the end the war was won by a better-trained and well-supplied
E

army backed by unified political and military control in the hands of one man – General Franco. For this reason the military history of the war, set out in Chapters 9 and 10, is of great importance. So was the highly controversial issue of war supplies discussed in Chapter 11.

What emerges from these essays is the great effort the republican government put into organising a modern Popular Army – in some respects its organisation was superior to the 'organic' divisions which formed the original basis of the Nationalist Army. Tactically the republicans could never maintain an offensive; Franco nevertheless doggedly insisted on winning back any portion of lost territory, even if this meant the sacrifice of larger objectives: hence the bloody battles of Teruel and the Ebro.

The essays show the importance of Soviet aid – particularly in the air, until the 'aeronautical revolution' of 1936 put Soviet planes at a disadvantage. Supporters of the Republic will find it difficult to accept the conclusion that it was less aid than the moral unity and logistic superiority of the nationalists which was decisive in the long run. General Rojo's testimony, set down immediately after the war, is a damning verdict on the effects of political fragmentation on military decisions. It is important to remember, however, that this testimony reflects the débâcle and disillusionment of 1939, not the spirit of 1936. What Ricardo de la Cierva describes as 'spiritual unity' did prove a better cement in wartime than the political alliances of the Popular Front. Yet political alliances are a consequence of a democratic war effort. It was to conquer the effects of politics on war that the communists drove ruthlessly for unification, a unification which their political opponents saw *merely* as a hegemonical device. No one, on reflection, can avoid the conclusion that unity of political direction and military command in the hands of one man, General Franco, was a decisive relative advantage.

It remains to give a brief account of the growth of a monolithic political and moral structure in nationalist Spain; it was achieved almost at the very moment when the Republic was faced with internal civil war in Barcelona. Most republican accounts blame the overall lack of arms supplies – indisputably a crucial factor, though there were times (e.g. late 1936 and early 1937) when a better use of available supplies was inhibited by a lack of central control. Indeed, it was the emergence of the problem of priorities for scarce supplies between 'competing' army groups that inclined the generals to insist on the choice of a generalissimo.

General Franco, a devoted career officer, enjoyed exceptional prestige in the army in 1936. His hesitations had appalled the more resolute conspirators; his commitment ensured the support of the Army of Africa stationed in Spanish Morocco. Once this army was ferried across to the mainland it became the most powerful unit on the nationalist side. Franco's prestige, his military power and his seniority made him the inevitable choice as commander-in-chief; but he was also made head of state by his military peers.

The consequences of this latter step were certainly not evidence to his fellow-generals – some of whom were monarchists. The machinery of state Franco took over was improvised, its political support fragmented. The Carlists, who had risen in Navarre (the Basque provinces, though controlled by the Catholic and conservative Basque nationalist party remained loyal to a Republic which granted it autonomy) were traditional monarchists or right-wing authoritarians. The Falange was in origins a radical nationalist party, afforced by 'new shirts' who sought security in its ranks; its expansion had left it in disarray and the nominal leader, Hedilla, was confronted with a congeries of rival local chieftains. The mass of the nationalists were probably old *cedistas*, with no place to go in a military, non-parliamentary state, and conservatives of all brands, and those who happened to be caught in zones occupied by nationalist forces – the 'geographically loyal' who existed on both sides. These disparate elements were kept together less by what they supported than by what they rejected: the Republic of the Popular Front.

The administrative and ideological confusion of Burgos and Salamanca disturbed Serrano Suñer, Franco's brother-in-law. To him the nationalist state lacked a 'juridical' foundation. By April 1937 this had been found in Franco as head of state and leader of a single party. The party was erected by the destruction of the Carlists and Falangists as independent entities – a process helped by their internal quarrels and inept moves at independence. Thus the Carlists had sought to establish a military college of their own. In the Falange, Hedilla's group, which had sought to give the nationalist revolution a social content and mistrusted generals as old-fashioned conservatives, was in sharp conflict with the local chieftains. Armed brawls and seizure of offices in Salamanca allowed Franco to end the Falange as an independent party. The new party – the F.E.T. de la J.O.N.S. – more briefly the 'Movement', was to give Franco a firm political base.[4]

However he used it, Franco's monolithic political and military control must give nationalist Spain an advantage in war; it was the advantage Marlborough had enjoyed at the height of his career. Such a concentration of power could not be achieved in republican Spain, which remained democratic in theory (wartime censorship and party control of the press limited the theory in practice). Franco was an efficient professional soldier, with a good eye for ground and a will of iron – it was his commitment to unconditional surrender that prevented a compromise peace, which his German advisers sometimes thought inescapable when the war was going badly. His trained troops came to enjoy a comparative advantage in arms supply. Only massive arms supplies to the Republic without corresponding escalation from Germany and Italy might have reversed the verdict of war. After the northern campaign – the decisive military event of the war – industrial power passed to the nationalists and their logistical difficulties were solved.

What had been decided in April 1937 was to determine the future of Spain to this day. The Falange lost its social radicalism in return for control of organised labour in Franco Spain; the Carlists (and the Alfonsine monarchists who still retained some support in the army and among the rich) were to lose immediate hope of a monarchical restoration in return for a Spain where their interests and their religion would be safe from the left. Indeed, the *effective* ideologies of nationalist Spain, in the early years, were military order and the Catholic faith. The church had suffered terrible persecution in the first weeks of the Civil War and the Spanish clergy (Basque priests apart) supported the nationalist crusade with greater enthusiasm than the Vatican.

The Spanish Civil War, like the Carlist Wars of the 1830s, concerned the Great Powers and reflected the balance between them and their relative determination to pursue their interests. The democratic powers were revealed as weak; Germany, Italy and the Soviet Union as ruthless. 'Non-intervention (the voluntary acceptance of a pledge to help neither side in Spain) was a mechanism invented by France and Great Britain to avoid commitment and became a device to prevent a worsening of relations with Germany and Italy. It was consistently flouted by Germany, Italy and the Soviet Union. When Soviet aid dropped off, effective and continuous supplies came to the nationalists.

Has, however, the importance of the Civil War in European terms been overemphasised by historians? Were the relations between the powers significantly altered by their performance in Spain? Did it need Italian 'deceit' over 'volunteers' to prove to Eden that the pursuit of an Italian rapprochement by Chamberlain was misconceived? The weakness of France and Great Britain was evident elsewhere and the real tests were Austria and Czechoslovakia, not Spain. Italy was seriously weakened by its efforts in Spain; Germany, in the end, gained little apart from the economic concessions it wrung out of Franco as a price for continued military aid.

One might even argue that Hitler would have invaded a democratic Spain during the Second World War and that the balance of power would have been less favourable to the allies in the Mediterranean. General Franco's policy after 1939 was determined by a balance between his dislike of the democracies who had sympathised with his opponents, his awareness of the weakness of an exhausted Spain and his desire to be on reasonable terms with the victors after 1943. The result of his calculations was to keep Spain out of the war; to Churchill this balancing act was advantageous to the allies but it could not earn the pardon of the European left. Nationalist Spain was ostracised by the victorious allies in 1945.

The Spanish Civil War decided the political destiny of Spain. In retrospect its importance to the world outside Spain appears symbolic and domestically divisive. In a Europe that to the left appeared doomed to go down before fascism, the resistance of the Spanish Republic was a 'beacon of hope', and aid to the Spanish workers a moral imperative. The effect of 'aid to Spain' on domestic political debate in France, Great Britain and the United States was of great consequence. Inevitably, this debate and concern for Spain was reflected in the work of a generation of politically conscious writers; it provoked, in Arthur Koestler's words, the last twitch of Europe's dying conscience.

In Britain, most conservatives instinctively supported Franco against the 'reds'. The government was concerned not to align itself with Russia and to avoid a general war by appeasement of Germany and Italy. Hence the Spanish question was an embarrassment: non-intervention might seal off this embarrassment. However, conservatives divided: Churchill (who had remarked that his relations would have been shot in republican Spain) believed that Britain was sacrificing its interests as a Great Power in aiding the creation of a pro-Axis Spain; Eden came to distrust concessions to Italy when it openly flouted non-intervention by sending its divisions to Spain. The majority of conservatives shared Chamberlain's subordination of the Republic to the necessities of appeasement; a significant minority opposed him.

The labour party was likewise divided over Spain and the policy of the leadership – Ernest Bevin above all – was so cautious that in 1939 the left could accuse the leaders of 'failing to use the great resources of the labour movement' to help Spain. Why?

First the leaders were bitterly hostile to the communists, who for years had abused them as 'social fascists', i.e. a more dangerous brand of being than honest-to-goodness reactionaries. It was now the communist party that pressed for active aid to Spain via a Popular Front in Britain; to the leaders this appeared a 'Trojan Horse' policy by which their old enemies, the communists, would control the United Front. More fundamentally, Bevin was a realist: he believed that the British working class *as a whole* did not want to go to war over Spain, and he shared the belief that an unprepared and unarmed Britain was in no position to risk a policy that might result in general war. The leftists who were demanding action were at the same time the pacifists who opposed rearmament; Bevin rammed home this inconsistency. The leaders denounced non-intervention when it worked against Spain – Attlee's speeches are some of the bitterest in British parliamentary history; but there was little they could do beyond this verbal violence and expression of sympathy with the Republic.

Britain, then, was deeply divided by the Spanish question. Until these divisions were healed, Britain could have no coherent policy.

Important as the Spanish war was in revealing the impotence and divisions of Britain – and France – its impact on writers and intellectuals was tremendous. Since with few exceptions (Catholics like Evelyn Waugh, the poet Roy Campbell, the inhabitants of ivory towers like T. S. Eliot) most writers were broadly liberal, they saw in the support of the Republic at war the 'last cause'. That their commitment was ruthlessly organised and exploited by communists or that it was frequently emotionally and psychologically self-regarding, should not blind us to its genuine nature.[5]

All over the world men responded to this call precisely because they were liberals of one sort or another, shocked at the overthrow *manu militari* of a 'progressive' government; John Kennedy, in spite of his family Catholicism, recognised that the republican government was 'right morally speaking' in that 'its program was similar to the New Deal'. To capitalise this liberal sentiment, in the United States, the communist party turned to the heroes of American democracy. When Earl Browder, the communist leader, wished to criticise the administration for its neutrality policy which denied Spain arms, he demanded, 'Let us ask Jefferson where he stands on this issue.'

To help the Spanish resistance gave a generation of intellectuals in

Britain, beaten down by the depression, unemployment and the national government, the sensation of effective action. A sense of personal liberation can be felt in most of the writing on the Civil War. Before the inexorable end came in sight, intellectuals felt on the side of history for once; they identified with Spaniards 'fighting for freedom'. It is an uncomfortable phenomenon of identification in some ways. Gustav Regler, who joined the international brigades, observed, 'Only on this occasion have *I* known that sense of freedom and feeling of unconditional escape, of readiness for absolute change. . . . We don't write history now, we make it.' The time when the Republic looked like winning was to Hemingway and his friends 'the happiest period of our lives'. 'You are all bad,' growled Ezra Pound, more concerned about the ravages of usury than the issues at stake in Spain, 'Spain is an emotional luxury to a gang of dilettantes.'

Almost every writer of significance sympathised with the Republic. Hemingway wrote one of his best novels on the war; James Baldwin his first short story at the age of twelve. It posed, indeed, in an acute form the social responsibility of the author: 'Picasso's stand for freedom and democracy should deal the death blow to the unsound argument . . . that the artist has no concern with public affairs.' Benny Goodman played his incomparable clarinet at a republican benefit. When accused, in a different climate, of supporting the 'communists' in Spain, John Steinbeck could reply, 'What's good enough for Shirley Temple is good enough for me.' Whether the total commitment of authors produced great literature is another matter. It was Tolstoy's maxim that the tension necessary for a great work of art comes from understanding the motives of both sides. To Cecil Day Lewis, the English poet, the war was simply a 'battle between light and darkness'.

The most dramatic European – and here the French contribution was numerically the most significant – and American response was the formation of the international brigades. Ludwig Renn, a German novelist whose most powerful work was pacifist, felt that the time had come for writers to stop making stories and to make history; he fought in the 12th International Brigade, composed of German anti-Nazis and possibly the toughest unit in the republican army. The brigades were recruited and organised by the communist parties; they contained non-communists – ranging from a sprinkling of writers who found a sense of personal freedom in exchanging the typewriter for a gun, young and politically active workers, hardened anti-fascist political exiles, communist party members, to the unemployed of Europe in the depression years. Indeed, it was to find 'real' contact with the dispossessed that many middle-class intellectuals went to Spain. Since the international brigades were shock forces their casualties were appalling; of the English and Americans who went into action on the Jarama in February 1937, nearly half were killed.

The apoliticism and disillusion of the writers of the forties comes partly from the feeling of emotions expended in vain: the Republic lost. More significantly it comes from the realisation later of having been *used* for a political cause by the unscrupulous manipulators of the communist party; a sense of shame, for instance, that at the communist-organised writers' congress of 1937 a defence of social realism became an unscrupulous attack on the French novelist André Gide as a Trotsky-ite because he had written a book criticising the Soviet Union. 'You must say yes or no to Fascism,' said Koltsov, the Soviet journalist, at the conference – and this meant accepting his condemnation of left-wing dissidents as Trotskyites. A liberal position was impossible.

The effect on communists was curious. Both Gustav Regler and Arthur Koestler were on the verge of leaving the communists: the mystique of the Popular Front brought them back for 'a second honeymoon with the party', only to make ultimate disillusionment more complete. Koltsov is an even stranger and tragic case. One can feel in his *Diary* that he came to believe in the Popular Front that he preached: Spain was for him a truly liberating experience. Like so many other Russians who had been exposed to Spain, he vanished mysteriously on his return to the Soviet Union.

The response of the right can be dealt with more briefly. Franco found conservative apologists; the most extreme were prepared to call him 'perhaps a saint' and to swallow the 'red plot' as an explanation of the immediate origins of the war. British and French financial interests, with their large investment in mining and public utilities, thought the nationalists would win and that Franco's need of foreign capital would free him from any exclusively political dependence on Germany and Italy which could not provide the foreign exchange needed to rebuild the Spanish postwar economy. American companies provided Franco with oil, without which his operations would have been paralysed. Nevertheless, it is a reflection on the strength of the American progressive tradition that the financial press was, on the whole, hostile to Franco: the American workers were less enthusiastic supporters of the Republic than Wall Street.[6]

It was the observed ruthlessness of the nationalists in victory, particularly in the Basque country, that drove some Catholics to oppose the approbation of their hierarchy. This was most evident in France, where the 'red Catholics' like Maritain and Bernanos supported the Republic. Originally a supporter of Franco, Bernanos reacted as any sensitive man must to the shedding of blood; his book on the 'butchery' of the Falange and the Italian Rossi in Majorca created a scandal in Catholic circles; like all engaged in the war, he accepted propaganda at its face value. Just as British conservatives believed the 'red plot', so Bernanos swallowed the Nazi plot; in his view the generals were so bereft of any widespread support that only the *previous* assurance of German and Italian aid could explain their rebellion.

In the United States a considerable proportion of the American laity did not follow their bishops – again an indication of the strength of the American progressive tradition. What strengthened the resistance of American Catholicism was the nature of the attacks on Franco supporters made by American Protestants. The Black Legend of Spain was part of American tradition; it delighted in the sound of broken images and readily believed that, as in the 1830s, priests acted as snipers from their own steeples.

It was the acceptance of the propaganda of one's own side that nauseated Orwell. To him the contrapuntal lying of committed newspapers, the dreadful simplifications of the propaganda of the communists which classed its enemies to the left 'beasts of prey', the sickening repetition of atrocity stories by the right, seemed a return to the monumental *suppressio veri* of the Great War. There was a 'cesspool of abuse' fed by 'screaming liars'.

Propaganda is nauseating; but more was at stake than the stomachs of the liberal left. Liberalism is a doctrine of compromise and as such it rarely survives the touch of the barricades. The dilemmas were real. How could pacifist socialists, who were fighting rearmament, advocate a degree of support for the Spanish Republic which might entail a general war? How could Roosevelt, who came to regard the arms ban on republican Spain as a moral error, attack non-intervention when his whole policy depended on friendship with France and Great Britain, the creators and proponents of non-intervention? How could American Jewish liberals – Goebbels had said all Jews supported the Republic – and Negroes demand from the administration a stand against Franco when it was the Catholic vote which had helped to bring their standard-bearer, Roosevelt, to the White House? How could liberal Catholics support the conquerors of Ethiopia and those who had brought about the decline and fall of the League of Nations?

Two last painful questions. How much did socialists and liberals, familiar with the international politics of Europe but ignorant of Spain, really care what happened in Spain, provided the reaction in their own country was in their favour? 'I shall reach Berlin through Spain,' said one German communist international brigadier. How deep were the political and emotional reactions? The 'grass-roots' reaction – did it go beyond the active minority? Between 20 and 30 per cent of Americans had 'no opinion'. Was it a reaction of the establishment, literary and political? Was Bevin's sense of the shallowness of the general reaction correct? George Orwell remarked bitterly that for two and a half years the British working classes saw their Spanish comrades 'slowly strangled and never aided them by a single strike'. True they raised money for Spain; but their contributions 'would not equal 5 per cent of the turnover of the Football Pools during the same period'.[7]

NOTES

1. For Professor Chomsky's views, see his *American Power and the New Mandarins* (Penguin edn, 1961), pp. 62 ff.

2. The decline is evident from the statistics published in Jose M. Bricall, 'Algunos caracteres de la economía catalana durante la guerra civil española', in *Moneda y Crédito*, cix (1969), 59 ff. As a judgement on collectivisation such statistics are irrelevant. The decline took place also in non-collectivised areas and any judgement on collectivisation as such is 'impure' because of the increasing government control of essential war industries.

3. The most modern treatment of the difficulties of the C.N.T. is contained in C. M. Lorenzo, *Les anarchistes espagnols et le pouvoir 1868–1969* (Paris, 1969).

4. The most detailed account of this infighting, though biased in favour of Hedilla, is contained in M. García Venero, *Falange Hedilla* (Paris, 1967). The memoirs of Serrano Suñer, *Entre Hendaye y Gibraltar* (Madrid, 1947), reflect the views of one of the architects of union.

5. A good account of British reactions is contained in K. W. Watkins, *Britain Divided* (London, 1963).

6. For the general intellectual and political background, particularly in America, see S. Weintraub, *The Last Great Cause* (New York, 1968), and A. Guttman, *The Wound in the Heart* (New York, 1968).

7. Cf. the remarks of Riesman and Glazer in *The Radical Right*, ed. D. Bell (Anchor edn, New York, 1964), pp. 123 ff. The opinion polls of the thirties revealed the conventional notion of the rich as conservative in government, labour and distributive policy as correct 'but false in the realm of civil liberties and foreign policy, when the greater impact of mistrust and fear of the strange and the stranger among the poor came to light'.

8. The Parties of the Left and the Civil War

BURNETT BOLLOTEN

ON the eve of the Civil War in July 1936 the left was riven by discord. The socialist party was split into irreconcilable factions, its internecine feud exacerbated by Largo Caballero, the leader of its left wing, whose new-born amity with the communists had led to the fusion of the socialist and communist youth movements into the J.S.U., a merger trenchantly denounced by Indalecio Prieto's centre faction as the 'absorption of the socialist youth by the communist party'. Furthermore, while Prieto had hoped to bolster the moderate Popular Front government and to restrain the disturbances that had convulsed the country, Largo Caballero – a reformist before 1934 – had called for proletarian dictatorship.

The dissensions of the left were compounded by the rivalry between the two labour federations, the socialist U.G.T., headed by Largo Caballero, and the anarcho-syndicalist C.N.T., inspired by the F.A.I., whose immediate goal was the establishment of libertarian or anarchist communism. For years the anarcho-syndicalists had reviled Caballero, and his recent call for proleterian dictatorship and the fusion of the two labour organisations only increased their animosity, for they condemned him as a 'dictator in embryo' whose 'crooked aim' was to absorb the C.N.T.

As for the communists, with a membership in July of only 40,000, although they hailed Caballero's collaboration, they declared that they would resist 'every attempt to break up the Popular Front prematurely'.

At the root of this cautious policy lay the Kremlin's fear that Germany's military strength, encouraged by the West, might be directed against the U.S.S.R. To avert isolation the U.S.S.R. concluded defence agreements with France and Czechoslovakia, which led, in August 1935, to the Comintern's moderate Popular Front line.

The Civil War came therefore at an embarrassing moment; for the failure of the military to achieve the expected walkover precipitated a far-reaching social revolution, threatening the Soviet Union's hopes for rapprochement with the democratic powers.

In the principal cities the state fragmented, as garrisons surrendered and the police disintegrated. The moderate, middle-class cabinet of José Giral possessed only the trappings of power; for power was scattered among workers' committees, which organized police squads and militia, prisons and tribunals, highway and frontier patrols.

In some of the provinces where the military rebellion collapsed, the unions appropriated a major portion of the economy. Landed properties were confiscated, some collectivised, others divided among the peasants. Railways, trams and buses, public utilities, industrial plants and mines were seized. Likewise, the property of handicraftsmen, small manufacturers and tradesmen was sequestered. In the countryside, the zealots imposed their will on small farmers, and, in the name of libertarian communism, established parochial dictatorships in many villages. Libertarian communism, they asserted, would raise the peasant's standard of living, banish 'hate, envy and egoism' and establish 'mutual respect and solidarity'.[1]

Aghast at these events, the urban and rural middle classes were without direction, for the leaders of the republican parties were either immersed in torpor or had fled the scene. Dismayed by their leaders' emasculation, the middle classes gravitated towards the communist party, which in accordance with its Popular Front line defended their economic interests:

. . . the small tradesmen and manufacturers [have] many things in common with the proletariat [affirmed *Mundo Obrero*, the party organ (27 July 1936)]. They are . . . as much opposed to the big capitalists and captains of powerful fascist enterprises as the workers. Hence, it is everyone's duty to respect [their] property.

In Valencia, 50,000 farmers joined the Peasant Federation, which the party formed for their protection.

We have . . . been within an ace of unleashing a civil war between the farmers and agricultural workers [declared the Federation's secretary]. Fortunately this has been averted, although at the cost of bursting our lungs in an intensive campaign of political education designed to secure respect for small property.[2]

In addition, the party – directed throughout the war by Comintern delegates – defined the political and social changes of republican

Spain after July 1936 as a 'bourgeois democratic revolution', thus appealing to domestic and foreign opinion. '[The] Spanish Communist party,' declared the French party, 'has asked us to inform public opinion . . . that the Spanish people . . . have only one aim: the defence of the republican order and respect for property.'[3]

Thanks to this policy, the Spanish communists ran foul of the social revolution. This meant violating venerable doctrines, but Stalin knew that as long as the Spanish government was recognised by the democratic powers it could insist on its right to purchase arms. He also knew that if Britain and France were to abandon non-intervention the Civil War might develop into a European conflict from which he would emerge the arbiter of the continent. It was therefore essential that President Azaña, morose and impotent, remain in office.

Although the left-wing opponents of the communist party charged it with planning to re-establish the old regime, its goal was far more subtle; for, under cover of a democratic superstructure, it aimed at controlling the principal elements of state power. This meant permeating the government, replacing the revolutionary police squads and militia by a state police and a regular army, establishing state control over ports and frontiers, destroying the collective farms, dissolving the workers' committees in the collectivised enterprises and, finally, nationalising the basic industries; for nationalisation, like decollectivisation, would enable the government to undermine the revolution at one of the principal sources of its power.

If by opposing the collectives in the urban areas the communists sought middle-class support, this was also their goal in the countryside. Through the ministry of agriculture, which they controlled, they used the decree of 7 October 1936 – which exempted from confiscation farmers who had not identified themselves with the military rebellion – to encourage those who had accepted collectivisation to demand the return of their land. Mariano Vázquez, C.N.T. secretary, accused the communists of 'stirring up egotistic impulses' in areas where the C.N.T. and U.G.T. had jointly established collective farms by inciting peasants to divide up the land.[4]

When Caballero became premier and war minister in September 1936, the communists held only two portfolios: agriculture and education. This did not reflect their mounting influence, for they soon became the strongest party in the left camp. While many of the new recruits hoped to salvage something from the wreck of the republican regime, an even greater number were swayed by the party's skilful propaganda, its organising capacity and the power it derived from Soviet arms and Soviet agents.

Hardly inferior as a source of strength was the impotence of the republican parties. Cowed by the violent reaction of the masses, wrote a politburo member, they allowed themselves to be influenced by 'our policy of discipline and order'. As for the socialists, many of Largo Caballero's most trusted aides had secretly or without disguise transferred their allegiance to the communists. Although Largo Caballero had encouraged the fusion of the two youth movements, believing he could control the J.S.U., he was quickly undeceived, for its leaders soon joined the communist party.

Furthermore, the libertarian movement, lacking cohesion and weakened by differences of principle, was an unequal match for the monolithic party. Fearing that the state might destroy their revolutionary gains, some of the C.N.T.–F.A.I. leaders urged participation in the cabinet. Although this meant jettisoning their anti-governmental creed – 'All governments are detestable', they had preached – they were loath to relinquish the affairs of state to rival organisations. Hence, in November 1936, while asserting that circumstances had 'transformed the nature of the Spanish government', they decided – though not without an inner struggle with conscience and principle – to join the cabinet. 'What inhibitions, what doubts, what anguish, I had personally to overcome . . .' declared Federica Montseny, herself one of the new ministers.

Once inside the cabinet, the anarcho-syndicalists yielded to their opponents. According to Federica Montseny, the arguments were always the same: 'It was essential to give an appearance of legality to the Spanish Republic, to calm the fears of the British, French and Americans.' Even left socialist Premier Largo Caballero, while not ready to turn his back completely upon the revolution, had modified his revolutionary stance in the hope of securing arms abroad. 'The Spanish government,' he stated, 'is fighting not for socialism but for democracy and constitutional rule.'

Although Juan López, C.N.T. minister of commerce, held that the C.N.T., in entering the government, wished to legalise the revolutionary committees, the cabinet soon decreed their replacement by local councils in which all the organisations of the left were to be represented, thus threatening the libertarian movement's dominant position in countless towns and villages and deepening the divisions within the C.N.T. and F.A.I. on the matter of governmental collaboration.

Simultaneously, the cabinet took steps to dissolve the revolutionary police by reconstructing the state police, while Minister of Finance Juan Negrín, Prieto's erstwhile intimate but now a communist supporter, began to rebuild the carabineers into a powerful force of public order. 'You are,' declared his under-secretary, '. . . the guardians of the state . . . and those visionaries who believe that a chaotic situation of social indiscipline and licentiousness is permissible are utterly mistaken.'[5]

Aided by their supporters in other parties, the communists secured pivotal positions in the police corps. Lieutenant-Colonel Burillo became Madrid's police chief; Justiniano García and Juan Galán were made chief and sub-chief respectively of the interior ministry's intelligence department, while two other communists were appointed to vital posts in the police administration, one becoming commissar-general in the *Dirección General de Seguridad*, and the other head of the training centre of the secret police, which formed the cadres of the new secret police corps. From the time of its creation this corps became an arm of the Soviet secret police, which established itself in Spain quite early in the war.[6]

While the communists were penetrating the police apparatus, they were calling for the militarisation of the militia units and their fusion into a regular army. It was of course essential to create a force of greater combat efficiency; but in the C.N.T.–F.A.I. units, in which there was no officers' hierarchy, militarisation encountered a philosophical impediment: '. . . every single militant had his share of scruples to conquer . . . and – why not admit it? – of illusions to be buried,' wrote C.N.T.–F.A.I. leader González Inestal.[7] For the communists, on the other hand, indoctrinated with the principles of leadership and control, militarisation caused no heart-searching. It was also a step towards the regular army which they planned to dominate.

The fear that a regular army might become 'the devourer of the revolution, the instrument of a party', was another reason why the anarcho-syndicalists entered the government, but they soon found that they had no say in military decisions. Although they agreed to militarisation, despite the warnings of the purists that 'if we sail along with the authoritarian current . . . nothing will remain of anarchist ideals',[8] they endeavoured to retain the integrity of their own units.

On the other hand, the communists were quick to dissolve their own militia, the 5th Regiment, and to weld its battalions with other forces into the new mixed brigades, thus controlling five of the first six brigades of the regular army.[9]

They also became firmly embedded in the general commissariat of war, which exercised political control over the armed forces. This they achieved largely because Alvarez del Vayo, foreign minister and commissar-general, secretly promoted the interests of the party by appointing an inordinate number of communist commissars. 'He labelled himself a socialist,' wrote Caballero, 'but he was unconditionally in the service of the communist party.'[10]

Another factor favouring communist influence in the army was the pressure of Soviet agents:

> The Spanish government [testifies Caballero] and, in particular, the minister responsible for the conduct of operations . . . were obliged to submit . . . to irresponsible foreign interference on pain of endangering the assistance we were receiving from Russia through the sale of matériel.[11]

A crisis arose when the Soviet ambassador demanded that Under-Secretary of War General Asensio, an opponent of the communists, be dismissed. Afire with indignation, Caballero cried:

> Get out! Get out! You will have to learn, Señor Ambassador, that although we Spaniards are very poor and need help from abroad very much we are too proud to let a foreign ambassador attempt to impose his will on the head of the government.[12]

Although Largo Caballero was forced to remove Asensio, he did not forgive his adversaries. For months he had watched their stealthy permeation of the state, yet fearing to forfeit Soviet supplies and to reveal to Britain and France the extent of Soviet influence, he had refrained from any overt censure. But he could no longer suppress his anger and publicly declared that around his feet 'serpents of treason, disloyalty and espionage' were coiled.[13]

He then took action against communist influence in the war ministry. He removed the head of the technical secretariat and the chief of the vital information and control department, and appointed six inspectors, all left socialists, to scrutinise the work of the commissariat of war. Still more threatening was his order dismissing all political commissars whose appointment and rank he had not confirmed by May 15.[14]

Thwarted by this measure and by Largo Caballero's refusal, at the request of Stalin himself, to promote the fusion of the socialist and communist parties, the Moscow delegation, at a meeting of the Spanish politburo, announced its decision to remove Largo Caballero. Supported only by José Díaz, the party leader, Minister of Education Jesús Hernández, opposed the move. But his arguments that Largo Caballero had been loyal to the communists, had helped them unite the youth and gain predominance in the army and had been 'docile' to Soviet advisers were disregarded; for, as Soviet chargé d'affaires Gaikins retorted, Largo Caballero had alienated himself from the party.[15]

A suitable opportunity was now needed to undo Largo Caballero.

This came with the eruption of an armed conflict in Barcelona, the capital of Catalonia. Tensions in the region had been mounting ever since the defeat of the rebel garrison on 19 July had made the C.N.T. and F.A.I. virtual masters of the city. The anarcho-syndicalists seized post offices and telephone exchanges, organised police squads and militia units, and, through their factory, transport and food committees, dominated the economic life of the city as well as a significant share of the economic life of the region. Furthermore, with other working-class organisations they assumed command of the Franco-Spanish border, a prerogative reserved to the central government. True, Madrid had been empowered by the Statute of Catalan Autonomy to take control of internal order if the interests of the state were threatened, but, itself a prey to revolution, it had neither the will nor the strength to exert authority.

Just as the republican Constitution had become an empty formula, so too had the Catalan Statute. The Statute had given Catalonia a parliament and an executive council – the government of the *Generalitat* – in which the *Esquerra*, the republican left of Catalonia, the strongest party of the Catalan middle classes, was dominant, but the practical significance of these two bodies had all but disappeared in the whirlwind of the revolution.

Addressing a group of triumphant anarchists Luis Companys, president of Catalonia and founder of the *Esquerra*, declared on the morrow of the defeat of the military rebellion in Barcelona: 'You have conquered and everything is in your power. If you do not need me . . . tell me now, and I shall become just another soldier in the struggle against fascism.'

Although the C.N.T. and F.A.I. could have abolished the *Generalitat* government, they did not do so. But the war could not be directed by a government without authority, so a Central Anti-Fascist Militia Committee was created, in which the C.N.T. and F.A.I. appropriated the key departments of war, public order and transportation.

Because the power of the Committee rested upon the revolutionary militia and police squads, it was the *de facto* executive body in the region. Not that the *Generalitat* government was destitute of power. It could rely upon remnants of the regular police and upon militiamen belonging to the moderate parties, but these were outnumbered by the armed revolutionaries.

Obviously, the urban middle classes could not be satisfied with the inferior position of the Catalan government and the power of the anarcho-syndicalists to collectivise at will; nor could the tenant farmers and sharecroppers of the *Unió de Rabassaires*. Having seized the land, they felt that the revolution had accomplished its mission. Not so the extreme spirits. In those villages where anarcho-syndicalist labourers were predominant or where the influx of C.N.T.–F.A.I. militiamen weighted the scales in their favour, individual cultivation was abolished and libertarian communism proclaimed.

Neither in the towns nor in the villages could the middle classes turn to the *Esquerra*, for it was timorous to the point of self-effacement. In contrast, the communists, who controlled the P.S.U.C., the United Socialist Party of Catalonia, and the Catalan U.G.T., boldly defended the middle classes.

It would be unpardonable [wrote *Treball*, the party organ, on 8 August 1936] to forget the multitude of small commodity producers and businessmen in our region. . . . They declare that nobody is concerned about their fate. They are elements who tend to favour any reactionary movement, because it seems to them that anything would be better than the economic system which is being instituted in our region.

It was the P.S.U.C., not the *Esquerra*, that opposed the C.N.T., defended the interests of the *Rabassaires* and organised 18,000 trades-men, artisans and manufacturers into the G.E.P.C.I., the Catalan Federation of Small Businessmen and Manufacturers. Because the P.S.U.C. allowed the G.E.P.C.I., an employers' union, to enter the U.G.T., it was criticised by Juan Domenech, the C.N.T. leader, who charged that the U.G.T., in order to increase its size, did not object to enrolling speculators, shopkeepers and merchants or to their exploiting the workers.[16]

Although only a small party – the result of the fusion in July of four groups aggregating 3000 members – the P.S.U.C. claimed 50,000 adherents by March 1937. Juan Comorera became the head of the united party, which was directed behind the scenes with extraordinary efficiency by Ernö Güero, the Comintern delegate, known as Pedro. 'Fifty thousand militants,' declared Comorera 'is almost a miracle. In Catalonia there is no Marxist tradition.'[17]

Backed by the moderate segment of the population, the P.S.U.C. urged the dissolution of the Central Anti-Fascist Militia Committee and the concentration of power in the hands of the Catalan government. In this it was aided by the central government, which discountenanced a revolutionary body that exposed to the world at large that its writ was ineffectual. '. . . we were told time and again,' claims F.A.I. leader Abad de Santillán, 'that as long as we persisted in maintaining [the Committee] . . . arms would not reach Catalonia.' There was therefore no course, he asserted, but to dissolve the Committee and join the Catalan government.[18]

In the new Catalan administration the anarcho-syndicalists held only three out of twelve portfolios. But although the dissolution of the Committee strengthened the Catalan government, it did not end the division of authority in the region; for the revolutionaries maintained their own police squads – the 'patrols' – as well as their militia.

To end this power became the goal of the Catalan communists in the coming months.

Their task was complicated by the P.O.U.M., the Workers' Party of Marxist Unification. An unrelenting critic of communist policy, of Stalin's trials and purges, the P.O.U.M. was denounced as 'Trotskyite'. Although some of its leaders, including Andrés Nin, the party secretary, had once been disciples of Trotsky, the P.O.U.M. was not a Trotskyite party. Nevertheless, in accordance with the tactic used by Stalin at the Moscow trials of amalgamating all opponents under a single label, the communists denounced the dissidents of the P.O.U.M. as Trotskyite agents of Hitler and Mussolini. The truth is that Trotsky had profound differences with the P.O.U.M. even before the war,[19] and his handful of followers, the Bolshevik Leninists, were later expelled from the party and organised the Spanish section of Trotsky's Fourth International.

The communists ignored these differences, for the P.O.U.M. was no less outspoken in its criticism of the Soviet Union and the party than the Trotskyites.

From the outset, it excoriated the communists and socialists for supporting the democratic Republic:

> [The international bourgeoisie] knows perfectly well . . . that the issue in Spain is one of revolution or counter-revolution, of socialism or fascism. The socialists and the communists in their efforts to deceive the republican bourgeoisie at home and abroad only deceive the working class.[20]

On 18 November 1936 *La Batalla* warned that the communist leaders had been instructed to liquidate those organisations that did not submit to their authority. 'That applies to us as well as to the C.N.T. and F.A.I. They feel that we are more difficult to defeat in the theoretical field and wish to destroy us first.' Indeed, on 26 November Comorera had proposed to the C.N.T. and F.A.I. that the P.O.U.M. be excluded from the government. At first the anarcho-syndicalist leaders refused, but, never sympathetic to the P.O.U.M. because of its attempts before the war to infiltrate the C.N.T., and not feeling personally endangered, they finally yielded, according to a prominent anarchist, because the Soviet ambassador made military aid dependent on the ousting of the P.O.U.M.[21]

The opening in January 1937 of the new Moscow treason trial added fresh acerbity to the press polemics when the P.O.U.M. declared that the accused were neither guilty nor Trotskyite *agents provocateurs*:

> Stalin knows perfectly well that, with the exception of one or two of the accused, the others are not Trotskyites. . . . We are also accused of being Trotskyites. We are not. . . . The accused in Moscow are charged with [being] agents of the Gestapo. . . . The same is said of us. . . . Fortunately Spain is not Russia, but an attempt is being made to put Spain under Russian control, which we oppose with the utmost vigour.[22]

Having removed the P.O.U.M. from the government, the P.S.U.C. turned its attention to the C.N.T.–F.A.I. food committees that had attempted to monopolise the wholesale trades at the outset of the revolution. In an attempt to re-establish freedom of trade, Juan Comorera, the P.S.U.C. leader and food councillor in the cabinet, ordered their dissolution. The committees, he alleged, shortly before issuing his decree, had replaced the middle men 'to the prejudice of society', and were responsible for the enormous increase in the cost of food.[23] Although the anarcho-syndicalists argued that the committees prevented the rich from speculating at the expense of the workers, it is clear from the C.N.T. and P.O.U.M. press that the committees 'in the name of "Liberty and the Revolution" ' were guilty of 'a thousand and one abuses'[24] and 'in most cases perpetuate the vices of the bosses and speculate just like them'.[25]

But it was a far cry from the publication of the decree to its enforcement so long as the power of the revolutionaries remained unshaken. To undermine this power the P.S.U.C. applied unremitting pressure to end the duality of police powers in the region, divided between the Assault and National Republican Guards[26] under the control of Police Commissioner Rodríguez Salas, a P.S.U.C. member, and the patrols under the authority of the C.N.T.-dominated *Junta de Seguridad*. Backed by the P.S.U.C. councillors, the *Esquerra* councillor of internal security decreed on 1 March the dissolution of the patrols and of all other forces of public order. Police duties were to be performed by a new corps formed of members of the dissolved organisations, but all positions of command were to be held by officers in the Assault Guard and National Republican Guard.

As the C.N.T.-F.A.I. councillors did not denounce the decrees, the P.O.U.M. declared:

> If other organisations . . . do not react as the situation demands, they will make themselves responsible before history. . . . Our party has one mission with regard to these decrees: to denounce them publicly and tirelessly and to see that the working class imposes its own order and its own police forces.[27]

Although the C.N.T. councillors had not publicly denounced the decrees, the feeling of the libertarian movement was reflected in *Solidaridad Obrera*, which condemned them as 'completely alien' to the aspirations of the working people (4 March 1937). As a result, the decrees remained dormant on the pages of the *Diari Oficial*.

Meanwhile, the P.S.U.C. kept up a tireless campaign for the enforcement of other measures, such as the militarisation of the militia and compulsory military service, which had been approved in October 1936 but had remained unheeded. On 21 February 1937 *La Batalla*, the P.O.U.M. organ, declared:

> The only guarantee the working class can have as to the fate of the revolution is its own army. And the army of the working class can be

no other than . . . an army recruited from the militia. . . . It is absolutely necessary that control be maintained by the revolutionary organisations.

At the end of February the P.S.U.C. set up a Committee for the People's Army, which in street demonstrations and military parades demanded the enforcement of the draft and the fusion of the militia into the regular army. But the libertarian movement was opposed to permitting the government to draft its members. While *Tierra y Libertad*, the F.A.I. mouthpiece, declared that behind the campaign for the regular army there lay a 'policy of aggression against anarchism',[28] *Solidaridad Obrera* demanded an 'army that defends the revolutionary conquests of the working class'.[29]

In view of these disparate attitudes, a governmental crisis was inevitable. The libertarian movement had tried to protect its interests by temporising and by feigning acceptance of the government's decrees, but now all pretence had ended and the C.N.T. defence councillor in the cabinet, Francisco Isgleas, resigned.

The P.S.U.C. declared that '. . . a government must be formed that will carry out its obligations and enforce its decrees'.[30] On the other hand, the F.A.I. maintained that no solution was possible unless the decrees on public order were immediately rescinded and the defence council was authorised to 'prevent by every means at its disposal military parades and demonstrations and whatever undermines the will to fight'.[31]

Andrés Nin, the P.O.U.M. leader, welcomed this stand. Concession would mean 'tomorrow . . . a violent struggle to put an end to the bourgeoisie and the reformists'. (*La Batalla*, 11 April 1937.)

Despite the intransigence of the contending parties, neither the C.N.T. nor the P.S.U.C. considered that the moment had arrived for a violent showdown, and a stopgap cabinet was formed. But the problems of military and police control remained in all their intractable complexity.

The reaction of the P.O.U.M. to the patched-up crisis was one of disappointment. After criticising the C.N.T. for not taking power in the early weeks of the war, *La Batalla* added on 17 April:

> The comrades of the C.N.T. did not know what attitude to adopt towards the problem of power. . . . [Instead] of urging the working class to seize it completely, they preferred to regard it as a simple question of collaboration.

Although the C.N.T. leadership had agreed to paper over the crisis, the real mood of the libertarians was evident from their press: '[The C.N.T.] has appeared flexible and accommodating in the extreme on many occasions. But beware! Let no one . . . think that the Spanish anarchists will allow themselves to be trampled underfoot by their so-called comrades.'[32] 'If [certain political parties] want to repeat in Spain what they have done in other countries, they will find us on a war footing.'[33]

In the midst of the heightening tension came the murder of Roldán Cortada, a P.S.U.C. member and U.G.T. secretary of the Municipal Workers' Federation. On the initiative of the P.S.U.C. a giant procession was organised on 27 April, the day of Cortada's funeral.

'It was not merely a funeral,' said *Treball*, 'it was a plebiscite. . . . A plebiscite has been held and it shows that the present situation cannot continue a day longer, that the anti-fascist masses must unite . . . against the enemy within, against those we call uncontrolled elements.'

Fast on the heels of Cortada's assassination came the killing of Antonio Martín, the anarchist leader in the border town of Puigcardá, in an encounter with Assault and National Republican Guards. Shortly thereafter truckloads of carabineers, dispatched by Finance Minister Juan Negrín, were moved to the border to wrest control from the revolutionaries.

Knowledge of the death of Martín, of the activity of the carabineers, of attempted disarmings by the Assault Guards under Rodríguez Salas, the communist police commissioner, and of raids by his men into the anarchist strongholds of Hospitalet and Molins del Rey in order to flush out Cortada's alleged killers, raised the political temperature of Barcelona to boiling point. On 1 May *La Batalla* demanded action by 'all the workers' to enforce 'control, but absolute control by the working class'.

In this explosive atmosphere Rodríguez Salas, acting in concert with the *Esquerra* councillor of internal security, made a daring move. On 3 May, accompanied by three truckloads of guards, he raided the central telephone building held by the C.N.T., sparking off the worst street warfare in Barcelona's history. 'Thousands upon thousands of workers have returned to the streets with arms in their hands,' declared the P.O.U.M. 'The spirit of July 19 has again taken possession of Barcelona.'[34]

All over the city, barricades were erected and the battle was on.

That same night the executive committee of the P.O.U.M. met with the regional committees of the libertarian movement:

> We stated the problem in precise terms [testifies Julián Gorkin]. . . . Either we place ourselves at the head of the movement in order to destroy the internal enemy or else the movement will collapse and the enemy will destroy us.

The anarcho-syndicalists, however, rejected this proposal.[35]

Nevertheless, *La Batalla* on 4 May urged the workers to keep in a state of 'permanent mobilisation' and to 'intensify the offensive that had begun'. 'It is imperative to demand and obtain the resignation of the police commissioner. . . . It is imperative to demand and obtain the abrogation of the decrees on public order.'

During the ensuing days the C.N.T.–F.A.I. leaders appealed to their followers to return to work. But there were forces intent on stoking the conflict. Not only did Rodríguez Salas's guards engage in new offensive actions, but the Bolshevik Leninists and the Friends of Durruti, a group of dissident extreme anarchists, hostile to the C.N.T.'s policy of accommodation, were extremely active. 'No compromise!' declared a leaflet distributed by the Bolshevik Leninists. '. . . This is the decisive moment. Next time it will be too late!' 'A revolutionary junta!' demanded a leaflet signed by the Friends of Durruti. 'No surrender of the streets. The revolution before everything. We greet our comrades of the P.O.U.M. who have fraternised with us.'

Meanwhile, in Valencia – the seat of government since November 1936 – Largo Caballero, fearing that his opponents might exploit the fighting to topple his government, summoned the leaders of the C.N.T. The Catalan councillor of internal security, he told them, had requested 1500 Assault Guards, but he could not comply because it would mean 'giving forces to persons who may have had a hand in provoking the fighting'.[36] He therefore suggested that they hasten to Barcelona to resolve the conflict.

On their arrival they appealed for a cease-fire. Mariano Vázquez, secretary of the C.N.T., urged his embattled followers to remember the neighbouring Aragon front where 'the fascists might attack at any moment'. García Oliver, the F.A.I. leader and justice minister since November 1936, declared:

> Think of the anguish . . . of those anti-fascist workers in that part of Spain dominated by Hitler and Mussolini when they learn . . .

that in Catalonia, we are killing one another. . . . Everyone should
. . . stop fighting, even though provoked by persons interested in
preventing a solution.[37]

The next day Mariano Vázquez again appealed for a cease-fire.

In Valencia the communist ministers threatened to provoke a cabinet
crisis unless the government assumed police and military control in
Catalonia without delay. 'For four hours comrade Frederica Montseny
led the opposition against the communists and republicans,' reported
the C.N.T. national committee. '. . . It was a tumultuous debate which
we lost when the vote was taken.[38]

Under duress, Caballero then appointed General Sebastián Pozas –
one-time commander of the Civil Guard and now a secret communist
convert – to the military command in Catalonia, and instructed his
interior minister to dispatch several thousand Assault Guards to the
region. But, in deference to the anarcho-syndicalists, whose political
support he needed, he appointed as their commander Lieutenant-
Colonel Torres, a sympathiser of the C.N.T.

The unenviable task of facilitating the entry of the Assault Guards
into Catalonia fell to the F.A.I. leader García Oliver, now back in
Valencia:

> It is indispensable [he said to Federica Montseny and Mariano
> Vázquez in a teletyped message] that the Assault Guards reach their
> destination to relieve the police who are . . . inflamed by the conflict.
> . . . It is imperative that you understand this and . . . make it clear
> to the comrades and villages through which these impartial, abso-
> lutely impartial forces of appeasement have to pass. They are strictly
> impartial, because the cabinet knows that otherwise the conflict . . .
> would spread to the whole of Catalonia and the rest of Spain and
> would result not only in its political downfall but also in its military
> defeat.[39]

The C.N.T. leaders agreed that a truce should be called the next day,
7 May, from 6 a.m. to 9 a.m. so that the Assault Guards could enter
Barcelona without incident. Several hours before dawn, there were
signs that the ardour of the anarcho-syndicalists had spent itself. A
feeling that it was futile to continue the struggle against the will of the
leaders had overwhelmed them and disillusion was widespread.
Numerous armed workers withdrew from the barricades and disappeared into the darkness. Seeing that further resistance was useless,
the P.O.U.M. instructed its followers to leave the barricades.

In the evening the guards entered the city unopposed, accompanied by a force of carabineers sent by Finance Minister Juan Negrín.

In Valencia, the communists now brought their struggle against Caballero to a head. Exploiting the fighting, they demanded the suppression of the P.O.U.M.

> Our principal enemies are the fascists [declared party secretary José Díaz on May 9]. However, these not only include the fascists themselves but also the agents who work for them. . . . Some call themselves Trotskyites. . . . If everyone knows this, if the government knows it, why doesn't it treat them like fascists and exterminate them pitilessly? . . .[40]

At a cabinet meeting the communist ministers demanded the dissolution of the P.O.U.M. Caballero retorted that the P.O.U.M. was not a fascist organisation and that he would not serve the political interests of any party. The communist ministers then left the room. Caballero would have continued the dispatch of routine matters, but Prieto informed him that the withdrawal of the communist ministers signified that the government coalition had been broken. When Caballero attempted to form a new cabinet, he found the communists, republicans and Prieto socialists unanimous in their demand that he relinquish the war ministry:

> I declared at the time that, as a socialist and a Spaniard, it was my duty to remain in the war ministry and that otherwise I would not accept the premiership. . . . I had the firm intention of fighting it out with the communist party and all its accomplices. This I could do only from the war ministry.[41]

As Caballero would not budge, President Azaña asked Juan Negrín to form a new cabinet. Although Prieto's own man, and recommended by him to head the finance ministry in Caballero's administration, Negrín – who was gradually to free himself from the bonds that tied him to the moderate socialist leader – had long been favoured as Caballero's successor by Arthur Stashevsky, the Soviet trade envoy, at whose suggestion he had shipped more than half the Spanish gold reserves to the U.S.S.R. The son of a middle-class family and professor of physiology at Madrid University, he was, to quote Walter Krivitsky, head of Soviet intelligence in Western Europe, 'just the type to suit Stalin's needs. He would impress the outside world with the "sanity" and "propriety" of the Spanish Republican cause; he would frighten nobody by revolutionary remarks.'[42] As politburo member Jesús Hernández remarked to Negrín, 'If you were a communist we could not propose you for the premiership. We want a premier who is a *friend* of the communists – nothing more, but nothing less.'[43]

As both the anarcho-syndicalists and left socialists declared that they would not join any government in which Caballero was not premier and war minister, a new cabinet was formed without them. Negrín, the communists' candidate, became premier and finance minister, and Prieto – Caballero's perennial foe, who, according to the communist minister of agriculture, Uribe, 'wanted to take revenge on Largo Caballero . . . for frustrating his ambition to become premier in May 1936[44] – occupied the defence ministry, combining the departments of war, navy and air.

Largo Caballero had now been defeated and the communists had triumphed. Not only had the communists despoiled him of his authority in the J.U.S., in the Catalan U.G.T. and in the Catalan federation of the socialist party – as a result of the creation of the P.S.U.C. – and taken over *Claridad*, his organ in Madrid, not only had he been betrayed or forsaken by some of his closest collaborators but he had now been ousted from the government. On the other hand the communists, through their penetration of the machinery of state, had risen from a position of insignificance to one where they virtually controlled the destinies of the left camp.

Despite the moderate complexion of the Negrín cabinet, and the fact that the communists held only the two seats they had formerly occupied, this was deceptive, for, in addition to retaining all the pivotal positions in the police administration they had previously held, Colonel Antonio Ortega, a party member, was named director-general of security.

As for the military apparatus, Alvarez del Vayo kept his post as commissar-general, while Caballero's order dismissing all political commissars whose appointment and rank had not been confirmed by 15 May was shelved, leaving the communists entrenched in that vital body. Furthermore, Antonio Cordón, whom Caballero had removed from the technical secretariat, was made chief of staff of the Eastern Army in Aragon, where the C.N.T. and F.A.I. militia were dominant, while Díaz Tendero, who had been dismissed from the information and control department, was reappointed to that key post.

The May events in Catalonia strengthened the communists still further. General Pozas, who had assumed control of Catalan military affairs, openly joined the P.S.U.C. and gave the party free rein, while Lieutenant-Colonel Torres, commander of the Assault Guards, was replaced by Lieutenant-Colonel Burillo, the communist police chief of Madrid. In succeeding weeks the story of Catalonia was one of mass arrests, of detentions in clandestine jails, of tortures, kidnappings and assassinations. The patrols were dissolved. The P.O.U.M. leaders were arrested on charges of espionage[45] by Colonel Ortega, acting on orders from Orlov of the Soviet secret police, while Andrés Nin, the party leader, was abducted and assassinated in Madrid after torture had failed to extract the required confession. Special tribunals were instituted and a rigorous radio and press censorship imposed. The anarchist terror of the early days of the revolution had now given way to the more sophisticated and more fearful terror of the communists. The C.N.T.–F.A.I. committees in the Catalan towns and villages were replaced by local municipal councils, on which the P.S.U.C. and the *Esquerra* were represented, and on 29 June, as a result of an adroit manœuvre by these two parties, the C.N.T. was eliminated from the *Generalitat* government.

Meanwhile, throughout the left camp the agrarian revolution was in sharp decline. Encouraged by Uribe, the communist minister of agriculture, the tenant farmers and sharecroppers who had not identified themselves with the military rebellion but had been forced to accept collectivisation, now demanded the return of their former holdings.

These attacks on the collectives damaged rural economy and morale, for while in some areas collective farming was anathema to the peasants, in others it was undertaken voluntarily. As the campaign against the collective farms reached its peak just before the summer harvest, the agricultural labourers abandoned their work in many places.

The minister of agriculture then issued a decree promising help to the collectives to avoid 'economic failures that might chill the faith of the land workers in the collective forms of cultivation they chose freely when they confiscated the land'.[46] But no sooner had the crops been gathered than the government dissolved the anarchist-controlled defence council of Aragon, set up in the early days of the revolution, and appointed, as governor-general of the region, a member of the left republican party, José Ignacio Mantecón, a communist supporter. Using the 11th Division commanded by the communist Enrique Lister, whom Prieto had previously dispatched to Aragon to ensure the fulfilment of the measure,[47] Mantecón broke up the collective farms.

While evading personal responsibility, the communists later admitted that this was a serious error:

> This measure was a very grave mistake. . . . Under cover of the order issued by the governor-general, those persons who were discontented with the collectives – and who had good reason for being so, if the methods employed in forming them are taken into account – took them by assault, carrying away and dividing up the harvest and farm implements without respecting those collectives that had been formed without violence or pressure, that were prosperous, and were a model of organisation. . . .[48]

To redress this situation the communist party was compelled to restore some of the collectives. 'The recognition of the rights of the collectives,' Silva added, 'and the decision to return what had been unjustly taken away . . . brought things back to normal.'

But, in truth, the hatreds and resentments generated by these events and by the severe repression that followed were never dispelled.

The attempt by the communists to remedy the situation, it should be stressed, stemmed not only from the damage to rural economy, but from friction with Prieto, the defence minister. A masterful character with great prestige among the middle classes, he had infinitely more in common with the liberal and even conservative republicans than with the communists or left socialists. If he had supported the communists for his own ends against Largo Caballero, he soon made it clear that he was not their puppet, for he bluntly rejected an offer by the politburo to provide him 'every day with suggestions, ideas and views on military matters'.[49] He also informed Gaikins, the Russian chargé d'affaires, that he would not support the fusion of the socialist and communist parties, to which the Russians replied by withholding a much-needed shipment of matériel. 'That', said Prieto, 'was the punishment I received.'[50]

Furthermore, while Stalin hoped that a moderate course would induce Britain and France to raise the arms embargo and that the prolongation of the conflict would keep Germany away from Russia's borders, Prieto hoped that Anglo-French aid would counteract the mounting influence of Russia. 'The Western democracies,' he declared after the war, 'fearful of communism, did not realise that this movement grew in Spain as a result of their own lack of assistance.'[51] Increasingly pessimistic, Prieto, like President Azaña and Julián Besteiro, the right-wing socialist, looked more and more to mediation to end the conflict. Many were the feelers put out in 1937 and 1938, but General Franco, backed to the hilt by Germany and Italy, would consider nothing but unconditional surrender.

Meanwhile, provoked by the proselytism of the communists, Prieto – within a few months of his entering the defence ministry – removed Alvarez del Vayo, the commissar-general, and a number of communist political commissars and high officers. Ignoring Soviet threats, he discharged Major Durán, the head of the Madrid section of the S.I.M. – the military investigation service he had formed on the advice of the Russians to investigate alleged spies and traitors.

It was at this juncture that the communists halted their attacks on the collective farms. Although this was partly for economic reasons, Prieto's hostility now impelled them to seek a temporary accommodation with the C.N.T. For, much as the communist party needed the support of the rural and urban middle classes, it could not allow them to become too strong, lest with the backing of the moderate socialists and republicans – now emboldened by the recoil of the revolution – they should attempt to take the reins of government into their own hands. In order to guide domestic and foreign policy the communists had to be supreme, and this was possible not only by controlling the police and army but also by a skilful balancing of the various factions and class forces.

In a conciliatory gesture towards the C.N.T., party secretary José Díaz declared that 'those who say that we cannot talk of revolution because we are at war are totally mistaken'. A few days later, El Campesino, the communist leader, embraced Cipriano Mera, a prominent anarchist, at a public meeting in Madrid. 'This embrace,' commented *Frente Rojo*, the communist organ, on 5 October, 'should be extended to all the workers of our Fatherland.'

At the same time, fearing that their opponents might rally around Caballero, who as secretary of the U.G.T. executive had negotiated a provisional alliance with the C.N.T., the communists delivered a death-blow to the socialist leader. Acting in agreement with the moderate socialists – who after the fall of the Caballero government had seized *Adelante*, his mouthpiece in Valencia – they formed a new executive on 1 October, with González Peña, a former *Prietista* but now a *Negrinista*, as president. The new vice-president and treasurer were also former adherents of Largo Caballero but now communist supporters. On 19 October Caballero denounced the communist party at a mass meeting, but was prevented from further activity and on 30 November he was divested of the newspaper *La Correspondencia de Valencia*, his last daily medium of communication. The conflict over the two rival executives boiled on until January, when it was settled by Léon Jouhaux, the French trade union leader, at the expense of Largo Caballero,[52] ending his political career.

Ignoring the fact that the communists now controlled the U.G.T., the C.N.T. – in defiance of some of the F.A.I. leaders – started negotiations for a pact with the new executive, and on 18 March 1938 signed a formal alliance. By recognising the authority of the state in such matters as nationalisation and the regular army, the document was a complete negation of anarchist doctrine.

Strengthened by their negotiations with the C.N.T., the communists were ready for the coming showdown with Prieto. On 9 March the nationalists had undertaken on the Aragon front their biggest offensive of the war. There was no organised resistance, and the enemy reached the coast on 15 April, splitting the republican territory in two.

At a special meeting of the cabinet held under Azaña's chairmanship, Negrín declared, according to Interior Minister Zugazagoitia, that he had rejected an offer by the French ambassador to initiate peace negotiations. Azaña, knowing that Prieto was as pessimistic as he, asked his views, which inevitably reinforced his own conclusion that the war was lost.[53]

Meanwhile the communists, with the support of the C.N.T., had organised a demonstration in which Assault Guards and military forces participated. Cries of 'Down with the treacherous ministers!' 'Down with the minister of defence!' were heard by the assembled ministers.

A few days later, after a meeting during which Prieto, according to Negrín, 'completely demoralized' his cabinet colleagues, the premier decided to remove him. Although Negrín affirmed that this decision was his own, Prieto asserted that the premier had 'yielded to the demands of the communist party'.[54]

While the governmental crisis was still unresolved, Moscow instructed the communist ministers, Hernández and Uribe, to withdraw from the cabinet. This tactic, Comintern delegate Togliatti explained to the politburo, was aimed at convincing 'English and French opinion that the communists are not interested in the conquest of power'.[55] Hernández opposed the move. 'The hatred and hostility for our party and Negrín,' he confessed some years later, '. . . were shared unanimously by all the forces of the Popular Front. Negrín could govern only by relying completely on the communist party's military and political power. To withdraw our ministers would have meant the death of the resistance policy.'[56] A compromise was reached: Hernández alone would withdraw. 'This demonstrates once again,' said Hernández at the time of these events, 'the dishonesty of all those persons [who are seeking] to impress foreign opinion with blustering threats of communist influence in the state machinery.'[57]

Although they held only one portfolio, the communists now controlled more levers of command than hitherto. Premier Negrín – whom Hernández describes as 'Moscow's man of confidence'[58] – took over the defence ministry, appointing party members or sympathisers to posts of great importance. Although Zugazagoitia, the moderate socialist, was named defence secretary under Negrín, this post was purely decorative,[59] for the under-secretaries obeyed only the communist party. Moreover, 70 per cent of the army command posts were in its hands.[60]

This power the communists could never have achieved without the active support, the connivance or unsuspecting good faith of others. As 'El Campesino', a prominent communist who left the party after the war, asks:

... how many Spanish politicians and military men were there who did not welcome the communist agents with open arms and did not refuse to play their game? At least I was a convinced communist and my attitude had some logic to it; but what logic was there in the attitude adopted by the others? Without the lack of understanding and the complicity that were almost general, would it have been possible, in the course of a few months, for a party as weak numerically as the communist party to penetrate – and nearly dominate – the whole governmental apparatus?[61]

As for the interior ministry, although Paulino Gómez, a moderate socialist, headed this department, the communists retained their key positions in the police apparatus. Through Soviet agents they also controlled the S.I.M. with its secret prisons and torture chambers for political opponents of the left and right.

The finance ministry went to Negrín's intimate, the left republican Méndez Aspe, who appointed a P.S.U.C. member to head the carabineers, the most powerful force of public order, characterised by its opponents as 'Negrín's 100,000 sons'. Furthermore, Alvarez del Vayo returned to the foreign ministry and gave Negrín's close collaborator, Sánchez Arcos, a party member, the under-secretaryship of propaganda, a key post.

The roles of the other ministers, including Basque nationalist Irujo and Jaime Aiguadé of the *Esquerra*, were inconsequential. In any case, they resigned in August 1938 in protest at the growing impingement on Catalan autonomy by the central government, which had moved to Barcelona in October 1937 hoping to ensure the political and economic control of this industrial region. No less trivial was the role of Segundo Blanco of the C.N.T., named minister of education as a sop to the libertarian movement, which was now so divided that some of its leaders, like Abad de Santillán, favoured a return of anarchist orthodoxy, while others, including Horacio Martínez Prieto, former secretary of the C.N.T., convinced that *apoliticismo* was dead and libertarian communism only a distant goal, advocated the creation of a libertarian socialist party, which would participate in every organ of the state;[62] thus demonstrating anarchism's insoluble dilemma that to survive it must compete for power yet, by so doing, it betrays itself.

From that time on [testified 'El Campesino', who left the communist party after the war] morale at the front and in the rear continued to decline. . . . The hatred of the communists by the mass of the people was such that a politburo leader had to admit: 'We cannot retreat. We must . . . stay in power at all costs, otherwise we shall be hunted like predatory animals through the streets.'[63]

To reinforce their position, the communists were compelled to rely more and more on their military and police power. At the fronts, cajolery, coercion and violence grew from day to day. '. . . thousands upon thousands of our comrades,' said an F.A.I. report issued in October, '. . . confess that they are more afraid of being assassinated at the fronts by the adversaries at their side than of being killed by the enemy they face.'[64] And, in the rear, the dread of the S.I.M. and secret police silenced all but the faintest criticism.

From now on Negrín, backed by communist propaganda and Russian supplies, became the symbol of resistance. Russian aid, limited by logistics and by Stalin's resolve not to become too enmeshed in the conflict, was predicated on the belief that Britain and France would eventually be forced to intervene in defence of their own interests. '[Moscow] will try by every means to avoid isolation, to force the Western democracies to fight Hitler, if war is the only course,' Comintern delegate Stepanov had told the Spanish politburo just before the fall of Prieto.[65]

In keeping with its resistance policy, the Negrín government

F

attempted to conciliate foreign capital. On 27 April it decreed that the foreign hydroelectric enterprises, operated by the C.N.T. under the name of *Serveis Electrics Unificats de Catalunya*, be dissolved[66] with the object of returning the plants to their original owners. This measure, commented a foreign observer in Barcelona, 'suggests that the Government is taking drastic steps to conciliate . . . the important financial interests which exert so much influence on the foreign policies of Britain and France'.[67] But, confident of Franco's ultimate victory, the companies involved ignored the gesture.

Simultaneously, government supervisors were appointed to decollectivise and nationalise certain Spanish enterprises, while others were returned to their original owners. Although these concerns were few – because many owners had been killed or had fled to nationalist territory – the communist-controlled foreign press censorship, which in the past had attempted to conceal the revolution, allowed foreign correspondents to make great play with the restitutions.

> If the loyalist republic ever were really 'Red', as its enemies call it [said another report from Barcelona], the great work of handing back factories and mines to their original owners certainly shows that the label cannot now be properly applied. . . .[68]

In the hope of influencing the Western democracies, Negrín enunciated, on 1 May 1938, a thirteen-point programme which included the promise of a Spain free of all foreign interference, with full civil and political rights and with freedom of religion. There was also an assurance that private property 'legitimately acquired', and 'the property and legitimate interests of foreigners' who had not helped the military rebellion, would be respected.

But the Thirteen Points made no impression on the democratic powers. 'Not a day passed until almost the end,' wrote Alvarez del Vayo, 'when we did not have fresh reasons to hope that the Western democracies would come to their senses and restore our rights to buy from them. And always our hopes proved illusory.'[69]

In spite of these disappointments, in spite of the immolation of Czechoslovakia by Britain and France in September 1938, in spite of the disastrous Ebro battle and the swift collapse of Catalonia without a struggle in February 1939, leaving only the central and south-eastern parts of Spain to the Republic, Moscow – prior to negotiating its non-aggression pact with Hitler in a last but successful attempt to turn German military might against the West – instructed the Spanish

communists to continue the resistance policy. But the war was lost and
Stalin knew it. Nevertheless the Spanish politburo declared on 23
February:

> The international situation has never been more unstable than it is
> today.
>
> Furthermore, the successes of the fascist invaders in Catalonia have
> increased their boldness, encouraging them to reveal still more
> clearly their plans of conquest, plunder and war, and this in turn . . .
> increases the possibilities of direct and indirect aid for the Spanish
> people.[70]

If the hopes of a European conflagration entertained by the communists and other parties were disappointed, it was not because Britain
and France were blind to the possible dangers of a Franco victory. If
they refused to challenge Germany in Spain, it was because they hoped
to avoid engaging the West until Germany had weakened herself in the
East. Hence the policy of Britain and France throughout the war was
determined not only by their hostility to the social revolution and subsequent communist domination – of which they were fully apprised
despite the efforts at concealment – but by the larger field of foreign
politics. Hence no attempt at dissimulation, no attempt at curbing or
even rolling back the revolution, could have modified their policy.

On 27 February Great Britain and France officially recognized the
Franco regime as the legal government of Spain. President Azaña, who
had crossed into France after the Catalan débâcle, immediately resigned, rejecting Negrín's request to return to the central zone and
liberating himself from his puppet role as constitutional cover for the
revolution. Martínez Barrio, the leader of *Unión Republicana* and
speaker of the Cortes, who should have succeeded Azaña, also declined
to return, as did other prominent republicans, socialists and anarchists.
Even General Vicente Rojo, chief of the central general staff, who had
enjoyed the confidence of the communists, refused to return to Spain,
convinced that the war was lost.

When the communist leaders arrived in the central zone, accompanied
by Negrín and members of his government, they found that the factions
of the left had coalesced against them. Embittered by political injury
and oppression, demoralised by the attacks on the revolution – as were
the left socialists and anarchists – and exhausted by a protracted war,
they execrated the Negrín government – which one leading socialist
described as the 'most cynical and despotic' in Spanish history[71] – as

much as they detested its resistance policy, which they now believed served only Russian ends.

> Resist? What for? That is the universal question [wrote Zugazagoitia, the moderate socialist]. . . . The front-line troops see the relaxation of discipline and desertions increase alarmingly. Those who do not desert to the enemy leave the trenches and find their way home. . . . The persons who surround the premier are, like the premier himself, tied to his resistance policy: they are communists[72].

It was in this climate of dissolution that Negrín, at the request of the politburo, promoted two leading communists to the rank of general and appointed others to command positions. Fearing a communist *coup*, Colonel Casado, the commander of the Centre Army, who for some time had been conspiring with socialist, anarchist and republican leaders to overthrow Negrín, formed a National Defence Council in the hope of negotiating a surrender without reprisals. Within hours Negrín and his communist entourage, including Comintern delegates Togliatti and Stepanov – all of whom had prudently avoided establishing themselves in Madrid and had kept close to an airport near the village of Elda – escaped by plane. So swift was their departure that no directives were given to the Madrid party organization, which, aided by communist military units, tried unsuccessfully to overthrow the Defence Council.

Hernández, who was in close touch with Negrín and communist leaders during those dramatic hours, held that Negrín's measures were intended to spark off an anti-communist rising.[73] 'The Casado group,' said Comintern leader Manuilsky in a discussion in Moscow after the war, at which Hernández himself was present, 'fell into the trap . . . and spared the party the responsibility for the final catastrophe.'[74]

In face of General Franco's insistence on unconditional surrender, the efforts of Casado to negotiate a settlement without reprisals aborted. By the end of March the forces of the left were in full retreat and the war was over.

In a 'valedictory' to Joseph Stalin, Enrique Castro, a member of the party's central committee who, like Hernández, lived through the final agonies of the Negrín government and left the party after the war, declared:

> Stalin! Comrade Stalin!
> We have prolonged the war for thirty-two terrible months.
> More than one and a half million Spaniards have lost their lives.

The towns and villages, the fields and ports of Spain have wounds
that will take years and years to heal.

We have poisoned the people with anguish and hatred that will
take fifty years to overcome.

Are you satisfied, comrade Stalin? Of course you are! What else
matters? We still believe in you! We continue to love you! The
Second Republic is dead. But you exist! The Soviet Union exists!
The great hope exists! Long live Stalin, our leader and great teacher!
Viva!

Vivaaaaaaaaa![75]

SUGGESTIONS FOR FURTHER READING

No earnest student can expect to master this complex subject unless he is
prepared to read Spanish. Even more important than the vast body of literature
is the imposing array of newspapers and periodicals published in the territory
controlled by the left during the Civil War and in exile after the war. The
author's *The Grand Camouflage* (1961) includes an exhaustive examination of
the left-wing press, but embraces less than one year of the conflict and barely
touches upon the revolution in Catalonia. Hence, in spite of an impressive and
growing literature, much work remains to be done by historians of the Spanish
revolution.

The following books by Spaniards who participated in the war are recommended. Diego Abad de Santillán (the F.A.I. leader), *Porqué perdimos la guerra*
(1941); José Peirats (a C.N.T.–F.A.I. member), *La CNT en la revolución
española* (1951–3) and *Los anarquistas en la crisis política española* (1964) are
indispensable for an understanding of the external and inner conflicts of the
libertarian movement. Official communist policy is delineated in the collected
speeches of José Díaz (the party secretary), *Tres años de lucha* (1947), and in
Freedom's Battle (1940) by Julio Alvarez del Vayo, the pro-communist socialist
leader. Two hostile books, written by prominent ex-communists, are valuable:
Enrique Castro (a central committee member), *Hombres made in Moscú* (1960)
and Jesús Hernández (a politburo member), *Yo fui un ministro de Stalin* (1953).
For an appreciation of the strife among the factions of the socialist movement,
the following are recommended: *Epistolario, Prieto y Negrín* (1939), an exchange
of correspondence between the two socialist leaders; Indalecio Prieto, *Cómo y
porqué salí del ministerio de defensa nacional* (1940), a transcript of his denunci-
atory speech before the national committee of the socialist party in August
1938; Julián Zugazagoitia, *Historia de la guerra en España* (1940), a cautious
but valuable work; Largo Caballero, *Mis recuerdos* (1954), ¿*Qué se puede hacer?*
(1940), and *La UGT y la guerra*, (1937) a transcript of his revealing speech in
October 1937. For the role of the P.O.U.M. and the Bolshevik Leninists
(Trotskyists), see Julián Gorkin (the P.O.U.M. leader), *Canibales políticos* (1941)
and Munis (the Trotskyite leader), *Jalones de Derrota* (1948). Finally, a first-
rate memoir by a liberal republican, honest and fearlessly outspoken, but sadly
ignored by republicans, is Jesús Pérez Salas, *Guerra en España* (1947). Two
books in French by non-participants which should be consulted are P. Broué
and E. Témime, *La révolution et la guerre d'Espagne* (1961) and the recent work

by César Martínez Lorenzo, *Les anarchistes espagngols et le pouvoir* (1969). Martínez Lorenzo, the son of Horacio Martínez Prieto, a former secretary of the national committee of the C.N.T., sheds fresh light on the infighting within the libertarian movement.

NOTES

1. For a documented account of the social revolution, see Bolloten, *The Grand Camouflage* (New York, 1961), pp. 35–76.
2. *Verdad*, 2 Dec 1936.
3. *L'Humanité*, 3 Aug 1936.
4. *Castilla Libre*, 10 April 1937.
5. *Verdad*, 27 Dec 1936.
6. For more information on communist control of the police, see Bolloten, op. cit. pp. 173–4.
7. M. González Inestal, *Cipriano Mera, revolucionario* (Cuba, 1943), p. 60.
8. *Ruta*, 28 Nov 1936.
9. Bolloten, op. cit. p. 227.
10. F. Largo Caballero, *Mis recuerdos* (Mexico, 1954), p. 212.
11. Quoted from Caballero's unpublished memoirs by Luis Araquistain, *El comunismo y la guerra de España* (Carmaux, 1939), p. 25.
12. Ginés Ganga, *Hoy* (Mexico), 5 Dec 1942.
13. *Claridad*, 27 Feb 1937.
14. *Gaceta de la República*, 17 April 1937.
15. J. Hernández, *Yo fui un ministro de Stalin* (Mexico, 1953), pp. 66–71.
16. *Solidaridad Obrera*, 8 April 1937.
17. Speech before the central committee of the Spanish communist party, *Cataluña, en pie de guerra*, p. 15.
18. *Porqué perdimos la guerra* (Buenos Aires, 1940), p. 116.
19. *Unser Wort* (Brussels, May 1936).
20. *La Batalla*, 15 Sept 1936.
21. Rudolf Rocker, *Extranjeros en España* (Buenos Aires, 1938), p. 91.
22. *La Batalla*, 27 Jan 1937.
23. *Treball*, 22 Dec 1936.
24. *Solidaridad Obrera*, 21 April 1937.
25. *La Batalla*, 23 April 1937.
26. In August 1936 the Civil Guard was renamed National Republican Guard.
27. *La Batalla*, 3 March 1937.
28. 6 March 1937.
29. 5 March 1937.
30. *Treball*, 30 March 1937.
31. *Tierra y Libertad*, 3 April 1937.
32. *Solidaridad Obrera*, 17 April 1937.
33. *Tierra y Libertad*, 17 April 1937.
34. *La Batalla*, 4 May 1937.
35. *Canibales políticos* (Mexico, 1941), pp. 69–70.
36. Report of the C.N.T. national committee, *Cultura Proletaria*, 19 June 1937.
37. *Solidaridad Obrera*, 5 May 1937.
38. *Cultura Proletaria*, 19 June 1937.

39. A typewritten copy of this teletyped message, now quoted for the first time, is in the Hoover Institution and War Library.

40. Speech reprinted in J. Díaz, *Tres años de lucha* (Toulouse, 1947), pp. 350–66.

41. Largo Caballero, *¿Qué se puede hacer?* (Paris, 1940), pp. 20–4.

42. *In Stalin's Secret Service* (London, 1939), pp. 100–1.

43. Hernández, op. cit. p. 87.

44. *Mundo Obrero* (Paris), 25 Sept 1947.

45. During the trial a year later, the charge of espionage could not be proved, but the P.O.U.M. leaders were condemned to various terms of imprisonment for their participation in the May events. Caballero and Montseny, as well as Zugazagoitia and Irujo, interior and justice ministers respectively at the time of the P.O.U.M. leaders' arrest, testified in their favour. 'The trial,' wrote Jesús Hernández after he had left the communist party, '. . . was a crude comedy based on falsified documents' (op. cit. p. 127).

46. *Gaceta de la República*, 9 June 1937.

47. Lister claims that Prieto, hating both communists and anarchists, wanted 'to kill two birds with one stone': Lister, *Nuestra guerra* (Paris, 1966), p. 156.

48. J. Silva, *La revolución popular en el campo* (Ediciones del Partido Comunista de España, 1937), p. 17.

49. *Cómo y porqué salí del ministerio de defensa nacional* (Mexico, 1940), p. 37.

50. *El Socialista* (Paris), 9 Nov 1950.

51. *Inauguración del círculo 'Pablo Iglesias' de Mexico* (Mexico, 1940), p. 13.

52. See Caballero, *Mis recuerdos*, pp. 233–4.

53. J. Zugazagoitia, *Historia de la guerra en España* (Buenos Aires, 1940), pp. 371–6.

54. *Epistolario, Prieto y Negrín* (Paris, 1939), pp. 16, 23.

55. Quoted in Hernández, op. cit. p. 166.

56. Ibid. pp. 165–6.

57. *La Vanguardia*, 9 April 1938.

58. Ibid. p. 157. Because too many people, in a position to know otherwise, have seemed blind to Negrín's services to the communists (see, for example, Claude Bowers, U.S. ambassador to Spain during the Civil War, who wrote that Negrín was 'as remote from communism as it is possible to be': *My Mission to Spain* (New York, 1954), p. 358), the interested student is referred to the abundance of opposing evidence adduced by Bolloten, op. cit. pp. 121–2, n. 9. Added to this is the fact that Negrín relied heavily upon his personal secretary, Benigno Rodríguez, a party member, and former editor of *Milicia Popular*, organ of the 5th Regiment.

59. Jesús Pérez Salas, *Guerra en España* (Mexico, 1947), pp. 194–5; also Zugazagoitia, op. cit. pp. 408, 417, 423–4.

60. Hernández, op. cit. p. 144. Peirats (of the C.N.T.) claims that by mid-1938 80–90 per cent of the command posts were in communist hands: *La CNT en la revolución española* (Toulouse, 1953), p. 223.

61. *Solidaridad Obrera* (Paris), 11 March 1951.

62. See article in Timón, as given in Horacio M. Prieto, *El anarquismo español en la lucha política* (Paris, 1946), pp. 28–35.

63. Valentín González, *Comunista en España y antistalinista en la URSS* (Mexico, 1952), p. 72.

64. Quoted by Peirats, op. cit. iii, p. 251.

65. Quoted by Hernández, op. cit. p. 159.

66. *Gaceta de la República*, 28 April 1938.

67. *New York Post*, 16 June 1938.

68. *New York Post*, 15 June 1938.

69. *Freedom's Battle* (New York, 1940), p. 66.

70. *Mundo Obrero*, 26 Feb 1939.

71. Luis Araquistain in a letter to Martínez Barrio, 4 April 1939, as given in A. Saborit, *Julián Besteiro* (Mexico, 1961), p. 398.

72. Op. cit. pp. 534–5.

73. Op. cit. p. 187.

74. Op. cit. p. 256. In spite of his many services to the communists, Negrín years later became their scapegoat. Writing in exile as party secretary, Dolores Ibarruri ('La Pasionaria') stated: 'Deep down within himself Negrín was hoping for a catastrophe that would free him from all governmental responsibility. . . . Although he has very often been accused of being a communist tool, it was we who were the victims, because . . . of our support without reservations of the resistance policy, which was the only just one at the time': *El único camino* (Paris, 1962), p. 433. See also ibid. pp. 445–6, in which she claims that Negrín's military measures were counter-productive and caused 'profound indignation among the conspirators'.

75. *Hombres made in Moscú* (Mexico, 1960), p. 739.

9. The Growth and Role of the Republican Popular Army

RAMÓN SALAS LARRAZÁBAL

1. Origins and Uprising

THE deep divisions which caused so much conflict in Spanish society in the months leading up to July 1936 were expressed, as was to be expected, within the armed forces. The officer corps had lost that unity of thought and action characteristic of armies, and began to split into factions representing irreconcilable points of view, thus generating the spirit of civil war; the apolitical, neutral standpoint of the great majority of officers was shifting gradually towards direct action – a course still anathema to many of them. At the extremes of the divided Spanish military family two minority factions held diametrically opposed activist views. The views of the right found expression in the U.M.E. Initially regarded with the utmost suspicion by the rest, this group gradually gained more influence despite its small number of active members. On the left the U.M.R.A. numbered among its members hundreds of officers, some of them of the highest rank.[1]

The army consisted of the metropolitan army and that of Africa. Stationed in Spain itself were eight organic divisions, one cavalry division, three mountain brigades and other ancillary forces grouped in three general inspectorates. The military command of the Balearics and of the Canaries were held by divisional generals (as was the case with the organic divisions), but their full strength was no greater than that of a mixed brigade. Lastly, in Africa, the pacification forces were equal to two divisions, but because of their superior organisation and training they were far more effective than those stationed in Spain. They were light, mobile forces, weak in artillery but well-trained and ready for action, so that their relative value greatly exceeded that of the peninsular forces, who were poorly trained and ill-prepared for action.

The rising, which initially began at the Melilla garrison, was a daring blow that paralysed all possible counteraction by the local organs of government, represented in this instance by the high commissioner, himself a professional soldier. He and the two generals in command were arrested and the rebels soon gained control of the whole Protectorate. But not only the highest ranks opposed the rising: a considerable number of staff officers were arrested or had to flee. The air force opposed the rebellion and the aerodromes were seized. There were frequent incidents in the garrisons, but the rapid and concerted action of the rebels left no room for opposition.

According to the plan of General Mola, the Spanish-based garrisons were to follow up the action begun in Africa on the next day; but internal resistance caused some deviation from this plan, and the risings in Spain took place over a period of four days. Thus the element of surprise – the decisive factor in Africa – was completely lacking. Already on 17 July the government, though apparently quite calm, was on the alert. The assurances received from divisional generals were a comfort; moreover, the uprising seemed localised, so all that was needed was to isolate it. To this end the war minister and navy minister ordered the air force and the fleet into the Strait of Gibraltar in order to bomb the African garrison cities and blockade the ports.

The political organisations and unions of the revolutionary left did not share the government's optimism. These bodies ran organised militias (the M.A.O.C. – Anti-fascist Workers' and Peasants' Militias), though these had not been joined by the Anarchist Youth who formed the syndicalist militia. The period following the electoral victory of the Popular Front in February 1936 had seen a massive growth of militia activity. By 17 July long-cherished aspirations had become urgent demands, and the militias clashed with the government over its refusal to supply them with arms. But in Madrid workers' unions were in the streets with their militants, armed or unarmed. The soldiers of the U.M.R.A. took over the ministry of war, where they set up their own permanent committee, and took charge of the guard on the presidential palace, preparing at the same time to arm the militias. On the afternoon of 18 July contradictory messages were received in Madrid; two general-inspectors, García Gómez Caminero and Núñez de Prado, were sent off in haste to join the divisions and clear up the situation. But their mission was a failure.

In Madrid the short-lived moderate government of Martínez Barrio had to step down in favour of one led by Giral, with General Castelló as minister of war and General Pozas at the ministry of the interior. On the morning of the nineteenth, Castelló and Pozas ordered the militias to be armed. Hours before, Lieutenant-Colonel Gil, chief of the artillery park, had anticipated this order and on his own initiative had handed over 5000 rifles. Thus equipped, five newly formed battalions immediately occupied Madrid, and patrolled the city along with the Civil Guards and the Assault Guards.

During the next two days the uprising spread to almost all divisional headquarters, and in spite of opposition from those who should have been its natural leaders, the risings were successful in various parts of Aragon, Castile, León, Navarre, Alava, Galicia and in Seville.[2] In San Sebastian the rebels soon found themselves besieged and in a difficult position; and the same thing happened in Oviedo, Gijón and Albacete. In Barcelona and Madrid the uprising was very badly organised and the rebels soon had their backs to the wall. There was a great deal of internal discord within individual units, tending to weaken their resistance. In Valencia the garrison managed to maintain a neutral position, but the delicate balance was upset by the end of the month.[3] The fleet stayed with the government as a result of a bold decision by a telegraphist in the navy ministry.

By 21 July the government was still in control of a vast territory divided into two zones and embracing the three main cities, almost all the industry and the most varied and productive agricultural areas, together with the administrative and financial apparatus of the central government. In the military sector, it retained control of the 1st, 3rd and 4th Divisions, the 1st Mountain Brigade and the 2nd Cavalry Brigade; important sections of the 2nd and 6th Divisions, and a fraction of the 2nd Mountain Brigade; the artillery parks of Madrid, Barcelona and Valencia and the arms factories of Toledo, Murcia, Trubia, Reinosa Eibar and Plasencia. In round figures all this was equivalent to half the metropolitan army's actual quota of men and most of its equipment. As the forces of public order took sides, things became even more weighted in favour of the government, who retained 55 per cent of the Civil Guard, 60 per cent of the carabineers and 70 per cent of the Assault and Security Guards.

In Spain itself, then, the government enjoyed a clear superiority, but always on condition that the Army of Africa and the rebel Spanish garrisons were kept isolated – which was made easier since the whole fleet and three-quarters of the air force were under government control. As for equipment and personnel, at the outset the government had at its disposal 250,000 rifles, 400 field guns, 75 coastal defence guns and 40 anti-aircraft guns. Out of the 15,167 officers on active service, over half were in the zone controlled by the Popular Front, and out of these approximately 3500 supported the government. This figure, along with the (approximately) 1500 who rejoined after retirement, leave or long absence from the service, added up to a total of nearly 5000. So it was a delicate situation, but some optimism was permissible. It should be noted that in Madrid, Barcelona and Cartagena – towns where the immediate outcome of the *coup d'état* was decided – the regular forces and armed services loyal to the government resolved the situation. The militias, poorly armed, and lacking organisation and training, were never more than an active chorus supplying all the traditional atmosphere of Greek tragedy. Thus, the effectiveness of the popular militias, had they been fully armed from the outset, still remains an open question.

2. The Military Consequences of the Revolution

In the republican zone the state collapsed, not because of the rebellion but because of the revolution it produced in the republican zone. This phenomenon is historically unique. The revolution was not aimed against the government; it simply ignored it. Nor did the revolution try to seize formal power, it was content to exercise it. In Azaña's masterly analysis: 'All over we find committees, representing groups, parties, trade unions; representing provinces, regions, towns and even just private individuals. All of these usurp the functions of the state, and leave it without defence or form.'4

But the government carried on. It was needed, after all, to keep up the appearance of legality within the revolutionary situation. It was essential for international relations, and for keeping those armed forces loyal to the Republic under control. So the Popular Front did not suppress the government, but made it the subordinate agent of its own forces.

At first the government itself assisted the revolutionary dismantling of the state by dissolving military units and simultaneously discharging the troops. It quickly discovered how damaging this measure was, and at the end of July 1936 it ordered the reorganisation of the armed forces and a call-up of those due for military service in 1934 and 1935. This order was widely disobeyed. Only in Madrid was the order carried out fully, and to a lesser extent in Murcia and Cartagena. In Andalusia, Catalonia and the north mobilisation took place, but the militias rather than the army attracted most of the reservists.

In this atmosphere of contradiction and disorder the first military operations began. The central organs of government controlled to a greater or lesser degree the columns organised in Madrid and Cartagena, but lacked authority over the rest. In Valencia the so-called Popular Executive Committee retained the power it had seized, ignoring the Junta appointed for the whole of Levante by the cabinet. In Catalonia the *Generalitat* (the autonomous government of Catalonia created by the Statute) supplanted the Spanish state and was in turn supplanted by the Committee of Anti-Fascist Militias. Valencia decided to take Teruel; Catalonia made Aragon and the Balearic Islands her objectives. The same fragmented pattern prevailed in the north.[5]

Militias throughout the whole republican zone were now being armed, draining the reserves in the armouries. However, the glamour of the militias went hand in hand with their military ineptitude, and records are full of military leaders' dispatches stressing this ineffectiveness: thus General Riquelme speaks of 'a disruptive element'; Colonel Salafranca remarks on 'a total lack of spirit in all matters'; Lieutenant-Colonel del Rosal complains that 'the militiamen abandon their posts on the slightest pretext', General Miaja, 'I have but a few useful militias', Captain E. M. Ciutat, a communist, that 'looting, pillage and murder are growing to such an extent that this will soon be a focal point of attraction for all those dangerous elements more or less affiliated to workers' organisations'. The same feelings were expressed, sometimes even more harshly, by other military leaders during the summer of 1936.[6]

Faced with this situation, the government attempted to subject the militias to some form of control or discipline. It created the National Inspectorate of Militias but immediately came up against opposition from political parties and unions; only the communists supported the government move, though they insisted that the foundation of the new army must be the M.A.O.C. In order to encourage recruits, the government fixed the militiamen's daily pay at ten pesetas. This was higher than the average wage at the time, three times that of the nationalist legionaries, and twenty times previous army pay. The measure was highly successful in the rural areas, where day-wages were meagre and insecure, but it had little success in urban areas, where men could earn their daily bread without going to the front; here the main weight of the military effort still fell on the regular army units and forces of public order.

Once Mola's advance on Madrid had been checked, and with government efforts in Aragon and Andalusia held up, it seemed that a balance of forces had been reached. To break this balance, on 18 August the government created the Voluntary Army, to be manned by reservists, officers and other ranks in retirement, with recruitment the responsibility of a government delegate committee based on Albacete. The workers' organisations disapproved of the measure, but it began to have some effect, which was more than could be said for an abortive attempt to organise officers' courses. These were immediately vetoed by the workers' organisations.[7]

In the south the military situation was deteriorating. The Army of Africa was being ferried into Spain by air. The government committed a grave strategic error in underestimating the effectiveness of the airlift, and also in ruling out the plans of the commander of the fleet against Algeciras. On 5 August a naval squadron was unable to stop Franco's convoy; the Soviet Admiral Kuznetsov remarked that the republican ships 'proved incapable of doing their duty'.[8]

3. The Battle of the Columns and the Advance on Madrid

The advance of the African column towards Madrid steadily overcame the resistance of militias along its route. Once it had joined up with Mola's troops (at Merida, 11 August 1936) Madrid, Valencia and Ciudad Real sent out regular troops and militias against it.

Catalonia, considering it her own affair, had meanwhile begun the conquest of Majorca, an objective of great strategic importance. The whole operation was well organised but, unaccountably, it failed. A large body of land forces took part, supported by the navy and the air force, supreme on sea and in the air. The presence of only three enemy fighters and as many bombers was enough to precipitate defeat. After the event both the central government and the *Generalitat* denied responsibility for the operation, thus revealing their lack of strategic foresight.[9]

The advance of the African columns was a continuing threat. Partly as a consequence of repeated defeats of republican efforts to check it, Giral resigned as prime minister in favour of Largo Caballero, who also took charge of the war ministry. Prieto became minister in charge of the navy and air force. Events now favoured the military attitudes of the communists, who demanded a disciplined army under a single command with the slogan: 'War now, Revolution later.'

A few days earlier the first Soviet ambassador had arrived in Spain, surrounded by an experienced group of assistants and military advisers who set to work straight away, concentrating particularly on the navy and air force. The Soviet Union would doubtless have preferred to have stayed on the sidelines, but found herself obliged to intervene in the conflict. In September the first deliveries of war materials were made and from October onwards they were to reach a high rhythm. This helped the government's military effort, because the Soviet equipment was of a better quality than the French, and there was more of it, particularly aircraft.

This material aid could not have come at a better time, it turned out, because the military situation was rapidly deteriorating. The loss of Talavera coincided with the fall of Irun, which closed communication lines between the northern zone and France. Hoping to check Mola's advance northwards, Prieto ordered the fleet to Bilbao. The organisation of the fleet had improved, the seamen's committees had lost much of their overriding power and the ships were once again under the command of professional officers, with Kuznetsov as an adviser.

With the guard on the Strait of Gibraltar substantially weakened, nationalist cruisers were able to slip in, sink one destroyer and chase off another, effectively breaking the blockade. This enabled the African column to come to the aid of the nationalists besieged in the Alcázar of Toledo and set them free. These were hard blows to republican morale; but, paradoxically, resistance grew even fiercer, with fresh columns taking the place of those defeated. Gradually an implicit priority emerged: the saving of Madrid. Two columns, called 'Liberty' and 'Land and Liberty', were moved from Catalonia to Madrid, along with a third of the Civil Guard, now called the National Republican Guard. From Valencia came combatants of all ranks, regular troops and militiamen. Almost all the battalions of the newly formed Voluntary Army were sent from its headquarters in Albacete, and from Alicante and Cartagena came forces of the army and the navy. The line of resistance hardened and Varela, in command of the advance on Madrid, found the going hard.

No longer were the communists, who had sent some of the best mountain brigades to the Tagus valley, the only ones to demand the formation of a single army. Moreover, their own prestige was in the ascendant. Their militias were of a higher standard than most, and from their ranks sprang improvised military leaders, well-versed in the arts of propaganda. The whole communist military effort revolved around the 5th Regiment, which provided them with a strong base and a source of considerable political influence.[10] Largo Caballero shared the communists' strong views on military unification, views which gradually

came to be reflected in legislation and to exert, however slowly and
arduously, some influence upon reality.[11]

4. First Phases in the Emergence of a New Army: The Mixed Brigades

On the very day he took over the presidency (4 September 1936), Largo
Caballero set up his general staff and reviewed the deployment of
forces on the various fronts. In place of the committees, he relied on so-
called 'civilian elements' to represent the political parties and the
unions on the general staff. He himself took supreme and direct command of the armed forces, within which military units and militias were
to be amalgamated. The militias were henceforth to be organised along
military lines and each battalion would be identified by a number, without any reference to party affiliations. Militia officers would be confirmed in their previous posts and in future would be recruited through
special training schools. To provide the new body thus created with a
corresponding new look, a different badge was introduced – a red five-
pointed star – together with a new salute (that of the clenched fist) and a
control mechanism consisting of the political commissars.[12] Thus the
new army was the incarnation of a new idea – the instrument of the
Popular Front; and the political commissars were supposed to make it an
effective tool. The commissariat already existed in the units of the 5th
Regiment, and its forerunner in the non-communist militias had been
the *responsable* or political delegate. The function of the commissariat
was to 'exert a constant influence upon the main body of combatants
and to make certain that they are ever mindful of the spirit which should
animate them all'.

The new army was of a strongly revolutionary character; so much so
that at first there was not a single republican among its political leaders.
The pro-communist socialist Alvarez del Vayo was appointed commissar-general; the posts of sub-commissars-general were filled by Gil
Roldan (C.N.T.), Mije (communist), Bilbao (socialist) and Pestaña
(syndicalist). The socialist Pretel was appointed general secretary, and
he soon went over to the communists. So communist influence was
dominant in the new set-up.

The office of information and control was given the task of 'purifying'
the army. This body had grown out of the corps committees active
since 18 July, and the government relied on it to determine whether
military personnel were loyal to the regime or not, retaining at its head
Major Eleuterio Díaz Tendero, founder of the U.M.R.A. It was he who

declared that 'people have frequently alleged lack of officers to justify what is basically the product of general disorganisation . . . there has never been a problem nor is there one now, since we have more than enough officers and always have had'.

This office classified all military personnel, putting an 'F' (fascist) by the names of those it considered disloyal, an 'I' by those whose attitude smacked of indifference and an 'R' by those it considered faithful republicans. Without the 'R' there was no command or hope of promotion. Those marked 'indifferent' were kept on in the army but were not allowed to occupy posts of responsibility; neither could they be promoted. Those the office considered opposed to the cause were expelled from the army, almost invariably imprisoned and frequently eliminated. All those considered loyal republicans were immediately promoted to higher rank.

Largo Caballero also ordered considerable basic reforms within the army. All the former columns were now reorganised into mixed brigades, named thus in view of the fact that they incorporated elements from various branches of the armed forces. The process of reorganisation started with certain carabineer units in training and with regular army battalions and militia battalions which happened to be stationed on the bases of the Voluntary Army near Albacete. The 5th Regiment and units of international volunteers were organised along the same lines. Thus six Spanish and two international brigades were born in October 1936, and plans were laid for the immediate creation of ten more Spanish and four other international brigades. The communists, with their eager acceptance of the idea of militarisation, which they quite justifiably considered their own, occupied a privileged position within the new army. Out of the six original mixed brigades, four were under the command of militant party men. And the international brigades have been rightly called by David T. Cattell 'a Soviet force in Spain'. The Spanish brigades were generally commanded by professional officers; the staffs of the international brigades were usually composed rather of professional revolutionaries.

This feverish reorganisation of the Republican Army spread out from Albacete over the entire zone. Tanks, artillery and aircraft began to arrive at the bases set up by the Russians in the province of Murcia. Supremacy in the air had been the government's until September, but now it passed to the enemy. The arrival of German and Italian equipment had started to make up for the supplies the government received from France, inferior in quality, if not in quantity. With the arrival of aid from the Soviet Union the scales tipped once more, and the position was similar with regard to armoured equipment. At first the government had the upper hand, but this changed in October with the arrival of the first Italian tanks and the German Panzer-1s. These were not very powerful, lacking the armour-plating and gun complement of real tanks, and seemed hardly more than reconnoitring vehicles; but even so they could be quite impressive unless confronted by the powerful Russian T-26s and TB-5s.[13]

But would the Russian tanks arrive in time? On 10 October fifty tanks reached Archena and together with later consignments they were formed into the Krivoshein Detachment. Thirty-nine Y-15s, called *Chatos*, were assembled on an adjacent improvised airstrip, and thirty-one SB-2 *Katiuskas* not far away in Albacete and Tomelloso. As many *Natachas* and *Rosantes* were ready for action by the end of October, and further vital consignments of equipment were on their way. Crews to man the forty-eight new batteries were being trained at Almansa and Chinchilla, and the Albacete centre was equipping men with Russian Maxim machine-guns.

There was a brief resurgence of optimism in the government ranks. Sizeable forces, in the form of columns, with which to withstand the advance on Madrid were aided, just in time, by the Krivoshein tanks and Russian bombers (which were swifter than the nationalist fighters). On 28 October Largo Caballero gave the general order to attack. This assault, aimed at the right flank of the nationalists, ended in failure, but it did prevent Varela from digging in his right flank on the banks of the Jarama river. Varela reached the suburbs of Madrid on 4 November.

5. *The Struggle for Madrid: Testing-Ground for a New Army*

On 4 November a new government including C.N.T. representatives had been formed in Madrid; it took over in an atmosphere of profound pessimism and immediately withdrew from Madrid. It left the city in the hands of General Miaja, commander of the 1st Division and, from that moment, president of the capital's defence committee, with delegated but virtually absolute powers. Pozas, who had succeeded Asensio, dismissed under communist pressure, remained in command of the whole Army of the Centre. The mixed brigades, except for the 1st and the 3rd, remained at his disposal, but he could neither use them nor hand them over to Miaja without express orders from the minister of war, who was hoping to use them as part of a larger unit to destroy

Varela's forces when the time came. The government's departure made it easier to unify the effective command of the defence of Madrid, organised with great skill and clear-sightedness by General Miaja. With the assistance of his chief of staff, Lieutenant-Colonel Rojo, a highly respected soldier of proven ability, Miaja managed to restore the morale of the resistance. The forces at his command consisted of some 25,000 infantry, initially backed up by eighty heavy guns and thirty tanks. According to Rojo's estimate, which turned out to be accurate, Varela was about to attack with about twenty-nine battalions and twenty-six batteries; some 30,000 men in all. The real difference in strength was in fact much greater, since Varela was up against not only Miaja but also Pozas, whose forces were drawn up along the Jarama–Tagus line. The disproportion was enormous.

Varela's campaign plans happened to fall into Miaja's hands by accident, and the latter immediately shifted his centre of gravity towards the right, bringing up the 11th International Brigade so that access was barred to the university suburb. The nationalists came up against fierce and unexpected resistance.

Confident that he had the upper hand, Miaja prepared to attack. Pozas was to attack simultaneously along the Jarama line, with the 12th International Brigade, which had arrived the previous day, going into battle alongside him. This counter-attack failed utterly, one of the most notorious defeats on this day being that of the 12th International Brigade at the Cerro de los Angeles. In face of this crisis all the mixed brigades, the newly arrived anarchists led by Durruti, and all the tanks placed themselves under Miaja's central command. Miaja ordered an offensive, but this was reduced to a simple surrounding manœuvre aimed at dislodging the nationalists from the woodlands of the Casa de Campo, which lay on the western approaches to the capital. On the very day chosen for this action, Varela too chose to attack and a terrible struggle ensued. Durruti, in the vanguard, gave ground and his forces retreated, soon to disband completely; the nationalists broke through on the right and by nightfall had occupied a good part of the university suburb, but without consolidating a new front line. Miaja reacted swiftly and effectively, and for the next few days the centre of battle was the university suburb, where the front stabilised after the seventeenth.

Half-way through November the struggle entered a critical phase because of the exhaustion of the combatants, and thereafter it gradually subsided into little more than a series of duels in the air. On 16 November the Nationalist Air Force was strengthened by the arrival of the German Condor Legion, consisting of about a hundred aircraft which at first were none too impressive,[14] pitted as they were against the powerful Russian fighter planes. The Russian planes usually did rather better, but were none the less unable to prevent the nationalist bombing raids, which were particularly harrowing in the latter half of November. But the morale of the defenders remained firm.

The defence of Madrid resulted in surprisingly few casualties on the government side: 266 dead and 6029 wounded. The militias gave a better account of themselves than ever before; yet almost every enemy breakthrough was due to some short-sightedness or failure on their part. The weakness of the anarchist fighting force in particular has been greatly exaggerated; but the other militias in their sector did not fight any better than the anarchists did, and indeed the communist troops of the 5th Regiment broke in front of the Hospital Clinico. If Madrid held fast, it was thanks to the effectiveness of the mixed brigades. It was Miaja's great achievement to issue clear instructions and to keep up morale. He was ably seconded by his right-hand man Rojo, while the Soviet advisers contributed towards the victory, but to a lesser degree. The battle of Madrid was no great miracle of military science; it was little more than a head-on clash between two ungovernable wills, in which courage rated higher than technique. The government troops failed every time they tried to launch any sophisticated manœuvre; the international brigades fought well on the defensive, but only moderately when it came to attacking. One of their most outstanding leaders, Lazar Stern of the 'Kléber' Brigade, hinted at weaknesses which were to be plainly demonstrated in successive battles. He also caused political trouble which led to his subsequent removal, somewhat delayed by communist propaganda which had made him out to be a hero. The 'defence committee' served its purpose of underpinning the armed forces and reducing any internal disagreements to a minimum; at the start of the battle, a wave of terror was unleashed, reaching its peak in early November. Miaja was able to call on considerable relief forces, who bore the brunt of the fighting, and he also had more regular officers than the other side, particularly in the higher ranks, though it is true that many of them had been relegated to administrative posts. The people were anxious and eager spectators, playing far less of an active part in the battle than has been claimed by propaganda. As General Rojo said, 'the vast reserve of manpower we thought we had behind us on the night of the sixth turned out to be not so great after all'. The defence forces of Madrid were more than doubled between

10 and 16 November, and continued to swell later on; but the extra help came from outside, from Catalonia, Levante, La Mancha and in particular from Pozas's army. Madrid, the capital itself, was only just capable of supplying a couple of battalions. The famous 5th Regiment sent but a single battalion. With the help of its agitprop organisation, the communist party was able to create a false impression of a popular uprising which never in fact took place, in spite of all the meetings and demonstrations. The battle was fought by Miaja's forces on the one hand and those of Varela on the other.

The Republic learnt its lesson at Madrid and no longer resisted the idea of militarisation. Even the C.N.T. was persuaded to change its mind. The government stuck firmly to its plans; though it must be noted that these were not intended to be put into action immediately, but were rather a general outline to be adapted to concrete situations. The centralisation of military planning and control in Madrid helped to strengthen the government, whose only link with the city was, paradoxically, through Miaja. Before the month ended, the Army of the Centre had begun the reorganisation of its militias and columns into mixed brigades. Throughout, the republican armies were hard pressed by the forces of Orgaz, who had taken over from Varela and was struggling to improve his position around Madrid. By the end of the year, all the troops under Pozas and Miaja had been organised into mixed brigades and numbered consecutively, carrying on from those formed at Albacete. By February all the mixed brigades were linked together in twelve divisions, also numbered consecutively. Two of these divisions, the 4th and the 11th, were under the command of communists who had emerged from the ranks of the 5th Regiment, namely Modesto and Lister. The others, like the vast majority of the mixed brigades, were commanded by regular officers.

These new units were born of a combination of voluntary and compulsory recruitment. The former militias, since their incorporation into the new brigades, had improved considerably both in effectiveness and morale, as they showed in the January fighting along the Corunna road. A new army, which was better equipped to resist attack and to achieve a military equilibrium, was emerging.

6. The Militarisation Process on the Battlefield: Teruel, the Jarama, Malaga

Half-way through December 1936 the Army of the South was set up under General Martínez Monje, but it did not really get past the planning stage because, from July onwards, the Malaga zone was in the hands of anarchist committees, which foiled all attempts at organisation. On the Teruel front, all the columns were unified under the command of Colonel Velasco, but he was dependent upon a Popular Executive Committee from which the government gradually took over. At the end of the year these units, reinforced by the 13th International Brigade and the 22nd Mixed Brigade, opened fire in the first battle of Teruel, described by Malraux in *L'Espoir*. In spite of an overwhelming superiority – both on the ground and in the air – their attack was a failure. It was at about this time that Largo Caballero was complaining bitterly to Companys, president of the Catalan *Generalitat*, that with his 40,000 men he (Companys) did not seem able to make things difficult for the enemy's 10,000 men; this justified complaint ignored the fact that exactly the same thing was happening at Teruel.[15] By January the reorganisation of columns on this front was complete. Only the picturesque anarchist columns of Teruel rejected all reform. Reorganisation took place throughout the rest of the central region, while in the nationalist zone the restructuring of the army along modern lines was proceeding at a much slower pace. While for the republicans the efficient mixed brigade was commonplace by now, the nationalists still clung to the basic battalion-type unit. In February 1937 there were already twelve government divisions; on the other side not a single one had materialised.

Well aware that the new military structure was far more effective, the republicans planned an offensive that would put the new brigades to good use and would be a repetition of the manœuvre planned after the battle of Madrid. The main attack – coming from the Jarama line – would be launched by Pozas with 15 brigades and 25 batteries; the secondary attack would involve Miaja with six brigades. The aim, as in the previous November, was to destroy the nationalist forces which were putting pressure on Madrid. Pozas was to intercept the routes to Andalusia, Toledo and Estremadura and then join up with Miaja to the rear of General Orgaz. Preparations for the battle made slow progress because of arguments between Pozas and his number two, Miaja, whose opinion was that nothing and nobody must leave Madrid. Meanwhile the nationalists, who had prepared for an offensive in exactly the same spot, decided to advance and attack. A fierce encounter ensued, and it looked as though Orgaz would reach Arganda and Morata. Since Miaja refused to send reinforcements, and since the nationalist attack took place precisely in the area where Pozas and

Miaja were supposed to link up, the government decided to put Miaja in charge of the entire zone, giving him command of the newly created Second Army and promoting him to equal rank with Pozas. Now Miaja felt responsible for the battle of the Jarama and poured in the reinforcements he had refused to Pozas. While Pozas held the nationalist offensive at bay, Miaja mounted a counter-offensive with four newly created divisions. Thus the battle of the Jarama, the toughest fought up to that time, had two distinct phases: the first, a defensive phase led by Pozas, was successful; the second, an offensive phase led by Miaja, failed, despite the firm and enthusiastic fighting of the Popular Army and despite their superior armoured equipment (a tank brigade under the Russian Pavlov) and their Douglas aircraft.

Meanwhile Malaga, the militia town, crumbled practically without resistance before the onslaught of the various nationalist columns and a detachment of Italian Black Shirts. If the defenders, undermined by the civilian and military anarchy prevailing in the whole province, were able to prolong the engagement, it was only thanks to the terrain and their equipment. The town fell on 7 February, and the front was reconsolidated at Motril by the 6th Brigade and the 13th International Brigade.

The fall of Malaga sparked off a massive political and military crisis. The communist party and its incongruous allies, the moderate republicans and socialists, unleashed an all-out attack upon Largo Caballero. But he was in a very strong position, so they took his military colleagues only as their targets, accusing them of treason. Largo was thus obliquely charged with protecting the disloyal. Colonel Villalba was tried; General Asensio, General Martínez Cabrera and General Martínez Monje, along with Colonel Hernández Arteaga, were deprived of their commands. People forgot that those long responsible for the situation in Malaga were the political commissar and the secretary of the executive committee – both militant communists – together with the Russian Colonel Kremeig. Largo rode the crisis but suffered a grave loss of political prestige. Another important consequence was the end of resistance to militarisation, since those militias which did resist found that they received neither arms, money nor food.

At the beginning of March 1937 an Italian army corps of 30,000 men, the *Corpo Truppe Voluntarie* or C.T.V., excellently equipped with artillery and partially motorised, attacked via Guadalajara. It was then that Miaja set up the 4th Army Corps under Lieutenant-Colonel Jurado, composed of the 11th Division under Lister, the 12th under

Lacalle and the 14th under Cipriano Mera. At Guadalajara, the government air force and the magnificent defensive action of Jurado's brigades and Pavlov's tanks managed to halt the Italian advance, which was made vulnerable by neglect of their flanks and generally shaky morale. Eventually they were obliged to retreat. Throughout, the republican side was in the throes of extensive reorganisation, both at the front and in the rear; no less than twenty-two new brigades were formed by calling up reservists who had done their military service in the years 1931–7 and arming them with Russian equipment. The tank brigade was divided into two, and an independent regiment of heavy BT-5 tanks emerged. The fighter force now numbered twelve squadrons, not counting those of the north. These measures completed the militarisation of all the forces of the centre, the south and Levante, putting them under the direct command of the minister of war. Only Catalonia and the north were exempt from this centralisation.

In fact, a separate but similar path had been followed in Catalonia. In September 1936 the anarcho-syndicalists had joined the *Generalitat* government and the notorious Anti-Fascist Militias' Committee, which had challenged the autonomous government's authority was finally dissolved, though the C.N.T. retained its organs of control. In December the *Generalitat*, which had encroached on the central government's powers much as the syndicalists had encroached on its own, set up a separate Catalan army (*L'Exércit de Catalunya*), raising three divisions by means of new conscription of reservists. The forces already at the front were divided into four divisions and four independent regiments. In order to stress the difference between these forces and those controlled by the central government, the Catalan army adopted the regiment rather than the mixed brigade as its basic unit.[16] The militarisation process tended to strengthen the authority of the regional government at the expense of the political organisations. The P.S.U.C. (the Catalan branch of the communist party) embarked upon a campaign against their 'fraternal enemies' of the C.N.T. In March 1937 the workers' and soldiers' committees were dissolved by order, and the rearguard militias and patrols suffered the same fate. Public order was made the responsibility of the ministry of the interior, which also took command of whatever forces of the Civil Guard and detachments of the Security Corps were based in the area. C.N.T. reaction was violent, and the Catalan government stepped down. After a month of negotiations the crisis was sorted out and the controversial measures suspended though not revoked. When the commissioner for public order, Rodríguez

Salas, attempted to enforce them none the less, it was the signal for battle. The anarcho-syndicalists, backed by the P.O.U.M., held sway in the streets and seemed ready for a repeat performance of 20 July – imposing their will without actually seizing power.

The central government and the autonomous government both wanted to find a compromise solution, but the communist, republican and socialist members of the cabinet, guided by Prieto, felt that the only way to solve the problem was the suppression of the rebel element. Largo Caballero chose a middle way: negotiation from a position of strength. With public order and military command once more the responsibility of the central government, he hoped to solve the problem by sending detachments of the army, the navy and the air force to Barcelona. The syndicalists accepted the truce, and the C.N.T. lost its position of overriding power. The councils of defence and of the interior set up by the autonomous government all but disappeared. The anarchists, the separatists and Largo Caballero himself were the big losers of the 'May Days'; the prime minister was accused of vacillation and partly lost the support of the syndicalists. The communists won the day and acquired a firm foothold in Catalonia, where they had previously been poorly represented. They soon became, throughout the whole country, the arbiters of the situation, and very soon they provoked a crisis, claiming that it was in fact caused by Largo Caballero's refusal to punish the rebels in Barcelona and by his obstinate decision to attack in Estremadura rather than in the centre, as the Russian advisers had urged.

7. The Battles of Summer 1937 and the Loss of the North

Throughout the spring and especially during the first few days of May, Russian convoys brought in massive loads of arms and defence equipment. Meanwhile the nationalists gave up their obsession with Madrid, and with good strategic sense turned to attack the republican north. This move increased the material superiority of the government in the central zone. In May 1937 there were 153 brigades organised or in process of organisation in this zone; there were 47 divisions and 13 army corps. The resignation of Largo Caballero and his replacement by Negrín on 19 May made a cancellation of the long-standing plan for an Estremadura offensive inevitable. Colonel Rojo became chief of staff in the central zone and Prieto minister of national defence. His ministry combined the old ministries of war, navy and air force. The C.N.T. left the government. The unions, which had been the heart and soul of the struggle, were swept aside to become mere bystanders. A campaign of repression ensued, cautious against the C.N.T. and pitiless against the Trotskyite P.O.U.M.

The army which Prieto inherited from Largo Caballero was unified, under a single command, and with no other political influences active within its ranks than those emanating from the commissariat. It was well equipped and reasonably well prepared for action. From December onwards the Popular Schools of Warfare were in operation and the system of military justice had been partially restored. In the main zone alone there were over 500,000 men, supported by 1465 guns and more than 400 aircraft. Enemy aircraft and artillery were tied up in the north, and it would take days to transport them to other fronts. On this basis, a series of well-planned operations were begun against Peñarroya, Teruel, Segovia, Huesca, Brunete and Saragossa. All these operations, which followed each other without a break from April to September 1937, ended in failure. While Largo Caballero was still in power, military action was usually carried out by local forces plus reinforcements (for example in Peñarroya, where the Andalusian forces were backed up by the 13th International Brigade), but the new chief of staff of the centre, Rojo, created an Army of Manœuvre with the best troops in the army. This force was ready in time to take part in the battles of Guadarrama and Huesca.

In the battle of Guadarrama – described in Hemingway's *For Whom the Bell Tolls* – the 31 March attack was led by two manœuvre divisions supported by local forces; it was launched in the direction of Segovia, which was poorly defended. It was a total failure, and the Republican Air Force (manned and commanded in this instance by Russians) did little or nothing to help. At Huesca the manœuvre force, composed of six brigades from the centre (among them two international brigades), together with two local divisions, was utterly defeated. The veteran leader of the 12th International Brigade, Maté Zalka 'Lukacs', was killed in the attack and was replaced by Kléber. All in all, the first attempt at diversionary offensive tactics had clearly completely failed to achieve its end, namely to weaken the nationalist offensive against the north.

In the decisive attack, on Brunete, the republicans were to wager their best troops and most carefully selected officers.

Throughout the Brunete offensive the Army of Manœuvre remained under Miaja's direct command, and the aim was to annihilate the

Nationalist Army Corps of Madrid. The republicans enjoyed overwhelming local superiority, and Rojo counted on this to have the whole action over before enemy reinforcements could arrive from their distant positions. Two basic factors contributed to the failure of this offensive: first, the defensive capacity of the local enemy garrisons, despite their reduced numbers, and their readiness for self-sacrifice; secondly, the great mobility of Franco's reserves, which arrived to take up their positions on the front much more quickly than Rojo had anticipated. On the other hand, tanks and aircraft once again put up a disappointing performance. It was in this battle that the German Messerschmitt fighters appeared for the first time; outnumbered by the *Moscas*, they were nevertheless much more effective.

The nationalist command made the mistake of accepting a wasteful battle which brought them no real gain; they struggled fiercely for three weeks simply to regain a ruined village of no tactical value, while their vital operations in the north were paralysed. It was because of the obsessive attraction of Madrid that such an operation, doomed from the second day, achieved, if not its primary then its secondary objective – to check the offensive against the north. Government troops complained that they were prevented by lack of reinforcements from carrying the operation through successfully, but at Brunete the republicans used in succession 11 divisions, 31 mixed brigades, more than 200 field guns, 200 tanks and armoured vehicles and 300 aircraft. Always superior to the enemy, their failure was due to general uncertainty and lack of confidence among both officers and men. The 13th and 15th International Brigades were soundly beaten; the Kléber Brigade's weakness was shown up at Villafranca del Castillo. All of them seem to have been overcome by an excessive fear of the enemy, and the obsessive concern with counter-attacks on their flanks held up the whole action. The Republican Manœuvre Force, apart from occasional minor routs, always fought more effectively on the defensive.

The next month's objective was Saragossa. For this attack the republican forces, under General Pozas, formed four groups attacking from as many points, all converging on Saragossa. Ten divisions took part, including two international brigades. Of all the great battles of the war, this was the one where the attacking forces had the greatest superiority and sustained the attack longest. The nationalist leaders did not make the mistakes they had made at Brunete; they neither called up their reserves nor halted their advance on Santander. They were content to contain the offensive. The self-immolation of the Belchite,

Quinto and Codo garrisons, whose men fought to the last, proved decisive.

After this, large-scale offensives in support of the northern front ceased, and with their failure the entire war changed character. The opportunity had passed. The republicans had not been able to take advantage of their local military superiority, which gradually diminished as the Army of the North disintegrated, leaving the enemy in a position of strength in the area.

The nationalists realised, albeit somewhat belatedly, that the final dénouement would come in the north. There, a powerful but isolated republican army would have to fight the bulk of the nationalist forces without any chance of assistance. These circumstances would enable the nationalists to achieve local superiority and with it to regain their lost advantage. By the end of March almost the whole Nationalist Air Force, the major part of their artillery and shock forces were flung into the offensive, leaving the nationalist forces on other fronts much reduced, but able to hold out on the defensive.

It was in the north that the government had its best troops. The Basques and the Asturians were politically motivated to a high degree; they were also better trained. In no other area were there so many volunteers (except in Navarre, on the nationalist side). Nowhere else was there such enthusiasm. Against this, one must take into account pronounced local separatist feeling which made co-ordination difficult. However, the north represented a considerable concentration of power, all the more so since it contained all the most important heavy industries, indispensable for the war effort. During 1936 and in the winter of 1937 the republican forces of the north had worn themselves out in attacks on Oviedo and Vitoria which failed because the local garrisons put up a stubborn resistance. Now they were on the defensive, aided to some extent by mountainous and difficult terrain.

In April 1937 the Army of the North, commanded by General Llano Encomienda, consisted of 150,000 men, 267 guns, more than 100,000 rifles, one armoured regiment and a plentiful supply of automatic weapons. Its weak point was air support, although at the beginning of the nationalist offensive it had thirty-five aircraft in service. At that time the bombers lacked the range to operate in the north from bases in the central zone, and it would have been suicidal to shift them north. Fighters and supply planes were sent instead. Many were sent (they amounted to a fraction of the total Republican Air Force), only to be destroyed in unequal combat. The decision to send them to the north was unfortunate but politically unavoidable. Their loss cost the government its air supremacy, which it never recovered. As a result, the general situation worsened, and there was no way of bringing relief to the Army of the North or of halting the continuous nationalist bombardment. The defence of the north depended heavily on the indirect support of diversionary offensives in the centre; when these failed, the Army of the North was doomed. In Biscay the battle was fought with courage and determination; the nocturnal counter-attacks of the *gudaris* gained them the wholehearted respect and even admiration of their enemies. Asturias and Santander came to Biscay's aid, so that her defence forces totalled seven divisions and twenty-seven brigades, thus outnumbering the attacking forces. Veteran leaders and Russian advisers hurried from Madrid to try and save Bilbao. They were unable to prevent the fall of the city, which took place on 19 June 1937. Disagreements between the Basque government and the central government, which had ordered the destruction of all industrial plants to deprive the enemy of their use, resulted in the last-minute defection of a considerable number of Basque units and the total demoralisation of the rest.

These facts, along with the poor performance in battle of the Santander forces, whose loyalty was highly suspect, and the growing superiority of the nationalists, made the Santander campaign an easy one for the latter. After the unnecessary Brunete episode, the Italian legionaries gained a victory as impressive as that of Malaga, though more costly, which helped to remove the bitter taste left by the campaign of La Alcarria. The situation of the Army of the North was becoming more and more desperate as its men were killed and its territory reduced. These losses called for successive reorganisations, and after the fall of Bilbao the Army of the North was completely integrated into the general organisation of the Popular Army. It still consisted of ten divisions with thirty brigades well-equipped with artillery and automatic weapons, but it was trapped in a tiny area with practically no protection from the air. A tough defence was mounted on this difficult ground, but on 19 October the nationalists entered Gijón. This was the end of the north, and the decisive turning point of the war. The government had lost 150,000 men, more than 100,000 rifles, 400 guns, 200 aircraft, thousands of automatic weapons and a powerful industrial base. The loss of 4 army corps, 16 divisions and 45 brigades added up to 25 per cent of all the republican forces. Nearly all these assets now passed to the enemy, who mobilised most of the prisoners and got industry moving, since it had not, as the central government wished, been destroyed. The nationalist superiority in men and equipment was finally achieved; the balance had been destroyed, to the republicans' cost.

8. *From Teruel to the Mediterranean*

After the fall of the north, which did not have the far-reaching political effects of the relatively insignificant fall of Malaga, the government reduced its military and political strategy to what Raymond Aron has called 'ne pas perdre'. The slogan of the day became 'Resistance equals victory'. The rearguard was breaking up. There were frequent cases of sabotage, and the famous fifth column, which had hardly operated before, became gradually bolder. Desertions, of which there had been few in the first phase of the war, reached alarming proportions with the mobilisation of reinforcements. Indalecio Prieto then set up an effective instrument of repression: the Military Information Service (S.I.M.), which was soon controlled by the communists and did more to cause dissension than to enforce discipline. Similarly the system of military justice was reformed. Permanent army and army corps' tribunals were set up, and discipline became much tighter. Political commissars were given authority to 'strip of their rank or cause the physical disappearance' of anyone who was suspect. Military power became more and more centralised, and even the C.N.T. bowed to the central military authority. To make up for its losses in the north, the government mobilised fresh reinforcements, creating four army corps, four new divisions and thirteen mixed brigades. The original distribution of units was thus reconstructed, but not their true strength. The new Armies of Levante, Andalusia and Estremadura emerged, and also the general headquarters of the Army of Manœuvre.

As always the job of reorganisation was made possible by the continuing flow of material aid from the Soviet Union. Up until half-way through 1937 this had mostly come by sea; thereafter it came via the French border, since the Nationalist Fleet, which had become a much stronger force in the Mediterranean after the disappearance of the northern front, was effectively blockading the Mediterranean ports. The equipment and supplies received by the government were in no way inferior to those received by their enemies from Italy and Germany: a tacit agreement – maybe a balance of fear – seemed to stand in the way of escalation. On both sides the volume of foreign aid, personnel and equipment reached its peak in spring 1937 and from then onwards decreased gradually and almost steadily.

The quality of aircraft, however, underwent a change – to the advantage of the nationalists. The year 1936 was crucial for the aeronautics industry in Europe: this year saw the switch from the slow biplane fighter to the fast monoplane, and to the stressed-skin construction giving bombers greater range and speed. From spring 1937 onwards, German and Italian aviation improved significantly with the advent of the new types. The Italian S-79s and German ME-109s and HE-111s were to win supremacy in the air from the Russian models. The government still had more fighter planes until the battle of the Ebro, but they had a smaller bomber force from spring 1937 onwards.

General Rojo, hoping to anticipate possible enemy action, returned in the autumn of 1937 to the old plan of attack in Estremadura, now known as 'Plan P'. But Franco's concentration of forces for yet another assault on Madrid was manifest, and Rojo decided to ward off the blow with a lightning diversionary attack on Teruel, after which he would return immediately to 'Plan P'. On 15 December 1937 he launched the offensive with a massive force (consisting of the 18th, the 20th and the 22nd Army Corps), and gained for the government its major victory – the taking of a provincial capital, Teruel. After persistent attacks on a narrow front, the nationalists finally decided on a broader manœuvre. After regaining Teruel in the battle of Alfambra, they broke through the Aragon front after 9 March 1938. Reinforcements, reorganisation, temporary regroupings: all were to no avail.

The defeat was beginning to look like a disaster. The way to Catalonia lay wide open after General Yagüe's daring crossing of the Ebro. Deserters arrived in Tarragona by the thousand. The Army of Manœuvre, in the south, put up a better resistance, but finally it retreated en masse. Lérida fell on 4 April, along with Gandesa. The recently organised Army of the East was disbanded and the International Brigades, reunited for a spell at Caspe, were scattered and practically wiped out. The political commissariat called for acts of heroism. Prieto, held responsible for the defeat, had to relinquish the ministry of defence, which was taken over by the president himself. Negrín now consolidated his position, and took a tough line with the backing of the army and the communist party. The syndicalists and the separatists toed the line, although internal dissent was undermining unity throughout the entire zone.

Just when the route to Barcelona seemed open, the nationalists made a surprise decision which greatly eased pressure on the defeated Army of the East, which, according to a central general staff report, was defenceless, having lost 70,000 men, despite the infusion of six divisions and nineteen mixed brigades.[17] The nationalist command called a halt in Catalonia and gave orders to push via the Maestrazgo towards the Mediterranean.

South of the Ebro the Army of Manœuvre, reinforced in its turn by three divisions and nine brigades from the centre, from Andalusia and Estremadura, stood firm against attack, and the 5th Army Corps in the Gandesa area prevented the nationalists from digging in their left flank on the river. Tagüeña's militia was particularly outstanding in these battles. The nationalists altered their advance slightly, and the Army Corps of Galicia, under General Aranda, broke through the centre once more and reached the sea on 15 April 1938.

Once again a nationalist decision, the most unexpected of the whole war, enabled the scattered republican forces to regroup. While they entrenched themselves hurriedly in the natural ditches along the Ebro and the Segre, the nationalists turned round to attack the Army of Levante and the Army of Manœuvre, aiming for the distant objective of Valencia. The fall of Valencia would not have been decisive, either politically or militarily, while that of Barcelona would virtually have ended the war then and there. By the time the nationalist advance on Valencia had got as far as Castellón, taken that town and passed on, two new army corps were drawn up along a new fortified front line called the XYZ, which blocked access to Valencia. The defence of this line was brilliant; but just when the nationalists were getting ready to launch the attack they hoped would be decisive, the attention of both armies, and of the world, was diverted once more to the Ebro.

9. The Ebro and the End

The Eastern Army Group under Hernández Saravia was composed of the Army of the Ebro and the Army of the East. What with the nationalists' apparent lack of interest in Catalonia, and fresh deliveries of arms and defence equipment, the Eastern Army Group reached, on the eve of the battle of the Ebro, a total strength of seven army corps, twenty-one infantry divisions and one assault division, sixty-four mixed brigades, one armoured brigade, the Northern Coastal Defence Group and some 200 batteries. Air support was considerably improved, and their fighter force was equal to that of the nationalists, thanks to the ultra-modern *Supermoscas* and *Superchatos*, piloted by Spanish crews trained in the U.S.S.R. There was also one squadron manned by

Russian pilots. The two government zones contained between them more troops than the nationalists, and although they had fewer aircraft and guns, their resources were more concentrated. They were handicapped, however, by the fact that they had been left in a poor strategic position after the division of their zone, the drive to the sea having divided government territory into two sectors which could not communicate. Franco, on the other hand, could call upon the whole of his force at once.

General Rojo decided upon an offensive, and on 25 July the Army of the Ebro, under the Militia Lieutenant-Colonel Modesto, crossed the Ebro in a well-executed manœuvre. Confronted by what was effectively a vacuum, the 5th and 15th Army Corps occupied a wide bridge-head. The nationalist response was immediate, and in a few days the front was stabilised and the breach plugged.

Then came another inexplicable nationalist decision. While in military terms it would have seemed logical to regard the whole incident as closed, to swing the Nationalist Army of Manœuvre round and attack the Army of the East, while surrounding the Army of the Ebro (which had a large river in its rear), the nationalists instead decided to take up the republican challenge and drive the enemy forces out of territory chosen by them.

This decision marked the beginning of the most bloody, the most long-drawn-out and least explicable battle of the Civil War. The battle, which favoured the defence, was eventually reduced to a series of confrontations, with the nationalist air and artillery support ever more decisively superior. Three and a half months of terrible struggle ended with the Army of the Ebro retreating to its original position. The republican forces fought well on terrain particularly well-suited to defensive action, for which Spanish soldiers have always shown a remarkable capacity. The resistance of the defenders, always courageous, took on at times during this battle an aspect of heroism; perhaps this was what facilitated subsequent glorification by propaganda. It was during the final phase of the battle that the foreign volunteers in the International Brigades were withdrawn. At that time approximately 40 per cent of the men in these units were Spaniards, and, along with the communist-controlled divisions, they formed the elite of the Popular Army: their presence in all the great battles of the war was an essential factor.

After the battle of the Ebro fresh conscription drives took place, but morale remained very low.[18] Despite everything, December 1938 saw the

G

organisation in Catalonia of two new divisions, seven brigades and four machine-gun battalions. When Franco's offensive began on 23 December, the breakthrough took some time, but when it did come there was no possibility of halting it. The successive defence lines L1, L2, L3 and L4 were hardly defended at all as the nationalists sailed through, and on 25 January they entered Barcelona. General Jurado took over command of the Eastern Army Group from Saravia, but to no avail. On 7 February 1939 the nationalists reached the French border.

In the central-southern zone, Miaja was given full military and civil powers – as in Madrid in 1936. On 23 January he was appointed supreme commander of land, sea and air forces (General Rojo did not come back after the fall of Catalonia). He declared a state of total mobilisation, as the army had always demanded and the politicians had always, until then, prevented. The Army Group of the Centre was put under the command of General Matallana. It still consisted of forty-nine divisions, an armoured division and three assault divisions with some 276,000 rifles, 8500 automatic weapons and a thousand guns. Its four armies, commanded by General Menéndez, Colonel Casado, General Escobar and Colonel Moriones, were still undefeated. In January, hoping to save Catalonia, Matallana launched a violent offensive, similar to the old 'Plan P', in the Peñarroya sector. In this offensive the Popular Army occupied the largest area of enemy territory in the whole war; it was its swan-song and perhaps its finest action to date. But after it was over – at the same time as the battle of Catalonia – the one desire left in the army was to end the war.

This desire – which had as its logical consequence refusal of obedience to a government which would fight on – was evident in the advice given to Negrín by the military leaders at a meeting at Albacete aerodrome on 16 February. Negrín, however, decided to resist them, and hoping to mollify them, he promoted Miaja and Rojo to the rank of lieutenant-general – abolished in 1931. He also promoted Colonel Casado and Colonel Cordón[19] and ordered an extensive redistribution of commands which never got past the planning stage. On 4 March a rebellion broke out in Cartagena, led by the 10th Republican Division. On the fifth, Colonel Casado openly rebelled against Negrín and together with General Miaja and the social-democrat leader Besteiro set up a defence committee in Madrid. The first measures taken by this body were aimed at removing all communist influence: all Negrín's promotion orders and appointments were cancelled forthwith, except for that affecting Miaja himself. The five-pointed star was removed from republican uniforms and the way was prepared for immediate negotiations with Franco. A communist rebellion was the immediate result. The situation was one of utter confusion, and in Madrid it was very serious indeed. Barceló, chief of the 1st Army Corps, took over the headquarters of the Army of the Centre and executed three colonels of the general staff and the political commissar. Casado found himself surrounded and asked the anarcho-syndicalist commander of the 4th Corps, Cipriano Mera, for help.

Mera set up a Corps of Manœuvre and sent it to Madrid while forces from the 65th Division set out from the Casa de Campo. The communists who had been the besiegers now were besieged themselves. Colonel Ortega, the communist chief of the 3rd Corps, accepted the mission of mediator between the two camps, and the communists eventually agreed to lay down their arms. Lieutenant-Colonel Barceló was shot. Casado, with the situation well in hand, proceeded to redistribute commands. These events had resulted in 233 dead and 564 wounded; astonishingly enough, the first figure was comparable to that occasioned by the battles of November 1936, which had decided the immediate fate of the city.

Once the peace negotiations had begun, Franco demanded as a prior condition the handing over of the fleet and the air force. When this could not be granted, he accused Casado of being unable to control his troops and therefore in no position to negotiate. He broke off the talks, demanded unconditional surrender and on 27 March ordered his armies to begin an offensive. The defence committee ordered that there should be no resistance. It was the end. By 1 April the nationalists had occupied the whole of republican territory. The Popular Army, ran the last general order of the war, was 'captive and defenceless'.

SUGGESTIONS FOR FURTHER READING

This study is itself a summary of an extensive work, provisionally entitled 'El Ejército Popular de la Republica', to be published by the author very shortly. Both are based on first-hand material in the Archives of the War of Liberation of the Military History Department in Madrid (S.H.M.–A.G.L.) and the Archives of the National Department of Documentary Information in Salamanca (D.S.D.).

The following books should be considered as a bibliographical introduction; not all of them have any intrinsic value, but together they give a picture of the republican Popular Army seen from many points of view.

Enrique Lister in *Nuestra Guerra* (1966) gives a history of the units commanded by himself during the war; its judgements on political questions follow the communist party line. Numerous errors do not detract from the interest of what is an important work.

The 'Russian Volunteers' in the Popular Army, led by Marshal Rodion Malinovski, have published in Moscow *Bajo la bandera de la España Republicana* – indispensable for any serious study of Russian intervention.

An understanding of the anarcho-syndicalist contribution to the war effort can be gleaned from José Peirats, *Los anarquistas en la crisis política española* (1964), and from Eduardo de Guzman, *Madrid rojo y negro* (1938).

Once artículos sobre la guerra de España, by Manuel Azaña, written after the war, corroborates some misleading theories (such as the disproportionate influence of the Germans and the Italians on the final result), but like all his writings during the Civil War is indispensable for those who wish to understand the internal causes of the fall of the Republic.

España heróica, by General Vicente Rojo (1961), is a good introduction to the military study of the war from the republican side.

The most fascinating introduction to a study of the political and military problems of the Republican Fleet is to be found in Manuel Dominguez Benavides's book *La escuadra la mandan los cabos* (1944).

For any study of the Republican Air Force, three complementary books should be consulted: F. G. Tinker's *Some Still Live* (1938), *Sangre en el Cielo*, by the republican pilot Francisco Tarazona (1938) and Jesús Salas's *La guerra española desde al aire* (Ariel, 1970).

The international brigades have been the subject of many books, among which one of the best, historically speaking, is Jacques Deperrie de Bayac's *Les Brigades Internationales* (1968).

The innumerable articles by Colonel José Manuel Martínez Bande in the periodicals *Ejército* and *Revista de Historia Militar* contain a great deal of data which are also contained in a different form in the four monographs on the military history of the Spanish Civil War published by the same author since 1968: *La marcha sobre Madrid*, *La lucha en torno a Madrid*, *La campaña de Andalucia* and *Guerra y Caida del Norte*.

J. Martin Blazquez's book *I Helped to Build an Army* (1939) is rather disappointing but his judgements should not be completely dismissed.

NOTES

1. The strength of both organisations, which was limited, has been greatly exaggerated; above all they were representative of states of mind. In the author's opinion neither the U.M.E. nor the U.M.R.A. contained more than 5 per cent of the total number of officers between the ranks of lieutenant and colonel.

2. Only one divisional general, Don Miguel Cabenellas of the 5th Division, joined the rebels; the rebels arrested the leaders of the 2nd, 6th, 7th and 8th Divisions. The commanders of the 6th and 8th were shot. Those of the 3rd and 4th stayed with the government, while the commander of the 1st Division was dismissed.

3. The documents preserved in the Military History Department in the Archives of the War of Liberation (S.H.M.–A.G.L.) on the Valencia and

Barcelona uprisings are particularly interesting for their portrayal of the mood among soldiers and garrisons throughout the country.

4. M. Azaña, *La Velada en Benicarló*, in his complete works (ed. Marichal), vol. iii. See also in the same volume *Once artículos sobre la guerra de España*, vii: 'La revolución abortada'.

5. The decree by which the Representative Junta was set up in Levante appeared in the *Gaceta*, 22 July 1936. The *Buletín de la Generalitat*, 21 July 1936, refers to the establishment of Citizens' Militias of Catalonia, whose title was changed under union pressure to that of Central Committee of Anti-fascist Militias. In the north, there were as many separate organisations as provinces.

6. See S.H.M.–A.G.L. records of the Defence Junta of Madrid, particularly those referring to the 12 December session, when the communist Diéguez declared that '120,000 rations are distributed daily while there are only 35,000 men at the front'. A report from the autonomous government of Catalonia states that wages were being paid to 90,000 militiamen though there were only 20,000 at the front (A.G.L. L556, C3).

7. *Gaceta*, 18 Aug 1936.

8. See S.H.M.–A.G.L. L477, C6 and L478, C4; Kuznetsov's version in *Bajo la bandera de la España republicana*, p. 160.

9. The documents referring to the Majorca operations are to be found in S.H.M.–A.G.L. L478 and 479.

10. The size of the 5th Regiment has been greatly exaggerated. Lister (*Nuestra Guerra*) gives the incredible figure of 70,000 men; no author goes below 50,000. The archives of the S.H.M. reveal that 15,000 were trained in Madrid and a smaller number elsewhere.

11. The militias were 'militarised' by an order of 19 October. By this and subsequent orders all militia forces came under a regional military command.

12. The commissariat was created by orders which appeared in the *Boletín Oficial*, nos 211 and 212 for 15 and 16 October. The new salute was officially introduced on 4 October and the new uniform by 31 October.

13. The German tank weighed 6 tons and was armed with two machine-guns. The Italian Fiat Ansaldo tank weighed 3·3 tons and had one machine-gun. The Russian T-26 tank weighed 8·5 tons and had a ·45 gun and two twin machine-guns; the TB-5 weighed 20 tons and had a ·45 gun and four twin machine-guns. According to H. Klotz in *Leçons militaires de la guerre d'Espagne*, those under eight tons were not much use in action.

14. The Condor Legion had 100 aircraft (JU-52 bombers, HE-51 fighters and HE-46 reconnaissance planes). It first appeared over the front at Madrid on 16 November. According to official government sources, bombing of the capital throughout the whole month of November caused 305 deaths.

15. Dispatch from Caballero to Companys, 23 December 1936: S.H.M.–A.G.L. L566, C6 bis.

16. The *Exércit de Catalunya* was created by a decree of the *Generalitat* on 6 December 1936, which provided for the formation of three new divisions from among the conscriptions of 1935 and 1934.

17. Details of these reinforcements are contained in General Rojo's report to the government, 1 April 1937 (S.H.M.–A.G.L. documentación del EMC Rojo).

18. The successive reorganisations of the Popular Army demanded fresh call-ups. By January 1939 general mobilisation of men between eighteen and forty-five was completed.

19. Both promotions appeared in the *Gaceta*, 25 February 1939. None of the others did; therefore, according to the Spanish legislation, they lacked any value.

10. The Nationalist Army in the Spanish Civil War

RICARDO DE LA CIERVA Y DE HOCES

As in the study of the republican zone, it is extremely difficult to isolate any survey of the Nationalist Army from an analysis of the history of the nationalist zone as a whole, as it concentrated its efforts on winning the war. It seems to emerge that in the nationalist zone the main war effort, in contrast to that of the government zone, was exerted rather in the main fighting army than in the rearguard. In this study we will summarise a series of more extensive analyses, some of them to be published shortly, of the military and socio-military aspects of the Spanish Civil War seen from the nationalist side.

1. The Complicated Process of Organisation

(i) *Division and Unity: the Problem of Morale.* Anyone approaching the subject of the causes of the Spanish Civil War in a comprehensive and balanced manner will find it difficult to ignore a fundamental pattern of attitudes and motives, both of individuals and of groups, throughout the period of history that had direct bearing on the conflict. This pattern can be summed up as the militant divisions of Spaniards regarding the future of their country, both in its own historical course and in its relations with the rest of the world.

For any explanation of the war one thing seems obvious: the essential factor in the many internal divisions in Spain was the split within the military forces. Various statistical surveys of this particular factor are being undertaken at this moment. One of the first of these has come up with the following results, which refer to the military personnel actually in the services on 18 July 1936.

Peninsular Army, including the Balearics and the Canaries

Generals, officers above captain, 4660 pro-nationalist out of just
    officers below lieutenant and   under 9000
    equivalent

Warrant officers	2750 out of some 7000
Subalterns	2010 out of some 4300
Ranks	14,175 out of 40,000

Army of Africa	Almost entirely pro-nationalist

Civil Guard

Generals and all officers	700 pro-nationalist out of 1500
Warrant officers	800 out of 2100
Ranks	12,700 out of 30,700
Total	14,200 out of 34,320

Carabineers

Generals and all officers	290 pro-nationalist out of 700
Warrant officers	450 out of 1090
Ranks	5300 out of 13,000

In the Security and Assault Forces (together totalling an estimated 30,000 members) the proportion of nationalists was roughly the same as in the other armed forces, although more exact statistics are not available at present.[1]

All grades of army officers attached to the air force took sides along much the same lines as the rest of the army. Out of an approximate total of 500 pilots (including civil pilots), 200 joined the government side, 200 the rebels, and a total of about 100 were eliminated on the two sides.

Statistics referring to navy personnel are more difficult to obtain. There were 19 admirals on active service on 17 July 1936; 224 captains (of battleships, frigates and corvettes); 251 officers and cadets. This information refers to the *Cuerpo General de la Armada* (General Corps of the Navy). The rest of the navy was served by 35 generals, 521 officers with the rank of captain or above and 667 officers with the rank of lieutenant or below. The figures for other ranks and seamen are uncertain, but the total number of ships' crews was approximately 11,000, with as many serving on land.

The relatively evenly balanced pattern of distribution between the two sides that can be detected in the other armed forces was not repeated in the navy, where approximately 80 per cent of the officers were for the rising, and 80 per cent of other ranks and seamen were on the government's side. This can be explained by the fact that class distinction was much more rigid in the navy than in the other forces;

extremist propaganda taking advantage of this had been quite successful. Of course, this phenomenon was not exclusive to the Spanish navy
at that time, and it is quite possible that, for example, in the British
navy the percentage of officers in favour of the rising in Spain was even
greater than in the Spanish navy, torn as it was by civil war.[2]

Given that geography does not play an exclusive part in people's
adherence to one side or another in civil war, it can and does still prove
a deciding factor, above all for those who are 'neutral'. It is interesting
to note that out of the 24,471 men serving in the Army of Africa on
17 July, 24,400 fought in the Nationalist Army. In the Peninsular
Army the difference between combatants and 'geographical loyalists'
in the two zones was considerably greater; but it should be pointed
out straightaway that victory or defeat for the rising in any particular
locality was, in every case, due primarily to the loyalties of the armed
forces at each point.

It is most important to realise from the start that the average age of
the military supporters of the rising was considerably lower than that
of those loyal to the government. We already know that on 17 July
there were in Spain eighteen divisional generals or their equivalent.
Out of these eighteen, only four joined the rising, which nevertheless
continued to be called 'the generals' rising': they were Cabanellas,
Queipo de Llano, Franco and Goded. In the note sent by Colonel
García Escámez to that great plotter of spring 1936, Mola, describing
the feeling in the garrisons, with a view to the projected rising, he says:
'The girls [officers from lieutenant down] O.K., the monitors [officers
above rank of captain] bad.'[3]

Some of the leading officers responsible for the July rising were
fearful, even before the event, of the possibility of a long and bloody war,
but the great majority hoped that victory would follow their *coup*
almost immediately. In any case 18 July was not, in principle, an anti-
republican outburst but a rebellion against the Popular Front and the
dangers that the rebels thought they could see in the revolutionary path
it was taking. This is neither the time nor the place to try to analyse these
dangers in depth, although we do consider that they were real dangers,
as we have attempted to show in other works.[4] We simply want to stress
the fact that not a few republicans, both soldiers and civilians, were
effectively involved in the preparation of the July rising. One of the aims
of the main organiser, General Emilio Mola, was in fact a 'republican
dictatorship'.[5] The most important manifesto of General Francisco
Franco (though not one of the most widely publicised) proclaimed the

need to defend 'order *within* the Republic'.

Other forces which helped in the rising were not, of course, so ready to defend such ideals, and perhaps for this reason efforts were made to avoid mention of the institutional question (i.e. monarchy versus a Republic). For the emergent organisation of the nationalist zone, the soldiers supporting the *coup* seized upon the ideal that was engraved on their memories and even on their subconscious; that of Primo de Rivera's dictatorship from 1923 to 1930, which many had served with enthusiasm. Between 18 July and 1 October 1936 General Emilio Mola was the main inspiration and pivot of the body that was set up in Burgos (as a successor to the 1923 Military Directory) – the Defence Junta.* Mola was the mentor of the Junta, despite the fact that his military rank (brigadier-general) prevented him from presiding. Generals Ponte and Saliquet were there as a gesture to the defunct *Junta de Generales* which had operated in Madrid between January and July 1936, and which had only managed to plan a couple of abortive uprisings. The colonels in the Junta were in turn members of another conspiracy organisation, equally ineffective in the field of decision-making but on the other hand highly effective in spreading subversive propaganda against the Popular Front within the army: this organisation was the U.M.E. or *Unión Militar Española*. The role of this body has been exaggerated and even regarded as of exclusive importance by more than one sensationalist historian. The simple bureaucratic fact that Emilio Mola was no more than a brigadier-general in 1936 had much more influence than people think upon the historic destiny of Spain.

On the very day that it was set up, the Burgos Defence Junta recognised the existence of two armies, one in the north, under General Mola, and one in the south, under General Franco. On 30 July the commander of the Nationalist Fleet, Francisco Moreno Fernández, joined the Junta, and on 3 August Franco joined, being officially recognised leader of the Army of Africa on 26 August. By 17 September Generals Queipo de Llano and Orgaz were already members of the Junta. Generals Gil Yuste and Kindelán (the air force chief) had joined well before that date. The Junta revealed in its workings the same mistrust as had Primo de Rivera's Directory towards all that smacked of bureaucracy or the civilian approach. One of the main

---

* Set up on 23 July 1936 with the following founder members: Generals Cabanellas (president), Saliquet, Ponte, Mola, Dávila; Colonels Montaner and Moreno Calderón.

results of its proceedings – which despite this prejudice were most interesting – was to stress in particular the need for a single command, once it was known for certain that the war would be both long and difficult.

It was the Burgos Defence Junta itself that appointed General Francisco Franco sole military commander at the end of September 1936. This occurred after the Army of Africa had given practical proof of its military efficiency, and on the eve (or immediately after, since the date has still not been definitely fixed) of the liberation of the Alcázar at Toledo, an event which, although exaggerated and misrepresented by all propaganda, was of prime importance for the progress of the Spanish Civil War. The combination of the headship of state with the supreme military command in one man presents certain historical problems of detail which are important only as academic issues, since, despite the distrust of more than one high-ranking military leader, the people of the nationalist zone accepted the supreme and overall command of Franco as something clearly desirable and necessary. It should not be forgotten that among the nationalists the one great desire in September 1936 was to win the war, to the exclusion of all other considerations. This was such an obvious aim that there was no need to proclaim it – as was the case in the republican zone. And to win a war you needed to be able to count on the best general available. The people knew very well who this general was, since, as one of his critics, Don José María Gil Robles, said of General Franco in spring 1935, 'the unanimous opinion of the army singled him out as indisputable leader'.[6] This same unanimous opinion, echoed beyond the ranks of the army, was that of all nationalist Spain in the autumn of 1936. Besides, Franco's 'promotion' was preceded and followed by an effective campaign of 'personality' propaganda, whose main mouthpieces were the hereditary monarchists of *Renovación Española* and *Acción Española*. And this propaganda was spread by the most important newspaper in the nationalist zone, the *ABC* of Seville.

The immediate effect of the unification of the military command under Franco was not felt so much in the tactical field (for in 1936 and part of 1937 the generals in charge of the larger sectors enjoyed considerable independence) but it was seen straightaway in the spheres of strategy and logistics. Political unification took much longer to come about, and in some areas, particularly in General Queipo de Llano's extensive sector, command seemed to be in the hands of an independent authority until well into 1938. The G.H.Q. of the generalissimo was set up from October 1936 to November 1937 in the bishop's palace at Salamanca; it was moved to Burgos on 4 November and remained there until the end of the war. The mobile G.H.Q. was known under the name of 'Terminus', and its most frequent location after the fall of the north was the Pedrola estate, near Saragossa. A short time after his appointment as supreme commander, Franco created an administrative Junta (*Junta Técnica Del Estado*), which began work with the same anti-bureaucratic prejudices as the Defence Junta. (The end of this tale was to be an excess of bureaucracy such as had never been known in Spain, but that is another story.) General Dávila was made president of the administrative Junta and chief of the general staff. At the end of January 1938 a ministry of national defence was set up, with three under-secretaries for the army, the navy and the air force. Both the administrative junta and the 1938 ministry dealt with military questions solely in their administrative aspects; the direction of military operations and of the war effort came under the strict control of Franco's G.H.Q.

The highly multiform nationalist forces that entered the Civil War were gradually transformed, throughout its course, by a powerful sense of unity which by the end of the war could be termed monolithic. But it could be seen emerging in the very first days of the war, when its existence and active influence could not be attributed to victories achieved in the field. It is impossible to understand the war effort and moral strength of the nationalist zone without previous acquaintance with the obvious fact that there existed there a progressively more unanimous confidence in victory. It was there from the start, but became daily stronger until, even in the summer of 1936, it represented the unbreakable certainty of a whole community. This cannot be attributed to a consciousness of superiority achieved by foreign aid. Confidence was even more in evidence at the fronts, where the political differences of the rearguard (which were never serious in spite of later exaggeration) were of very little consequence, with the exception we will note. A brave village-woman expressed perhaps better than many erudite authors one of the root-causes of the situation: 'The rich have managed to be poor, and the poor have not known how to be rich.'[7] There was everywhere a genuine spirit of sacrifice and disinterest. The Spanish aristocracy itself, which before 1936 had shown clear signs of degeneration, sacrificed a greater proportion of its sons for the victory than many other sections of society. In no republican newspaper of the time will you find the geographical concreteness that was common among the nationalists: no one spoke there of 'reaching Salamanca or Corunna one day', while on the other side banks were giving credit to the newly impoverished on property in Murcia or Catalonia.[8] The Italian planes that defended Majorca were not bought with the gold of Juan March but with the gold of public subscriptions; and the first act of refugees arriving in Irun from the enemy zone was to deposit the meagre treasures they had managed to save from the disaster at the aid stations set up by the Junta throughout the whole country. The reflections of General Vicente Rojo (republican chief of staff in the centre) on the causes of defeat and victory in the Spanish Civil War, set down with great sincerity, are of tremendous value to those who wish to study this in more depth.

The moral unity of the nationalist leaders came about even before political unity. When Franco managed to get his vital airlift over the Straits of Gibraltar he sent a telegram to Mola saying, 'We command the Straits. We are on top,' and sent him 600,000 cartridges which he desperately needed.[9] Despite the unavoidable resentment he was harbouring, General Queipo de Llano resigned himself to a secondary military role for the duration of the whole war. Nevertheless he made a much more effective contribution towards the military progress of the war than propaganda has made out.[10] The first official war dispatch from the united nationalist zone did not come until 16 October 1936. Up until then the effective co-ordination of the war effort had been more spiritual than material. This doubtless also brought about serious errors and setbacks; such as, possibly, the delays caused by the relief of Oviedo and the liberation of the Alcázar. It also gave rise to serious historical problems: why was the main force of the Army of Africa, which seemed to be marching on Madrid, not transferred to bases in the Sierra 40 kilometres from Madrid, once the link-up with the Army of the North had been made at Mérida? At such moments, no doubt, each of the generals responsible for a particular action relied principally on his own forces, and spiritual unification was as yet far from being reflected in unified objectives and unified direction of the Civil War.

(ii) *From Columns to Army Corps.* In a sense, metaphorically speaking, the divided Spanish officer corps of July 1936 fell into the two old feuding camps of 'Africanists' and 'committeemen'.* What is evident is that the military experience of the nationalist leaders consisted

---

* This division had grown up during the Moroccan campaigns and represented those who saw promotion in terms of service in the field versus those who regarded themselves almost as a branch of the home civil service.

mainly of experience in the Moroccan campaigns, where the basic tactical and all-purpose unit had been the column. For this reason columns formed the basis of the primitive nationalist military machine, and continued to function much longer in the nationalist zone than in the republican zone, where organisation of autonomous mobile units was much more up to date and efficient than in the nationalist zone, once the confusion of the first few moments had passed.

Those areas where the population had given most decisive support to the rising became, before July was out, centres of column organisation and recruitment. These columns – of extremely varied composition – formed themselves, on orders from the improvised officers in the zone, into groups, larger groups and fronts (which were little more than rather ill-defined lines marking off an as yet undetermined enemy zone), and then later, when organisation improved, into sectors. In their actions the columns revealed in the early days a strangely administrative mentality, and devoted themselves to making sure that those who commanded each capital had the support of the main areas of each administrative division, i.e. the corresponding province; this happened in both zones.

Once assured of overwhelming popular support, the columns quickly put a stop to their cleaning-up operations, and raised their sights to objectives at once more distant and more ambitious. For the nationalist zone Madrid was by far the most important objective of this kind. In accordance with the essential points of the conspirators' plan, Mola's first two columns set out for Madrid on the night of 19 July 1936, and on the following day; the column of the 7th (Valladolid) Division set out for the same objective on the same day. But the 5th (Saragossa) Division had to be satisfied with the job of organising resistance in Aragon against Catalonia, which had become a centre for the organisation of enemy columns. The Aragon (Nationalist) Front split up into spontaneous defence sectors called *circunscripciones*. These were manned by local forces with the help of select troops, and supported by mobile forces of Assault Guards. This system was highly effective, particularly around Teruel, and because of it the nationalists were able to hold out against forces four times greater than themselves, right up until the sector became an important theatre of operations in spring 1937.

Navarre, where the Carlist tradition was strong, was the chief organisation and recruitment centre for nationalist columns. During the first week of fighting no less than eleven columns were organised in Pamplona, varying from 200 to 2000 men. Of these, seven went out against the Basque province of Guipúzcoa (which was loyal to the government) and the rest set out for Madrid, or to reinforce the Aragon fronts. The Galician-based columns made the relief of Oviedo their prime objective, which was surrounded for the second time in two years by the implacable Asturian miners. The numerous, and usually small, local Andalusian columns, reinforced by African units, undertook the difficult task of patching up and uniting a wavering and broken front. But the most famous and effective columns were those which soon formed the Army of Africa, which had been largely ferried over by airlift, and which already had 5000 men on the march by 10 August 1936. At the beginning of November, after its impressive advance, the Army of Africa, under Varela got ready to attack Madrid. At this time it had five columns in the vanguard, two in reserve, two stationed along the Jarama–Tagus line and powerful supporting forces: nine air squadrons, two Moroccan *tabores*, seventeen batteries, three tank companies and two sapper companies. It was a miniature army corps, of great mobility, with a total of 30,000 men and twenty-six batteries.

When General Franco took supreme command on 1 October 1936, he joined the Army of Africa to the Army of the North, so that General Mola, in charge of the latter, took over responsibility for the advance on Madrid. On 3 October Mola reorganised the Army of the North on the basis of the old 'organic' divisions – administrative and territorial demarcations rather than large mobile units. The 5th, 6th, 7th and 8th Divisions were kept more or less to their traditional limits; to them was added the Soria Division, under Moscardó, the newly liberated hero of the Alcázar of Toledo. In addition, on 10 September, the commands of Cáceres and Badajoz were set up. Badajoz, like the whole of Andalusia, came within the territory of the Army of the South, under General Queipo de Llano. A new division was also quickly created, the Avila Division.

In fact the 'divisions' kept their 'organic' character and acted as bases and link-up points for the 'columns' networks operating in the corresponding region. In December 1936 the Reinforced Madrid Division was set up as an autonomous unit, but not until April 1937 were the first tactical divisions created. At this point the territorial divisions were turned into equally territorial army corps, and the old columns gave way to the new divisions. The operational army corps which had emerged in March 1937 in the government zone did not appear in the nationalist zone until October of the same year, except for the troops of the Madrid front, which were reorganised as an army corps in the April – and the Italian C.T.V., which was in operation from the March.[11]

While in the republican zone there emerged an efficient modern organisation based on mixed mobile brigades, in the nationalist zone the basic unit continued to be the battalion. Not even the Reinforced Division of Madrid was a large military unit in the modern sense. In the battle for Madrid it was composed of a variable and often fortuitous collection of 'brigades' which were nothing more than *ad hoc* groups of battalions; that is to say, a collection of 'columns'. Organisation into divisions began at the end of March, for example in the Army of the South, but it was not till November–December 1937, with the elimination of the northern front, that a general reorganisation of the nationalist army took place. This reorganisation affected above all the Army of the North under General Dávila. The Navarre brigades were formed into divisions and the divisions became the new army groups which began to go into action in the battle of Teruel. By the beginning of March 1938, when the great offensive drive towards the Mediterranean began, these army groups were those of Navarre, Castile, Galicia, Aragon, Morocco, the Valiño group (which became the Army of the Maestrazgo), and the C.T.V. Gradually and insensibly these army groups were converted into operational units, and increasingly – though never completely – they lost their connection with the regions which were the theoretical base of their organisation. During 1938 the Army of the Centre was composed of the 1st Corps and various division groupings which did not really merit the title of army corps. The Army of the South underwent various reorganisations: the most important of these took place in August and November. It was made up of the 2nd, 3rd and 4th Corps plus a reserve manœuvres group. In November 1938 the Army of Levante was set up with the Castile and Galicia Corps; on 1 December 1938 the Urgel Army Corps appeared.

We have some quite trustworthy figures for the total number of men in the Nationalist Army during its different phases. Half-way through August 1936, according to the calculations of Mola's secretary, Iribarren, the rebels had at their disposal some 100,000 men in the north and 60,000 in the south. Regular mobilisation began on the island of Majorca, and continued in those regions covered by the Armies of the North and of the South, according to the needs at a given moment in a particular region. This continued until, in March 1937, the M.I.R. (*Jefatura de Movilización, Instrucción y Recuperación* – Centre for Mobilisation, Training and Recuperation) was created. This formed

part of Franco's G.H.Q. and came under the supervision of General
Orgaz. During 1937 various age groups were called to the colours – in
all eleven. So by the first days of January 1938 the Nationalist Army
was about 500,000 strong. A total of 14½ classes continued to be called up
throughout the whole war, three of them remaining in the rearguard.
Most of the men who had served on the enemy side and had then
stayed in nationalist territory joined the ranks of their conquerors –
once they had been politically 'purified'. Their period of service in the
enemy forces was naturally *not* counted in their favour. Under this
system more than two-thirds of the Republican Army of the North
fought in 1938 – and with similar effectiveness – under the new flag;
this is an important fact that has not received the attention it deserves.
According to central general staff data made available in 1964, the total
figures for what was called the victorious army were (as at 1 April
1969) the following:

Infantry	840,000
Cavalry	15,000
Artillery	19,000
Engineers	11,000
Services	68,000
Moroccan troops	35,000
C.T.V.	32,000
Total	1,020,500

From the same source of information[12] we learn that their equipment
at the end of the war was as follows:

Small arms	1,090,000
Automatic weapons	35,000
Mortars	7,600
Artillery	3,244
Armoured vehicles (between 33 companies)	651

(iii) *'Selective' and Popular Elements*. Those who are familiar with
the history of the Republic, and above all with the lessons of the revolution of October 1934, will not be surprised at the predilection shown by
the nationalist leadership for elite military units. If, however, the
historian listens only to republican witnesses, they will almost succeed
in convincing him that the republicans were up against just legionaries
and 'Moors'. In a sense this exaggeration is understandable, since

General Franco, once he had managed to get across to Spain a large enough number of African troops, sent them to the most dangerous areas. Even in the summer of 1936 turbans and green caps popped up in Granada and Aragon, on the Madrid fronts and on the northern fronts, although the main body of the force remained united in the African columns advancing on Madrid. The total number of Moroccan troops to appear on the Spanish battlefields is probably somewhere near 80,000,[13] although many were sent home after a long stretch of service in Spain. The 'Moorish' soldier was generally excellent, showing blind obedience towards his Spanish officers. The Legion, contrary to the claims of romanticised folk-history, was, from the beginning, more than 90 per cent Spanish; and this percentage soon increased when the original *banderas* (battalion-type units) had to be renewed – this happened more than once in the course of the war. There were also, in addition, other experienced troops, the Civil Guards and Assault Guards being particularly outstanding. It was largely due to the military effectiveness of the former that resistance took place at all in the nationalist redoubts of Toledo, Oviedo and Santa María de la Cabeza. By virtue of their spirit and the military training that was taking root in their ranks, the *Requetés*, i.e. the Carlist regiments of Navarre can be placed among the most select troops. It was upon the *Requetés* that the nationalist leadership relied to strengthen many weak points on various fronts. Their achievements were particularly brilliant in Aragon.

The Nationalist Army was, to a high degree, a popular army. This thesis should not come as a surprise to those readers who have followed our previous analysis of the will to victory that reigned in the nationalist zone from the very first days of the conflict. And these were days (as Indalecio Prieto pointed out, in a famous speech) neither victorious nor hopeful for the nationalists. To the statistics already quoted (from Mola's secretary) should be added the fact that out of the total nationalist personnel in August 1936 only 80 per cent in the south were regular soldiers, and in the north little more than 40 per cent; local enthusiasm tended to blind observers who, far from the south, greatly minimised the number of volunteers in that sector.

Up to October 1936 about fifty volunteer battalions had been formed in the nationalist zone. Navarre alone had contributed eleven *Requeté tercios* and five falangist *banderas* (the *tercio* and *bandera* were battalion-type units). By about the same date another fifty regular battalions had been formed, but it is important to note that these were largely composed of volunteers. In March 1937 there were more than a hundred volunteer battalions. The African Army offered great advantages to recruits (although never material advantages, as on the other side, where the daily wage of the militiaman was ten times greater than that of the nationalist soldier), and by the end of 1936 it had created 20 light infantry battalions, 4 legion *banderas* and 25 *tabores* or regular units of Moroccan troops (the *tabor* was slightly smaller than the battalion-type unit). The regiments, of which twenty remained initially in the nationalist zone, became centres for voluntary and compulsory recruitment, and in many cases formed as many as six battalions (thus tripling their theoretical strength). Thus between October 1936 and January 1937, by one method of recruitment or another, some 200 battalions were created. The first reliable statistics on the voluntary army in the nationalist zone have recently been published. The Carlists and similar organisations produced a total of 62,722 volunteers throughout the whole of Spain, not only in Navarre, as has been mistakenly reported. The Spanish falangists formed 116 *banderas* with 207,933 men. There were units of the youth section of Gil Robles's party of *Renovación Española* and of the *Albiñanistas* (followers of Dr Albiñana, leader of the nationalist party, d. 1936).[14] All these militias were led, partly at least, by regular officers, cavalry officers in most cases, and it was due to this fact that the Cavalry General Monasterio was appointed direct head of armed militias, immediately after the political unification of April 1937. But this appointment turned out to be only a symbolic one, since the militias were responsible both before and after the unification to the local military commander; thus the delicate political problems which bedevilled the republican militia organisation never arose in the nationalist zone. Echoes from the small disturbances in the rearguard caused by the unification of April 1937 were scarcely heard at the front.

Only on the Madrid front was there a localised movement of revolt in some small falangist units, but this was immediately crushed by their own leaders, who did not regard their membership of the Falange as separate from their military careers and vocation. The official militarisation of the militias had been achieved quite a while before, by a decree of 20 December 1936 which made them subject to the code of military justice and to the authority of the military command. This decree was the official embodiment of an attitude which with rare exceptions had been prevalent from the first.

One of the most conclusive proofs of the popular character of the Nationalist Army is the famous scheme of provisional *alféreces* (officers below rank of lieutenant). Created by a decree of the Defence Junta of 4 September 1936, the famous *estampillados* ('rubber-stamps'), about whom there were all manner of sick jokes – 'provisional *alférez*, actual corpse' – were recruited from civilians and soldiers possessing some elementary education. After the creation of the M.I.R. General Orgaz, who was as good an organiser as he was a dubious commander, managed to set up twenty-two academies. The instructors were for the most part German officers, who carried out their task with singular efficiency. Payne calculates that by the end of the war the academies had turned out 22,936 *alféreces* and 19,700 N.C.O.s.[15]

On fronts which were far from central control and relatively stable for long periods, local militias organised themselves on their own initiative. This accounts for the 'nationalist crusades' of summer 1936 in Granada, and for the groups of gunners so effectively organised by Commandant Aguado in the villages round Teruel. As the war went on these 'unofficial' militias became integrated into more orthodox units, but not always. The most interesting exception to this rule are the guerrilla bands. No study of these has yet been undertaken, but a good starting point would be the documents on the 14th Republican Corps, which was set up expressly to check the activities of the nationalist guerrillas in the Sierra Morena region and the Montes de Toledo. Another mysterious and crucial guerrilla focus was in Catalonia, where the guerrillas were mainly the heirs of the ever-belligerent Carlists of Catalonia, who wanted to help 50,000 or so Catalans who were fighting determinedly in the Nationalist Army.

Things military were very much in fashion in the zone governed and controlled by the army. Many civilians who, for reasons of age or circumstances, were unable to sign up for the provisional officers' academies managed, by many and devious means, to gain the rank of honorary officers, by being appointed to auxiliary posts with the press and propaganda, or as legal assessors. One of the best known of these was Captain Luis Bolín, for a time chief of the nationalist press department. He had made the arrangements for sending a plane to Franco in the Canaries before 18 July. It was he who conducted his own private war with one of the most famous communist agents of the Spanish Civil War, Mr Arthur Koestler, whose cover, following a suggestion made by Willi Münzenberg – leading propaganda agent of the Comintern – was that of correspondent for the *News Chronicle*.

It is to Koestler, in fact, that we owe one of the first and most widely published accounts of a subject that has been difficult to treat because

of the frightened silence that has surrounded it in post-victory nationalist Spain, and because of adverse propaganda: namely, the subject of
repression in the nationalist zone. The present author is attempting to
explore this subject in monograph form and is as yet far from coming to
any real conclusions. So he will simply give an account of the lines of
investigation followed.

As in the republican zone, although with its own peculiar characteristics, repression in the nationalist zone went through various phases
which were not clearly limited to any particular place or period. A
terrible legacy of cruelty had been inherited from the nineteenth century, a cruelty that had never been exclusive to any particular side and
that (as history shows and as the course of the Second World War was to
confirm) was not really an exclusive characteristic of Spanish civil
wars. The first phase, already predetermined by Mola's crisp instructions before the rising, was to a certain extent a phase of uncontrolled
repression dependent upon the whim of the local militia chief or even
of the local political leader in sympathy with the rebels. This phase
continued, getting gradually less fierce, until General Franco took
over sole command and decisions on death sentences for suspected
enemies had to be submitted to G.H.Q. Here was established the war
tribunal of the Army of Occupation, whose members went with the
troops as they advanced and administered the most summary military
justice in the conquered territories. Alongside this system the old
system of spontaneous repression organised by local armed bodies or
political groups still functioned intermittently.[16]

One must take great care in evaluating eye-witness accounts published
during or immediately after the conflict; without a single exception on
either side, these accounts are vitiated by propaganda. From the first
reliable data we possess it seems to emerge that in the conquered
territories it was the harsh law of retaliation that decided whether the
death penalty should be meted out or not. The number of victims on the
nationalist side was equivalent to that caused by repression – both
spontaneous and controlled – on the part of the republicans. We have
begun a statistical analysis which, although incomplete, will certainly
enable us to come up with some revealing results. The total number of
victims of the repression, both in the nationalist and in the republican
zone, is much less than the exaggerations that have been so widespread.
The number of victims, which we cannot even begin to guess, is similar
for each zone. Injustice, over-hastiness and personal vengeance were
not lacking, unfortunately, in a cause which boasted of more elevated

spiritual ideals than its enemy, and which publicly based these ideals on the Christian faith, and did so, moreover, with complete sincerity. In some ways the history of the bloody Carlist Wars was being repeated. In the nationalist zone men were condemned to death for their ideas alone, or in reprisal for atrocities committed by the enemy side. This does not mean to say that repression in each zone was exactly equal; we repeat that we lack information, and that when we have it we will make it known with the same sincere intentions as we now reveal our uncertainty.

2. External and Political Implications of Nationalist Strategy and Tactics

(i) *The Effect of Foreign Military Aid.* The subject of foreign intervention in the Spanish Civil War is an inexhaustible mine of propaganda, whose output is given fresh stimulus year after year by the publication of memoirs and first-hand accounts by innumerable foreign observers and combatants who were in Spain between 1936 and 1939. Foreigners tend to see the Spanish Civil War through the intervention of their compatriots or of their country; it is for this reason that so many conflicting points of view still prevail. The day that both those who took part in, and those who comment on the Spanish Civil War decide to consider it as a primarily Spanish affair (this is the theme of Professor Gabriel Jackson's book), we shall have reached a proper basis for mutual understanding.[17]

A principle that seems to influence most historians is the principle of balance. Foreign intervention on both sides maintained a balance throughout the Civil War, as if there were a tacit agreement – there probably was – not to exert too overwhelming an influence on the final outcome. Both sides rushed to ask for military and economic aid from abroad. The newly opened archives of the Axis have shown that economic and military aid to the rebels was not forthcoming before the outbreak of war.[18] Today we know the exact dates of the arrival of equipment and the exact figures for aid to the nationalist zone throughout the whole war. Immediately after war was declared, emissaries of Franco and Mola went out in search of all kinds of armaments, above all aircraft more modern than they already possessed. But these aircraft did not come straightaway, and besides, the first ones did not come from fascist countries but from Great Britain. The famous airlift over the Straits of Gibraltar, vital for the implementation of the nationalist plan of campaign, went on for nine days (the crucial nine days during which the nationalists made sure of their hold on Seville, Cadiz and Huelva) with Spanish planes and crews. On 30 July the first armed Savoias arrived in Morocco, but for various reasons they were unable to fly until 4 August. During the first ten days of August there arrived eight Savoias-81s and nine Junkers-52s out of the twenty that the German government promised after considerable hesitation. The airlift became a joint Spanish–German operation, and from then onwards it was exclusively German. An average number of 500 men were transported daily, and by October (when the Nationalist Fleet gained clear supremacy at sea) 23,393 men had been brought across by the airlift, considerably more than were conveyed by sea in the famous 'victory convoy' of 5 August, which transported less than 2000. All the German and Italian aircraft of 1936 were inferior to their French equivalents, let alone the Russian models. Even so, with the arrival of the first squadrons of Fiats, and given the superiority of the nationalist, German and Italian pilots, the rebels seemed supreme in the air throughout September and October, only to lose their supremacy completely when Russian planes entered the fray at the end of October and beginning of November. With some local variations, the nationalists regained air supremacy at Brunete, thanks to the advent of the new German ME-109, HE-111 and DO-17 planes, and also the Italian S-79. From this moment until the end of the war, the nationalists enjoyed increasing superiority in the air.[19]

While the Italian contribution, in terms of air support, was thus very important, the same could not be said of their tanks. The Ansaldo 3·3-ton tanks with two machine-guns fore and no defence aft were fast and impressive to look at, but they were powerless against the heavy Russian models. Obviously the greatest contribution of fascist Italy to the nationalist side was in terms of manpower. It was a much-proclaimed contribution, swathed in the myths and propaganda of the time; but it was cordially and generously given and much appreciated by the Spaniards, despite the many stories in circulation about the Italians.

The first contingent of Italian infantry reached Spain at the end of September 1936: 16 officers and 160 men, who acted as instructors for the special equipment and took part in operations between 21 October and 26 November, when they were relieved. The really large-scale Italian intervention did not begin until 22 December, when 3000 Black Shirts landed at Cadiz, soon to be joined by 3000 more. In January 1937 the first volunteer brigade was formed, together with two mixed Italian and Spanish brigades – the 'Blue Arrows' and the 'Black Arrows'. The Volunteer Brigade performed brilliantly in the operation to destroy the republican salient at Malaga. After Malaga the erstwhile 'Italian Military Mission' became the official *Corpo Truppe Voluntarie* (C.T.V.), which provided four divisions for the battle of Guadalajara. Everyone knows the story of the defeat of the C.T.V. on the battle-fields of La Alcarría; the defeat has received definitive treatment at the hands of Colonel Martínez Bande in his recent book, the whole of which constitutes an important source.[20] The defeat was unequivocal, and in a sense beneficial: it convinced the somewhat conceited Italians that 'Guadalajara is not Abyssinia', as the song went at the time, and after the repatriation of a good number of its men the C.T.V. became more and more assimilated into the Nationalist Combat Army. From then on the Italians, ever more closely integrated with Spanish officers and men, fought calmly, effectively and courageously. In the battle of the north, three divisions totalling 27,000 men took part (at Guadalajara the number had been 31,200). In December 1937 the C.T.V. had two wholly Italian divisions and another two mixed ones. On 1 October 1938 the repatriation of Italian volunteers began, after more than eighteen months' service in Spain to their credit; the C.T.V. was thus left with one Italian and three mixed divisions, and in this form took part in the Catalonia campaign.

The main German contribution was undoubtedly the Condor Legion, which consisted of 100 aircraft with their respective aircrew and auxiliary personnel. These figures stayed almost constant for the duration of the war. More or less affiliated to the Condor Legion were the instructors and the experts on new weapons – of which the most effective in Spain was without doubt the 8·8-centimetre gun, also famous in the Second World War. Initially the 100 planes of the Condor Legion consisted of heavy JU-52 bombers, old HE-51 fighters and HE-45 reconnaissance planes. When the German factories sent to Spain the first models that had emerged from the 1936 aeronautical revolution, the old models were passed on to Spanish crews, and the total quota for the Condor Legion stayed invariably at 100 planes – or slightly less when the German government wanted to exert political or economic pressure on General Franco. The Condor Legion first entered the fray on 16 November 1936 over the Madrid front. Its leaders were Generals Sperrle, Volkman and Richthofen, and its crews and other personnel, working a much faster-changing rota than the Italians, never numbered more than 5000 men. The first Germans who eventually formed the Condor Legion arrived at the beginning of November. At the end of October two Panzer companies and one transport company arrived, together with a group of tank instructors. This particular Panzer was a modest 6-ton vehicle with two machine-guns, easy prey for the Russian T-26 and TB-5.

On 22 July 1936 General Mola requested the aid of the Portuguese government, via General Ponte. Their favourable reply came four days later. The government of Dr Salazar identified itself with the rising and gave it a great deal of moral support. Franco and Mola were making contact via Portuguese territory before the two sectors were joined. The Portuguese contribution to the ranks of the Nationalist Army has invariably been exaggerated by a great number of historians, who have found in a source as unknown as it is apparently convincing the fantastic figure of 20,000 men. Using all the Portuguese volunteers scattered throughout the whole Nationalist Army it was impossible to form even a brigade of 3000 men, even though there was a plan to do so.

From other more or less democratic countries came important aid for the nationalist cause, and these are worth a brief mention. The unlimited supply of fuel oil and lubricants on credit from oil companies in the southern United States, and the pressure of Catholic opinion there which kept the embargo on arms for the Republic had perhaps as important an effect on the course of the Civil War as other more highly publicised contributions. An enthusiastic group of French volunteers tried to form a 'Joan of Arc' company, and probably did so in 1937, but at present only a few fragmentary references to this are available. More familiar is the role of the Irish *banderas* formed by General O'Duffy; the nationalist commanders kept them occupied in dreary trench warfare that totally unnerved them. Other foreign contributions to the nationalist military effort seem to us to be pure fabrication.

(ii) *Political Strategy and Military Tactics.* This is not the moment to appreciate in military terms the development of the Spanish Civil War as seen from the nationalist side; studies published on this subject appear fragmentary when not applied to the exposition of some preconceived theory. As in the rest of this work, we shall indicate here the main lines on which a profitable investigation might be pursued.

The unity of the military command, and the spiritual unity of the nationalist zone were decisive factors in maintaining a tough, effective military discipline, which was perhaps the principal advantage of Franco's troops over their opponents, with their variegated political and personal leanings. 'Throughout the whole civil war,' as Payne writes with some conviction, 'the great advantage of the Nationalist command lay in the military discipline observed by their forces.'

When Vicente Rojo took over the main responsibility for military decisions on the republican side, Franco faced a leader of comparable intelligence and military background; but Rojo's function was solely an advisory one, and he had to submit to double military-executive and political control. This did not happen to Franco, who held all the reins of power in his own hands. The most important strategic decision taken by the nationalists throughout the whole war was, undoubtedly, when they gave up – temporarily – their obsession with Madrid, after bloody and repeated failures during the hard winter of 1936–7, and unleashed their campaign in the north, which altered the balance of human and economic resources to the advantage of the victors. The main credit for convincing the generalissimo's G.H.Q. of the appropriateness of this decision must go to General Juan Vigón.

General Franco had proved his tactical capacities in Africa and his logistic and strategic ability in crushing the 1934 revolution – something which has received little attention. It was primarily in the field of logistics that he consistently had the edge over his adversaries in the Civil War. A delicate communications network functioned with amazing efficiency, making possible the execution of plans for massive transportations of men and equipment, plans which were carefully prepared, tested and carried out. The Navarre Brigades appeared in the area of Brunete, in July 1937, forty-eight hours earlier than Rojo had expected, and there are many other such examples. While in the government zone many leaders fiercely resisted any suggestion that they should put their inactive reserves of men and equipment at the disposal of other fronts – a typical case was Miaja – Franco left garrisons in quiet sectors with the minimum quota of men, in order to deal his main blows with all the forces available. Trusting more and more in his logistical superiority, he sometimes left whole sectors thinly manned while he concentrated the last tank and the last plane on the point chosen for action. This logistical superiority was a much more decisive factor in the final victory than any superiority due to foreign arms and aid.

The advance on Madrid, the movement towards Santander, the battle of the Alfambra in the second phase of the second battle for Teruel and the exploitation of the break in the Aragon front during the first week – these, together with the clinching final offensive in Catalonia, were Franco's greatest and most brilliant tactical successes. At other times his strategic decisions and their tactical implementations were less easy to explain in purely military terms. One can detect in the decisions of the generalissimo's G.H.Q. a marked tendency to respond, blow for blow, to the enemy's actions, and in areas chosen by the enemy. It was the fact that weak garrisons were able to hold out in areas suddenly under surprise attack – in the last analysis human courage was at the root of Franco's logistical potential – that meant that reserves nearly always arrived in time to restore the situation. They arrived usually about three or four days after the attack: Brunete and the Ebro being classical examples. Even so, Franco was never satisfied with *restoring* the balance but always insisted on a massive counter-attack, and on the reconquest of the particular town or area – the symbol of the whole operation – even if this lacked, as at Brunete, the slightest military importance.

Without wanting to say that such decisions were completely justified, it must be pointed out that Franco ran his war – which after all he won, and for a general what matters is winning wars – with political and moral criteria as firmly held as purely military ones. The slight delay during the advance on Madrid caused by the successful relief of the Alcázar at Toledo was made imperative by the unanimous outcry in the nationalist zone: with the liberation of its heroes came a new and decisive dose of confidence in victory. Franco did not want to leave to the enemy a single square mile of the land he considered sacred and inviolable: God was on his soldiers' side and would never permit the final surrender of that square mile to the forces of Evil, as the enemy were officially termed. On other occasions, like the barely explicable decision to halt Yagüe's advance on Catalonia, the fear of international complications was what counted. The fall of Valencia, contrary to what has been said, was to turn out to be as important a factor in ending the war as the fall of Barcelona.

Franco never lost sight of the fact that he was fighting against Spaniards, and that these Spaniards would in the end have to live together in one Spain. For this reason some of his military decisions seem inexplicable to those who forget the domestic nature of the Spanish Civil War. For example, Franco was at one point seven kilometres away from the reservoirs on which Madrid depended for its water supply, yet he never attempted to destroy them, though it would have been child's play to do so.[21] The persistent desire to capture Madrid – which prevailed until the end of 1937 – is also proof of the symbolic and political preoccupations that always affected strategical and tactical decisions at G.H.Q. But the nationalists did not always give in to political temptations: Belchite, for example, was sacrificed to facilitate the much more important Santander victory.

The Nationalist Army was successful in manœuvre. Exactly the opposite was true of the enemy, and here is the root of the tactical superiority of the one over the other. On the defensive both armies gave proof of similar courage and skill.

The Spanish Civil War took place during the period 1918–39, and for this reason some of its aspects are particularly characteristic of the transition from one World War to another, though always on the small scale of a local civil conflict directed by the Spaniards themselves. In neither of the two zones, except on rare occasions, did foreign advisers supplant the Spaniards who were in charge of operations, or those responsible for the main strategic and tactical decisions. The main novelty was undoubtedly the use of the new weapons. The transition from the aircraft developed in 1914–18 to the 1939–45 models took place, effectively, in the sky over Spain. The Russians, at first so much better off in terms of equipment, clung stubbornly to old group-combat tactics, and entered the Second World War without learning the lessons of aerial combat furnished by the Spanish Civil War. The Germans tried out many prototypes in Spain, and a variety of aerial tactics, from dive-bombing (in restricted and near-secret experiments) to large-scale bombing of civilian populations, like the highly publicised case of Guernica.[22] As for artillery, apart from trying out rapid-firing guns, the Spanish war had few lessons to add to those of the First World War. The breaching of the famous 'Iron Ring' round Bilbao was an artillery rather than an air force operation.[23] On the other hand the 1936 airlift was a typical application of modern methods, here tried for the first time on a large scale.

During the conflict the fleets of both sides concentrated on the maritime supply lines to the republican zone, which led primarily through the Mediterranean: the one side concentrating above all on keeping them open, the other on blocking them. The Nationalist Fleet, though much weaker, turned out to be infinitely more effective than the Republican Fleet, which was hidden away in its naval bases, rotten with anarchy and dissension and commanded by officers who were highly capable but few in number, and who suffered from the general lack of confidence. The German and Italian fleets supported the action of the Nationalist Fleet, sometimes quite barefacedly, and made up for some of its material inferiority. But the action of the nationalist ships themselves was highly effective and resolute, and much more decisive than people have thought.

The effect of the air force on morale, especially during the first conflicts, was much more important than might be thought, given the small number of men and machines that nationalists had at their disposal. Their pilots turned out to be considerably more effective than those of the enemy, and learnt to their own advantage what their allies taught them. On 20 October 1936 20 out of 30 large aircraft were being flown by Spanish crews; also 10 out of 20 fighters, 50 out of 60 supply planes and all the 10 seaplanes. The arrival of the Condor Legion tipped the balance in favour of the foreigners, and the same thing happened when the new Italian aircraft came. But throughout the whole war Spanish crews increased in number and effectiveness.

Neither of the protagonists of the Spanish Civil War managed throughout its course to overcome the old ideas about tank warfare. The republicans took no advantage of the overwhelming superiority of their Russian tanks against the weak Panzer 1936 models and the small Ansaldos. Von Thoma's claim that his intervention via a tank attack at Brunete was decisive is pure fiction. During the whole of the Civil War tanks were used more as secondary tactical support, for undermining enemy morale, rather than in the independent action that was to become the norm in the Second World War. Anti-tank weapons – which on both sides ran the whole gamut from artillery to Molotov cocktails – were used with an unexpected effect which was quite in keeping with the character of the Spanish fighter.

These reflections should encourage those engaged in research to undertake or revise their studies of the Spanish Civil War, relying less on *a priori* deductive methods. No other modern war has proved so hard to classify, to synthesise or to make generalisations about than this difficult and still mysterious Civil War; and the Spanish themselves, succumbing to the many myths and legends that surround it, still disagree about its genesis and progress. Foreign hispanists are usually, at least at first, the victims of attitudes and folkloric prejudices that are amusing when the subject is the bull-fight, but sometimes tragic when applied to the study of this incredible internal explosion of 1936.

SUGGESTIONS FOR FURTHER READING

The only introductory study in existence on the subject of this article is by Stanley G. Payne, *Politics and the Military in Modern Spain* (Stanford and Oxford, 1967), in the chapter entitled 'The Nationalist Army in the Civil War'. The present author is intending to devote an extensive chapter to the subject in the second volume of his *Historia de la guerra civil española* (the first volume appeared in 1969). In his *Bibliografía general sobre la guerra de España y sus antecedentes* the author has devoted a large section of the index to military assessments of both sides in the war. Highly recommended are the monograph studies by Colonel Martínez Bande whose publication began in 1968 and of which three have already been published: *La marcha sobre Madrid, La lucha en torno a Madrid* and *La campaña de Andalucía*. More of these are in preparation, and all are of great interest for the volume of as yet unpublished documentary information that has been gathered together. For the republican point of view, General Vicente Rojo's books are full of interest, and for the topics covered in this article his *Alerta los pueblos*, written in 1939, is particularly useful. The *Revista de Historia Militar*, xvii (1964) has various basic studies on the subject. The archives of the Military History Department (S.H.M.) preserve all the key documents.

The best monographs are *Brunete*, by Commandant Casas de la Vega (Madrid, 1969), and the two volumes on *La Batalla del Ebro* written with great attention to detail by J. M. Mezquida (1963, 1967). The work of the brothers Jesús and Ramón Salas Larrazábal, now nearly completed, will shed new light on many points touched on in this study. A highly informative study on the Nationalist Fleet is *Memorias de Guerra*, by Admiral Cervera (Madrid, 1968).

NOTES

1. This statistical survey has been prepared by a group from the Military History Department (S.H.M.) in Madrid and appears with more detailed commentary in the present author's *Historia de la guerra civil española*, i (Madrid, 1969), 756 ff.

2. There is no complete and trustworthy account of the action of the two fleets during the Civil War. At present, apart from Admiral Cervera's book (see Suggestions for Further Reading), there is the biased but interesting *La escuadra la mandan los cabos* by Manuel D. Benavides (Mexico, 1944), which gives the republican version of the Civil War at sea.

3. *Historia de la guerra civil española*, p. 787.

4. See above, and also *Los documentos de la primavera tragica* (Madrid, 1967).

5. In his order of 5 June 1936, quoted in *Historia de la guerra civil española*, p. 780 (see n. 1).

6. J. M. Gil Robles, *No fué posible la paz* (1968), p. 235 n.

7. This was the first sociological evaluation of the Spanish Civil War to be received by the present author. It was made by an old woman from Roa de Duero.

8. The present author knows of at least ten cases preserved in the archives of the Banco Hispano Americano in San Sebastian.

9. There has been much imaginative speculation about the friction between Franco and Mola. There was between the two of them, and always had been, an absolute understanding and co-operation. It was Franco, as chief of staff in the centre in 1935, who appointed Mola commandant-general and head of the military forces in Morocco, a post he was relieved of by the Popular Front.

10. For proof of this thesis, see the masterly account by Martínez Bande in *La campaña de Andalucia* (Madrid, 1968).

11. Cf. R. Salas Larrazábal, *El ejército popular de la Republica* (now in preparation).

12. See *Revista de Historia Militar*, xvii (1964), 116 ff.

13. First-hand account of Don Francisco de Caveda, superintendent of native affairs in Morocco, which agrees with the details supplied by Payne, and with those given in *Revista de Historia Militar*, xvii.

14. These impressive figures, based on data and documents preserved in the Secretaría General del Movimiento – and relatively trustworthy as we have been able to prove – have been published in the over-modest book by J. M. Rosa, *Memorias de un requeté* (Madrid, 1968).

15. S. G. Payne, *Politics and the Military in Modern Spain* (Stanford and Oxford, 1967), pp. 388 ff.

16. Many eye-witness accounts – like that of Ambassador Cantalupo – confirm a number of unpublished documents (see Alfaro file in the S.H.M.) which record great efforts made by General Franco, from the July days, to control and suppress spontaneous repression. His comments on the events in Granada were not only harsh but effective. One officer, who was an honorary member of the war tribunal of the Army of Occupation from 1936 to 1939 is preparing a well-documented report which will be invaluable for the present author's monograph.

17. See G. Jackson, *The Spanish Republic and the Civil War* (Princeton, 1965).

18. See the latest contribution on this subject in David Kahn's interesting article 'Secrets of the Nazi Archives', in *Atlantic Monthly* (May, 1969), 50 ff.

19. Apart from works by the above, see the recent fundamental study by S. Rello, *La aviación en la guerra de España* (vol. 1 in a long series).

20. *La lucha en torno a Madrid* (March 1968).

21. See the revealing republican pamphlet *Canales de Lozoya, Aportación a la guerra* (1937), which proves exactly the opposite of what it sets out to prove.

22. Vicente Talón is in process of preparing an exhaustive account, both from documents and from first-hand accounts, of Guernica, the reality and the myth.

23. See Carlos Martínez de Campos, *Apuntes sobre empleo de la artilleria* (Madrid, 1942).

11. Foreign Intervention in the Spanish Civil War

ROBERT H. WHEALEY

THE outbreak of the Civil War in July 1936 revealed that Spain was threatened with anarchy; at the same time the international system could also be described as one of anarchy. The five Great Powers with the greatest interest in Spain – Great Britain, France, Germany, Italy and the Soviet Union – all pursued different and mutually conflicting policies.

In Britain the conservative government wanted to avoid another Great War at almost any cost. In July 1936 Foreign Secretary Anthony Eden thought he could best maintain peace by avoiding involvement on the Continent. For the British government, therefore, the Civil War in Spain was most unwelcome, and its immediate reaction was to impose unilaterally an arms embargo against both sides (31 July). France, Germany, Italy and the Soviet Union were all more likely than Britain to get involved in war with each other over the question of Spain's future. This tendency of Europe to divide itself into diplomatic and ideological blocs was something Britain wished to avoid.

However, the security of the £40,000,000 ($194,000,000) which British private citizens had invested in Spain was at stake.[1] Even more important for Britain's far-flung imperial interests was preservation of its sea base at Gibraltar. Therefore, the government remained officially silent as to whether it preferred the victory of the Popular Front government at Madrid, or the victory of General Francisco Franco. Many conservatives, in part because of their fear of Bolshevism, privately hoped Franco would win. The labour opposition, on the other hand, publicly denounced the revolt of the Spanish army officers: it was clear to them that the insurgents were anti-democratic.

The key to French foreign policy was the historic suspicion that Germany was the major threat to her security. By 1936, French diplomats were prepared to sacrifice almost anything for the sake of a com-

mon diplomatic stance against Germany with their British counterparts in Whitehall. Foreign Minister Yvon Delbos had inherited a
treaty system in eastern Europe: mutual assistance pacts with Poland
(1921), Czechoslovakia (1925), Romania (1926), Yugoslavia (1927) and
the Soviet Union (May 1935). In 1936 these five treaties were weak;
much of the living faith between allies that makes an alliance a reality
had disappeared. But on paper at least a formidable alliance system was
still directed against Germany. France's main problem was that Britain
was in no way committed to these five eastern allies of France, and was
not committed against Germany unless an attack moved directly across
the Rhine.

France's diplomatic problems were complicated by the Spanish
Civil War. Because of geography and economics, Spain was more
important to France than she was to any other Great Power, but
France's five eastern allies had no strategic interest in Spain. A victory
for a Spanish Republic dominated by the left might endanger France's
$135,000,000[2] investment in Spain and her imperial interests in Morocco
and Algeria as well. On the other hand, a Franco victory could mean a
falangist Spain allied to Nazi Germany and fascist Italy, aggravating
the threat to French frontiers in the case of war. In addition, a hostile
Spain would make it harder for colonial African troops to reach France,
while Spanish strategic materials like pyrite ore would be redirected
from France to the Reich.

In June 1936, a month before the outbreak of the Civil War in
Spain, France had elected a Popular Front government which was a
coalition of the socialist and radical socialist parties. The communist
party lent its electoral support in the chamber and in the press. Thus
the government in Paris was similar in ideological outlook to the
Madrid Popular Front government elected in February. French
Premier Léon Blum, a socialist, personally desired a Spanish Popular
Front victory over the insurgent generals. But conservative interests in
the French parliament, the army, the diplomatic corps, private business
and the Roman Catholic church, as well as elements within the radical
socialist party, which held the balance in the cabinet, and even pacifists
among the socialists, deterred Blum from any outright support of the
Madrid government. The July crisis in Spain showed the world that
major elements in the Spanish Popular Front were revolutionary; in
Paris the Popular Front was reformist. Open support for Madrid by
Blum might provoke the fall of his cabinet or even civil conflict in France,
as well as alienating Britain. Therefore, the French government, for

entirely different reasons from the British, regarded the outbreak of civil war in Spain with great alarm.

Unlike Blum or Eden, Hitler did not shrink from the dangerous threat to peace created by the Spanish crisis. He nursed grievances against the Versailles system and dreamed of an expanding Pan-German empire in eastern Europe, and he saw the Spanish issue in the light of these preoccupations. Thus, the French–Soviet alliance 'encircling' Germany could be weakened by labelling the Popular Front 'communist'. The prestige of the 'Jewish' anti-fascist Popular Front in France could also be weakened if Hitler and Mussolini succeeded in helping to destroy the Spanish Popular Front. Moreover, an ideological and political struggle enlisting the energies of both Italian fascism and French anti-fascism in Spain could only facilitate Hitler's own eastern ambitions by dividing any would-be anti-German coalition. Once involved in Spain, France would take her eyes off Czechoslovakia and take some of her men from the Rhine, while Italy would forget the German threat to Austria. Frightened over the 'Bolshevik menace' in Spain, Italy and perhaps even Britain might be won as allies of Germany on the basis of an anti-communist crusade. Although the British and French governments declared their hopes that foreign powers would not intervene in Spain, Hitler secretly dispatched twenty-six aeroplanes and eighty-six men, which arrived at General Franco's headquarters on 29 July.[3]

Like Hitler, Mussolini resented the French and Spanish Popular Fronts; both of the democratic coalitions stressed an anti-fascist 'crusade'. In July 1936 Mussolini was even more anti-British and anti-French than Hitler, because through the League of Nations those two countries had actively hindered his campaign against Ethiopia.[4] Since 1926 the Duce had toyed with the idea of competing with French naval interests in the Balearic Islands, for Mussolini had grandiose ambitions about reviving the Mediterranean Roman Empire; hence his interest in a 'friendly' Spain. Nine Italian Savoias reached Spanish Morocco to aid General Franco on 29 July, the same day that Hitler's planes arrived.[5]

Stalin's interest in Spain was ideological and political rather than economic or strategic. By 1936 he was devoting himself to building 'socialism in one country'. The U.S.S.R. was threatened by the imperial and racist dreams of both Hitler and Japan, so in the mid-thirties Stalin called for a world-wide anti-fascist front. This strategy required party alliances of liberals, socialists and communists; these were built in 1934 and 1935 in France and Spain by labelling the enemy 'fascist' instead of 'capitalist' or 'feudal'. To attract non-communist parties to

H

these alliances, the U.S.S.R. had to seek to destroy its image as a revolutionary power. The German communist Willi Münzenberg, an exile in Paris, built a world-wide structure of anti-fascist front groups. Münzenberg had great indirect influence among non-party journalists, writers and teachers in England and the United States as well as France. The communist front propaganda and espionage network was Stalin's one asset abroad.[6] The front groups would help protect the 'Soviet fatherland' diplomatically by bringing pressure on their governments to join the U.S.S.R. in opposing the fascist countries. In 1936 the Soviet Union was calling for an Anglo-French–Soviet coalition against Hitler; but the conservative diplomats of London and Paris still suspected communism's revolutionary aims.

After the Spanish generals' revolt, the basically liberal Popular Front government on 19–20 July armed the anarchist, socialist, Trotskyite and communist party militias. Confronted with a popular revolution, the Spanish communist party became the most cautious of the radical leftist parties, because Stalin hoped to build up an anti-fascist alliance in the liberal West.

In accordance with Stalin's programme, Etorre Togliatti, Italian representative of the Third International advising the Spanish communist party, and Willi Münzenberg from Paris, put out the line that the Spanish Republic was fighting for democracy not socialism. Stalin was thus applying the Menshevik line of 1917 to the Spanish revolution of 1936. Foreign Minister Litvinov advised the French and British to mind their imperial interests in Spanish waters and take a strong stand against Italy and Germany; France, not the Soviet Union, would suffer if the Spanish generals won the Civil War. It would be better for Stalin if Germany went to war in the West rather than the East. The conservative diplomats of France and Britain, however, countered by rejecting Litvinov's advice in the hope that Germany would move East rather than West.

While the Russian communists did nothing to aid Spain directly, the Western European communists, together with the liberals and socialists, set to work as early as 21 July quietly collecting money, men and second-hand arms for the Spanish Republic.[7] One of the first to volunteer was the pro-communist novelist André Malraux, who hired twenty pilots for Spain. Throughout Europe and America, Münzenberg created national Committees to Aid Spanish Democracy, and these propaganda committees drew together democrats of all varieties with communists to support the Spanish Republic. For Western leftists, the Spanish Civil

War became 'the last cause' for which intellectuals volunteered to man the barricades.

We have looked briefly at the varying national interests of the five Great Powers and their attitudes towards the Spanish crisis in July 1936. It remains to explore two themes: How much did foreign intervention prolong and affect the Civil War which began in Spain? And how did the Spanish crisis mould the relations among the five Great Powers and shift the European balance of power?

When Hitler received Franco's request for planes to fly Moroccan troops across the Straits of Gibraltar, he delegated the Spanish operation to his military and economic experts, headed by General Hermann Göring, air minister and Reich commissioner for raw materials. Hitler said nothing to Göring or Franco about fighting communism in Spain, and limited the mission to providing aviation services on credit, to be repaid with Spanish ores. Operation *Feuerzauber*, which provided six fighters to protect twenty Junker transports, was expected to last only a few weeks; it was considered that General Franco would capture Madrid within this time. This service would enable Germany to obtain valuable Spanish raw materials.

A second objective of this operation was for Hitler to consolidate his already good relations with Mussolini. Joint German–Italian military talks about Europe in general had been initiated in June and, after the outbreak of the Spanish Civil War, Hitler sent the German chief of military intelligence, Admiral Wilhelm Canaris, to talk with his Italian counterpart, General Mario Roatta. On 4 August they discussed coordinating German–Italian aid to the insurgents.[8] Italy and Germany were drawing together to attack the Popular Front and to pull the imaginary teeth of 'Jewish' France. A joint Italo-German mission conferred and observed battle conditions in Spain during September; as a result General Walter Warlimont, economic expert on the German general staff, and General Roatta recommended that Berlin and Rome expand their military and economic aid. Hitler's second step was the dispatch of arms on 29 September known as Operation *Otto*.[9]

Under Operation *Feuerzauber* German military efficiency had provided a more effective transport service for Franco than had Italy; three of the twelve Savoias dispatched by the Duce had crashed *en route* and never arrived in Spain.[10] The greatest significance of the German operation was its timing. From 29 July to 11 October the Germans transported 13,523 Moroccan troops and 270,100 kilograms of war material from Morocco to Andalusia;[11] and it was Franco's African forces, thus transported and supplied, which were a decisive factor in the war. Without the African Army it can be argued that the military rebellion might have been overcome in a few weeks.

During July and August German military aid to the insurgents continued to be more significant than Italian. As early as 2 August, Admiral Rolf Carls met Franco aboard the battleship *Deutschland* in Ceuta, Spanish Morocco. In September the Germans had 553 troops in Spain, compared to 413 Italians.[12] If Mussolini was going to assert his sphere of influence in the Mediterranean, he was going to have to move faster and farther. On 27 August Mussolini accordingly took a second step expanding the war. Two hundred Italians disguised as Spaniards landed on Majorca, largest of the Balearic Islands. From then on, Italians dominated the base at Palma de Mallorca, which became the major blockade headquarters for Franco's navy.

During September the Duce began taking the lead from the Führer as the major source of military aid to the nationalists. On 23 September Hitler sent Minister without Portfolio Hans Frank to Rome to confer with Mussolini and other fascist officials. Frank and Mussolini vaguely discussed the allocation of spheres of influence, agreeing that Mussolini would have a free hand in the western Mediterranean in exchange for a German free hand in the 'Baltic region'. Italian Foreign Minister Ciano visited Berlin on 23–25 October and signed a nine-point protocol, christened 'the Axis' by Mussolini. Italy and Germany agreed to joint recognition of nationalist Spain, which was carried out, at Hitler's suggestion, on 18 November 1936.

While the Duce proclaimed the newly formed Axis in a Milan speech, Hitler made his third basic move in Spain: *Winterübung Hansa*. On 31 October 1936 the Nazis began dispatching the *Legion Condor*, which comprised 3829 men and 92 aeroplanes, along with tanks, anti-aircraft guns and signal equipment.[13] Thus Hitler provided Franco with additional first-class technical service, bringing the grand total of Germans in Spain to 4523 men by the end of November. In view of the fact that Franco had begun his revolt with only five signal officers,[14] a handful of planes and no tanks, this aspect of German aid may have been decisive.

Mussolini answered Operation *Winterübung Hansa* by taking a third step of his own. Italian Chief of Cabinet Filippo Anfuso negotiated a treaty with the nationalists, which was signed on 28 November 1936. In it Mussolini was promised that Franco would work with Italy to modify Article 16 of the League Covenant – that hated article used against Italy during the Ethiopian campaign – and that Spain would be benevolently neutral in any future war involving Italy. Franco also specifically promised that no transhipment of troops of a third party would be allowed in Spain or the Balearic Islands, a move clearly directed at France. The Duce, with his eyes focused on France, thought he had won a diplomatic victory from Franco.

Actually, however, Hitler now had Mussolini on a string. The Germans pointed out to the Italians that, since Italian political gains in Spain were substantially greater than those of Germany, it was Mussolini's duty, not Hitler's, to furnish Franco any substantial increases in military aid. In December Hitler resolutely refused a large-scale expansion of the *Legion Condor*. He pointed out to his fanatical anti-communist ambassador in Spain, Wilhelm von Faupel, who seriously wanted to carry out a military crusade against Bolshevism, that Spain was a convenient sideshow which absorbed the energies of the other Great Powers,[15] thus leaving Germany a freer hand to pursue its ambitions in the East.

One additional German training unit sent on 10 December eventually trained 56,000 officers and non-commissioned officers for Franco. This German aid had no significance *vis-à-vis* Italy, but proved to be one of the most valuable of the specialised services the Germans provided for Franco. It was in December 1936 that the *Legion Condor* reached its maximum strength of 5000 men with over a hundred planes, a force maintained throughout the Civil War by periodic replacements. Hitler escalated the German operations in Spain no further, though arms for Franco's forces were sent from time to time. In all, 118,882 tons of weapons costing RM 510,000,000 ($250,000,000) were sent between July 1936 and March 1939.[16] Yet during the war Hitler never publicly acknowledged his aid to Franco.

The relations between Hitler and Mussolini drew ever closer during the Spanish Civil War, despite a certain under-handed and unspoken rivalry. They stimulated each other as 'Brutal Friends'. Unilateral *coups* by one were resented by the other, and yet admired by the loser as an example for his own future action against 'decadent countries'. The exchange of Axis military, propaganda, financial, police and party delegations increased markedly during these years. Though the relationship was loose legally, psychologically it was more effective than an alliance. Hitler held the initiative in his hands, but the world, and even the Duce, did not fully realise it. Mussolini was given the public credit as the founder of fascism, and he often boasted that he was saving Spain from Bolshevism. It was Mussolini who was the main defender of

Franco in London, where a committee of ambassadors tried to implement an ineffective agreement to cease intervention in the Civil War.
Yet when the war was all over, Italy was economically and politically
weaker, while German influence had increased throughout Europe.

In contrast to Hitler's clever exploitation of the Axis Agreement,
French diplomacy in 1936 was ineffective. France had legal commitments
with seven friendly states – the five eastern allies and Britain and Belgium
– but was psychologically bound to none. France and six of her seven
allies were countries of indecision and confusion in regard to Germany.
Stalin wanted to resist Germany, and Russia was potentially France's
most reliable anti-German ally. But the ideological breach of 1917,
Stalin's purges at home, the geographic remoteness of the U.S.S.R., all
created an image at the French foreign and war ministries of a Soviet
Union that was the least reliable of France's anti-German friends.

To an already overstrained and weakened France, the outbreak of
civil war in Spain simply added a new problem: should France allow
Italian fascists and German national socialists to get away unopposed
with their aid to General Franco?

The Spanish Republic had asked France on 20 July 1936 for twenty
planes. Minister of Air Pierre Cot and Premier Léon Blum had agreed.
Then after visiting London on 22–23 July, Blum was forced to reverse
his decision to aid the Republic.[17] Conservatives thought that France
could not afford to alienate the British government, already committed
to the notion of an embargo on arms supplies to Spain. Others, like
President Albert Lebrun, were concerned that right-wing opposition
to Blum's proposal might overthrow the recently elected Popular Front
government. The rightist view prevailed in the major French newspapers, in business and among 75 per cent of the army and navy officers.
The Roman Catholic church was also a formidable voice against the
Spanish left. Marshal Henri Pétain and former Premier Pierre Laval
even developed private intelligence contacts with General Franco. All
this put pressure on the right wing of the cabinet, the radical socialists,
to resist sending military supplies to the Spanish Republic.

On 8 August, therefore, the French government, following the
British example of 31 July, issued a unilateral arms embargo against
both Spanish republicans and Spanish nationalists. Meanwhile the
French communist party, with seventy-two votes in the chamber of
deputies but no members in the cabinet, was free to criticise. Maurice
Thorez, parliamentary leader of the communists, publicly attacked the
proposed international arms embargo on 6 August. The Soviet Union

announced the same day that it was sending $2,000,000 to the republicans. Malraux's pilots landed at Madrid with twenty French planes on 13 August.[18] Finally, the largest labour union in France, the *Conféderation Général du Travail*, approved a resolution on 21 August condemning the arms embargo. Officially, Paris agreed with London to maintain an embargo on the export of arms, but there were many loopholes in the French law. It did not prevent the departure of commercial planes, money, individual private volunteers or French weapons to Mexico or Belgium for transhipment to Spain. Thus French policy towards Spain remained as divided as French opinion.

It was the aid given by the unofficial France of the left that angered Mussolini, although in technical terms this illegal private French military intervention provided little competition for the organised units sent by Mussolini and Hitler. Germany adhered to the British- and French-sponsored Non-Intervention Agreement on 24 August, and Italy on 28 August, although both went calmly on breaking both spirit and letter of the agreement. Over the course of the war, Hitler violated the agreement at least 180 times by sending as many shiploads of war material and men to Spain, while Mussolini sent 134 shiploads.[19]

It was Italy, distrustful of the French, that first suggested establishing a committee to apply the international Non-Intervention Declaration. On 6 September this Non-Intervention Committee began meeting in London, a location more favourable to Franco than Paris would have been. The committee of ambassadors with its permanent British secretary and the subcommittee of nine which did most of the work kept up an uninterrupted flow of evasive talk which lasted until the end of the war.

The development of the non-intervention programme meant that Russian aid soon became as significant as the unofficial French aid to the possible survival of the Spanish Republic. Since the French and British governments were officially committed to an arms embargo, and twenty other European countries joined them, the Spanish left were forced to look to the Spanish communist party and the Soviet Union. Stalin was following a double policy. On 21 July he had permitted Western communists to organise the purchase of weapons in the West;[20] yet to co-operate with the governments of Britain and France, he allowed Litvinov to adhere to the Non-Intervention Declaration on 23 August.

On 13–14 September Stalin stepped up his intervention in Spain. Russian military advisers and equipment were to go to Spain in exchange for the Bank of Spain's gold reserve. Like Hitler, Stalin enforced the strictest secrecy on the project. The s.s. *Neva* arrived in Alicante on 25 September with the first Russian weapons,[21] while as early as 16 September a few Russian military and police advisers arrived by air in Madrid. Three Russian ships in September, seventeen in October and seven in November reached republican ports on the Mediterranean, while the first Russian aeroplanes went into battle as early as 6 October.[22]

The Soviet decision to intervene militarily entailed much heavier personal risks for the communists of fifty-two other nations than for citizens of the U.S.S.R. On 16 October André Marty, French representative on the Comintern, arrived in Albacete to organise the international brigades' training camp. By 7 November the international brigaders using Russian military supplies were defending Madrid from the threat of imminent nationalist capture. World attention was focused on the romantic heroism of the brigaders, who reached maximum strength of approximately 20,000 men by January 1937.[23] Only about half were communists, though the higher officer corps were all communist. The international brigades were shock troops whose losses (at least 25 per cent killed) were among the heaviest in military history.[24]

The brigades provided cover for the very few Russians actually in Spain. Russian armour and aviation specialists numbered only about 400 to 500 men, who assumed Spanish names and kept their national origin very quiet. However, Soviet advisers infiltrated the Spanish ministry of war through the communist system of political commissars. Thus Russians enjoyed a more important voice in the political decisions of the Republic than either Hitler or Mussolini could ever hope to exercise in Franco's councils.

By mid-December there were in Spain approximately 5000 Germans and 3000 Italians and, on the other side, possibly 18,000 international brigaders, close to the peak number for the entire war. But this substantial leftist strength was soon offset by Mussolini. In a fourth move he raised the number of foreign troops sent to Spain far beyond what Hitler or Stalin were willing to contribute. On 26 December the first group of 3000 Italians of the *Corpo Truppo Voluntarie* (C.T.V.) were dispatched to Cadiz, and by 30 January there were 28,700 Italian troops in the peninsula.[25]

Britain more than any other power was determined to cut back any direct foreign intervention. This was first evidenced as pressure on Italy. On 12 September the British Embassy in Rome had mildly protested against the Italian occupation of Majorca, and Ciano promised that the Italian troops would withdraw as soon as Franco won the war. But neither London nor especially Paris could trust this promise. Mussolini's wisest decision during the Civil War was to leave the Balearic Island of Minorca in republican hands, in order to allay British and French naval fears.

Nevertheless, as late as November 1936, or possibly as late as January 1937, Eden assumed that the U.S.S.R. was more responsible for prolonging the Civil War than any other foreign power. Rather than support the republican demand at the League of Nations for a restoration of free trade in arms, the British government was seeking to bring about a mediated peace in Spain and to secure (26 December) the withdrawal of all foreign troops already fighting on both sides in Spain. Nothing was done during January to implement the proposal, and nearly 25,000 additional Italians poured into Spain. On 20 February the five Great Powers agreed through the London Committee to stop the flow of volunteers. They set up inspection teams along the Portuguese and French borders. From 20 February until 1 July 1937 the French government, with the assistance of international inspectors, tightly controlled the border at the Pyrenees. The French communist 'underground railway' that ran from Paris to Barcelona and Albacete temporarily broke down. But nobody stopped Hitler, Mussolini or Stalin from resupplying by sea their units fighting in Spain, although a naval patrol of 111 observers (as it turned out, mostly pro-Franco Dutchmen) was stationed aboard a number of warships of the four Western powers.

From July 1936 to January 1937 the British and French, unsure of themselves and about Spain, were also confused as to what attitude they would take towards the three dictatorships overtly intervening in Spain.

The British foreign office was nevertheless becoming increasingly anti-Italian because of Spain. Anthony Eden, who had previously blamed the U.S.S.R. for intervention, in January 1937 began viewing Italy as the chief foreign culprit for continuing the Spanish war. Early in November, in order to offset Ciano's conclusion of the Axis Agreement in Berlin, Mussolini had offered to negotiate a bilateral agreement with Britain. Lengthy negotiations finally produced the Anglo-Italian Gentleman's Agreement of 2 January 1937, in which Mussolini promised not to alter the territorial status quo in the Mediterranean. But Eden quickly discovered that the Duce was no gentleman when British intelligence learned of the heavy troop landings of Italian Black Shirts in Spain. To Eden, Mussolini's signature of 2 January was rendered worthless by his actions.

At the same time the Spanish question was causing a worsening of Anglo-German relations. Eden disliked the Germans' violent reaction to the bombing of the pocket-battleship *Deutschland* (29 May 1937) by republican planes: the German navy retaliated by bombing Almería and the Italians and Germans used the incident as an excuse to withdraw from the naval patrol. On 19 June, in the decisive battle of the Spanish Civil War, Bilbao fell to the Spanish nationalist and Italian troops. The rich iron mines of Vizcaya had traditionally fed Welsh smelters, but henceforth much of that ore was redirected to Germany. Franco signed a secret commercial protocol with Germany on 12 July guaranteeing that the Germans would have the first chance after the war to conclude a comprehensive trade agreement. Hitler wanted the continued delivery of Spanish iron and pyrite ores to Germany at the expense of Britain.

Growing Anglo-German tension on the one side meant closer Anglo-French solidarity on the other. This understanding was not yet as solid as Hitler and Mussolini assumed; it was not as firm a relationship as the Rome–Berlin Axis. Nor was it necessarily directed against Germany or Italy, at least in Britain, where Neville Chamberlain had become prime minister in May 1937. Gradually regaining power to make foreign policy by taking away the independence Eden had exercised under Baldwin, Chamberlain was to be less favourable to France. Chamberlain hoped to preserve peace in Europe with a four-power pact including capitalist Italy and Germany and excluding communist Russia. Anglo-French co-operation was to Chamberlain only the first step towards a four-power concert.

The French, on the other hand, were aiming at a real *entente cordiale*, directed against the Axis. The Anglo-German tension of June 1937 was paralleled by growing French–Italian tension. Following the fall of the Basques, Paris ended the international control along the Pyrenees on I July, and on 13 July the border to Spain was tacitly reopened for the smuggling of arms and men. The bulk of foreign combatants in the opposing armies in Spain were Frenchmen and Italians. Press attacks on fascism (identified with Rome) and on anti-fascism (identified with Paris) filled the newspapers in France and Italy. Relations grew so bad that both countries withdrew their ambassadors.

Anglo-French divergency now appeared. Chamberlain countered the anti-Italian action of France by trying to negotiate directly with Mussolini through private letters. The conquest of Bilbao, which at first had increased Anglo-German tension, convinced the Chamberlain–Eden government, after further thought, that Franco's nationalists would probably win in Spain. With this eventuality in mind, and because British commercial interests had long exerted pressure on their government to grant some recognition to Franco, London decided in September 1937 to send a British 'agent' to nationalist headquarters in Burgos. The French government took no such step and still hoped for Franco's defeat.

Meanwhile the fascist bloc was gaining strength. In July Hitler's ally Japan had attacked China while Britain and Russia did nothing. In September the Duce visited Hitler in Berlin and was captivated by the Führer's hospitality. The basis of the Axis was reaffirmed when the two dictators agreed that Italy should have a sphere of influence in the Spanish area in exchange for a free hand for Germany in 'the East'. On 6 November Mussolini adhered to the German–Japanese Anti-Comintern Pact, and Italy withdrew from the League of Nations on 11 December. The three fascist Great Powers began discussing the formation of a tripartite military pact.

With ideological blindness, Chamberlain refused to recognise the threat which a tripartite pact would pose to British interests; he can be regarded as a victim of anti-Comintern propaganda. The Russians as a power factor were missing from Chamberlain's political calculations; he simply ignored them. Stalin felt increasingly insecure because of the behaviour of the capitalist powers and Chamberlain's determination to create a four-power Western pact excluding the Soviet Union. In early October 1937 the Soviets refused to pay their dues to the Non-Intervention Committee, whereupon Eden suggested to the Germans that the Russians be allowed to let their participation in the Committee lapse.[26]

In the summer of 1937 Italian submarines began attacking merchant shipping in an attempt to exclude all aid from republican Spain. The threat of joint Franco-British naval action against this 'piracy' of Mussolini's brought results. 'Piracy' stopped and the Italians began to talk seriously to the British about withdrawal of Italian troops from Spain in exchange for the withdrawal of the international brigades.

Soviet aid to the Republic was already declining. During the Italian submarine campaign, Soviet shipping to Spain fell from six vessels in July and five in August to none in September and only one in October.[27] In the meantime Russia's problems with her Far Eastern frontier were increased by the Japanese invasion of China, a move which was met with indifference by the Western Great Powers. In the autumn of 1937 Stalin apparently came to the private conclusion that Franco would win and began to seek adjustments. On 10 November the U.S.S.R. and

Nazi Germany initiated exchange of prisoners captured in Spain. The Soviet dictator's intervention in Spain from the beginning had been predicated on the assumption that the French government and maybe even the British would eventually be drawn into oppose Italy and Germany. Instead, an *entente cordiale* appeared to be developing against Russia, not Germany. The Popular Front strategy was not working. The possibility of a four-power capitalist bloc increasing the isolation of the U.S.S.R. seemed very real.

Republican Spain's survival was increasingly precarious. Its one chance of getting continued foreign aid was that the socialists of the Second International were, in the spring of 1938, co-operating more than ever before with the communist Third International. Spain was the principal reason. Mussolini's bombing of Barcelona, the continued sinking of British ships and Hitler's take-over of Austria on 12 March injected new life into anti-fascism among the leftists of Britain and France. This meant new hope for republican Spain. As a result of Hitler's march into Austria, Delbos was replaced in Paris by a more leftist foreign minister. The second Léon Blum government informed the British and the Russians that France would fight to honour its Mutual Assistance Pact of 1925 with Czechoslovakia. The French cabinet seriously discussed a plan to invade Catalonia, but shelved the idea in favour of renewed French aid for the Spanish Republic. French arms began to come to republican Spain from 12 March until 13 June 1938. Eight-four French planes were to be matched by eight-four Russian planes and sent through Marseilles to Barcelona.[28]

The long spring from March to June 1938 was thus in some respects the Indian Summer of the Popular Front. In early April 1938 Hitler, Franco and Mussolini all thought they had won the Civil War, but the renewed French and Russian military aid saved the Spanish Republic for almost another year. Then in May the seemingly defunct French–Soviet–Czech system of 1935 took on new life when the Czechs mobilised against German threats. Winston Churchill was now calling for a 'grand alliance' of France, Britain and the U.S.S.R. against Germany.

Meanwhile Chamberlain was working against these anti-fascist tendencies, so much so that Eden resigned as foreign minister in February 1938. On 20 March Chamberlain announced that Britain would neither aid Czechoslovakia nor back France in a war with Germany over Czechoslovakia. The British prime minister pursued his Italian negotiations in Rome; on 16 April he agreed to recognise Abyssinia as part of the Italian empire after the Italians withdrew 'a substantial' number of their troops from Spain. In reply Italy reaffirmed to Britain that it had no territorial, *political* or *economic* designs in Spain or in the Spanish colonies.

This unsigned declaration, in which Mussolini made sweeping promises he would not be likely to keep, was actually meaningless. It could not help Chamberlain's overall goal of winning Italy and then Germany to a four-power pact, because it was to take effect only when the 'Spanish question was settled'. Chamberlain believed that the end of the Civil War was only a few weeks away. He vowed to sceptical Britons that he would 'eat his hat' if Mussolini fooled him. He thought rather that he would fool 'the socialists'. But during that strange 'Popular Front Spring' of 1938, it was the 'socialists' who fooled Chamberlain by sending in fresh arms to the Spanish republicans. For a while the French government was willing to defy Chamberlain's views on both Spain and Czechoslovakia.

However, French Premier Edouard Daladier and Georges Bonnet, his more conservative foreign minister, soon ended the Popular Front politically by eliminating the French socialists from the cabinet. The Popular Front's Spanish policy met decisive defeat on 13 June when the French government, after much prodding by Chamberlain, again closed the frontier with Spain. For republican Spain the sealing of the border was a near-fatal blow.

The Russians reacted to the French shut-down of the communist 'underground railways' from Paris to Barcelona by preparing to end Soviet assistance to the Spanish Republic. On 17 June *Pravda* hinted as much, while *Izvestia* for the first time suggested that the Falange might win in Spain.[29] In the West the French–Czech–Soviet alliance of 1935 came unstuck; in the East, Japan and Russia began an undeclared war on the Manchurian border. On 23 June Litvinov told the Germans that a non-aggression pact with the Third Reich was possible.[30] During July the Soviet military advisers were secretly withdrawn from Spain, and the Russians dropped their opposition to the most recent British proposal for foreign troop withdrawal. But Stalin's retreat from the Spanish venture from June to August 1938 was due to events in Japan, France, Britain and Czechoslovakia; it had little to do with Spain itself.

If the opening months of 1938 had seen a 'Popular Front Spring', the closing months of 1938 brought a 'Four-Power Pact Autumn'. Urged on by Chamberlain, France's sell-out of Czechoslovakia at Munich was predictable. The conclusion of the Four-Power Pact at Munich on

29–30 September was in his mind another step in a new concert of Europe which ignored the role of Soviet Russia. More importantly, it would preserve peace between Britain and Germany, and thwart Stalin's alleged revolutionary aims. Official London believed that Stalin had been trying to provoke Anglo-German war in Spanish waters since 1936. The faster the Spanish turmoil could be brought to a close, the better were the chances for Anglo-German peace.

Munich constituted a major diplomatic defeat for the Soviet Union. The long build-up by Britain and France towards Munich encouraged Stalin's withdrawal from Spain. He got his men out, although continuing to send some supplies by sea. The Spanish communist party from October 1938 to March 1939 fought on stubbornly, as if nothing had happened. It encouraged that Republic to continue to resist with the faith that the international situation could suddenly reverse itself. They argued with the socialist Negrín that the Popular Front had not really died, and that the four-power concert would be unmasked as an illusion.

Following Munich, Chamberlain pursued two plans: first, a visit to Mussolini to develop Anglo-Italian rapprochement; second, continued encouragement of the French to improve their relations with Italy. Chamberlain was also anxious that the Spanish question should end with the victory of Franco.

Chamberlain's efforts in Rome failed. On 11–12 January in Rome Chamberlain and his foreign secretary, Lord Halifax, told Mussolini and Count Ciano that they hoped that the issue of the Spanish war could be quickly brought to an end by Italian withdrawal of their remaining 30,000 men. France could then begin its proposed discussions with Italy. Mussolini reiterated that he would do this after Franco won a complete victory. Later Mussolini confided to Ciano that the discussions had been a meaningless platonic exercise, and that he was determined to sign a military alliance with Japan and Germany directed against Britain and France. Mussolini also wanted French territorial concessions in Somaliland, Tunisia, Corsica and Nice. The idea of a concert of Europe maintaining the peace against the forces of social revolution seemed absurd to Mussolini, and he compared the bourgeoisie of Britain led by Chamberlain with Prince Metternich's system of one hundred years earlier. Mussolini, an ex-socialist, was no longer interested in the international proletariat, but he still regarded fascist Italy as a revolutionary, have-not nation compared with Britain and France. For the Duce, the essence of politics was struggle and war. As soon as his troops were withdrawn from Spain he wanted to send them to Albania to win more glory.

While Chamberlain and Mussolini talked in Rome, General Franco was opening his last offensive against Catalonia. Republican Spain began falling rapidly to his armies. From 12 to 27 January 1939 the French chamber of deputies endured an agonising foreign policy debate in which defeat in Spain was finally recognised by many socialists and radicals who had given their hearts to the Republic. The day after Barcelona surrendered, the Daladier–Bonnet government's policies of leaning on Britain for protection and abandoning eastern Europe and Spain to fascism was upheld by a vote of 374 to 228.

The first week in February saw the further disintegration of republican Spain in Catalonia. Bonnet sent Senator Léon Bérard to Burgos on 4 February to negotiate recognition and economic détente with Franco on the same day that President Manuel Azaña, symbol of the liberals in Spain and chief founder of the Republic in 1931, fled Catalonia. On 5 February the U.S.S.R. finally cut off all supplies. One hundred and thirty thousand refugees piled across the French border on 7 February. This was also the date that the British destroyer *Devonshire* docked at Minorca, evacuating republican refugees and landing Franco's troops. A secret British–nationalist deal had been made to save lives and ensure that the Italians would not seize Minorca. Franco reaffirmed to London his pledge that the three Mediterranean islands would not be fortified.

The false sense of security under which the governments of Britain and France had been living since Munich crumbled in March 1939. On 28 February Hitler informed them that he had no intention of guaranteeing the rump state of Czechoslovakia. The underlying philosophy of the four-power concert was as incomprehensible to Hitler as it was to Mussolini. On 15 March Hitler moved into Prague, thus ending Chamberlain's two-year dream of compromise with the Führer. The British prime minister emotionally denounced Hitler and undertook unilaterally to guarantee the integrity of all Poland. This was no help to the Spanish Republic, where Franco's troops took Madrid and officially proclaimed their victory on 1 April 1939.

A new power alignment emerged in 1939. Negrín and the Spanish communist party had been right in forecasting that the ephemeral four-power concert would not last; but when the British government finally awoke to the dangers of fascism, it was too late to help republican Spain. Negrín and the Spanish communists had forecast wrongly in believing in the Popular Front, which Stalin himself had abandoned in

June 1938. Stalin was a traditional Russian nationalist: Russia had to have allies in Europe – if not France, then Germany. Since France had sabotaged the 1935 Mutual Assistance Pact, Stalin would seek to revive the German–Russian Pact of Rapallo of 1922, which was technically still valid. On 10 March 1939 Stalin put out another feeler indicating that he was ready to make an agreement with Hitler, the basis of which would be the common German–Russian hatred of Poland. In the last analysis, Negrín's faith that some international crisis would turn up between October 1938 and March 1939 – a crisis that would save the Spanish Republic – proved to be an illusion. He would have had to fight on until 1941 when the British, Americans, Russians and a few 'free French' finally came together in the 'grand alliance' against Hitler.

The Spanish Civil War was a tragedy for Spain; it was also a tragedy for international peace. From 1936 to 1939 the U.S.S.R. wanted to let France take the lead in Spain, but France shifted responsibility to Britain, which in turn allowed the initiative to fall to Mussolini, who was determined to follow Hitler.

One must marvel at the stubborn persistence of the British leadership, which tried to ignore the issues in Spain for nearly three years. Throughout the Civil War, Britain kept asking Germany and Italy to adhere to a new four-power pact. She at last succeeded at Munich in September 1938, but the agreement lasted barely five months – just long enough to ensure the final defeat of the Republic. Although technically it was France which had proposed the international agreement to impose an arms embargo on both Spanish 'factions' on 1–3 August 1936, it was London that became the staunchest supporter of non-intervention. Between 4 December 1936 and 8 October 1938 the British proposed to the Committee at least thirteen plans attempting to mediate an end to the Spanish war, to restrict the delivery of weapons and men and to gain withdrawal of foreign troops.

The British government's attitude towards the Russians was similar to its treatment of the two Spanish camps – it ignored them as much as possible. Frightened of revolution, the English conservatives took the slogan 'the Bolshevik danger' all too seriously. Republican Spain was experiencing social revolution, but what the supporters of the national government did not realise was that the communists were not the main agents of revolution there; in fact, the Spanish communist party, at Moscow's behest, was trying to crush revolution in order to cement an alliance between the Western democracies and Russia. The trouble with the tories in 1936 was that they confused social revolution among the Spaniards with Stalin's reactionary bureaucracy and nationalist foreign policy. It was true that the influence of the U.S.S.R. was growing in Spain during the Civil War, but this was primarily because of Russian delivery of arms to the Republic which the Western powers refused to supply. Militarily the U.S.S.R. did less than Germany and Italy, while the U.S.S.R., given its geographic location, could hardly hope to succeed to the political, strategic and economic dominance which Britain and France had exercised in Spain since the eighteenth century. If the real danger to European peace was Soviet imperialism, then a four-power pact among the capitalist Great Powers was the right response. But the Nazi reality made this a nonsensical theory. Stalin wanted in July 1936 what Winston Churchill later called the 'grand alliance'. But in July 1936 Churchill still regarded the Soviet Union as an unworthy ally, and he refused even to talk with the Spanish republican ambassador in London until April 1938. Thus even Churchill, that prophet crying in the wilderness about the German danger, was unwilling to come to terms with 'Bolshevism'. The Spanish Civil War was seen by the governing conservative circles of Britain as a frightening social revolution. This made the conservatives far more prone to excuse German and Italian fascism for their support of the Spanish nationalists.

As the Spanish war progressed the British foreign office also sacrificed any faith in the League of Nations. In order to block the eight appeals that the republicans made in attempting to end the international arms embargo, Britain forsook the League in favour of the Non-Intervention Committee – a Committee that included the Italian and German representatives who had abandoned the League.

On the other hand, the Spanish Civil War caused the labour party, which had been pacifist in the early thirties, to become committed to an international war against fascism and to begin to see that such a stand made it impossible to resist rearmament.

It was Hitler, because of his great skill as a diplomat, because of his understanding that a conservative Europe could be frightened by talk about 'the Bolshevik danger', who won the international victories of the Spanish Civil War. From July 1936 to March 1939 he solidified relations with Mussolini and Japan, and completely disorganised the French security system in eastern Europe. While Italy and France carried on a propaganda war in the press, while French-backed international brigades fought Mussolini's troops in Spain, while the French and Italian fleets manœuvred about the Balearic Islands, Austria and

Czechoslovakia were left to fend for themselves. Hitler's pointing to Spain and reminding French and British conservatives that he was the 'bulwark against Bolshevism' helped thus to provide the psychological atmosphere for his bloodless victories in the East.

Hitler's strategy was most effective with Mussolini, who, encouraged by the Führer, maintained 40,000 men in Spain. Hitler limited his own contribution to 5000 men, so that Mussolini was fighting for warlike glory and took the military burden of the Spanish venture while Hitler took the mining rights. Mussolini infuriated the French, to the point that keeping the French–Italian conflict within bounds preoccupied the diplomatic energies of Eden and Chamberlain. Meanwhile, Mussolini thought the British senile for signing four declarations with him while he was bombing British shipping; despite the blandishments of the British right, Mussolini had no intention of stopping his military aid to Franco short of a complete nationalist victory. Nor did Mussolini think of breaking the ever-firmer Axis understanding with Hitler, although he was being used by Hitler. Mussolini got little out of Spain for himself. But for Franco, Mussolini's role was decisive. The Duce outfought both Hitler and Stalin with blood and treasure in Spain.

Stalin got the French communists to organise the 20,000-man international brigades, of which at least half were Frenchmen. He mistakenly thought that this might draw in the French government. He also sent 932 planes as compared with the 282 French planes sent to the Republic.[31] Official France lagged behind in Spain for fear of alienating Britain, whom they prized more highly as an ally than they did the U.S.S.R.

Within Spain itself Soviet policy was self-defeating. In republican Spain the 400 to 500 Soviet military advisers seemed to exert great influence because of the leverage of Soviet arms shipments. But this factor boomeranged. The machinations of the Soviet G.P.U. in Spain caused defections among socialists, liberals, anarchists and Trotskyites who were also Spanish patriots. Many of the international brigaders became disillusioned with Stalinism long before the Soviet pact with Hitler in August 1939. Stalin alienated the leftists by his reactionary purges at home and in Spain, while he alienated the conservatives because he still spoke the rhetoric of Marxism–Leninism. Hitler was able to defeat Stalin in Spain because he had the help of Mussolini. Mussolini was the one stubborn dictator whose pride was dedicated to nationalist victory. Stalin was therefore the first dictator to withdraw.

Militarily the Italian aid of 6,800,000,000 lire ($355,000,000) combined with the German expenditures of RM 540,000,000 ($216,000,000) just about equalled the $650,000,000 in Spanish gold charged by the U.S.S.R. and $85,000,000 in direct Soviet aid.[32] German and Italian money was more efficiently spent on men and military equipment, while the delivery of Russian aid was complicated by logistic problems. Nevertheless, Franco's 1200 Italian and German aircraft[33] were just about equal to the 1200 Russian and French planes which the Republic received during the war. In the last analysis, the Republic did not lose because it could not get enough foreign arms. It lost politically because too many of the political, ideological and economic interests of the Great Powers were against it. Not only were the Italians and the Germans openly against the Republic but also many private groups like the tory party, the Roman Catholic church, business corporations in Britain and France were passively against it. Latin America was solidly behind Franco except for Mexico. The isolation of the United States had the effect of endorsing the Non-Intervention Committee and virtually anything the government in London wanted to do.

The impact exerted by the Civil War on France and the French role in keeping the Republic alive are the most difficult to assess. After the First World War, the French had no clear concept about the role they should play in Europe. Only sometimes did France act as if she were still a Great Power. She maintained alliances with five eastern European countries and Belgium, a colonial empire in South-east Asia and in Africa and an interest in the Near East. At other times France played the role of a small power, dependent on Britain. This confused role is in part explained by the fact that French political parties were split between pro-German and pro-Russian factions.

Was France a Great Power in relation to Spain in 1936? The Civil War further confused an already anomalous situation. The French proclaimed a non-intervention policy, yet allowed extensive smuggling to go on. The conflict in Spain and its outcome definitely weakened France. Whether there was an alternative policy (either more or less intervention) which would have been better either for Spain, or France, or world peace, cannot be stated definitively.

It can be argued that forceful Anglo-French intervention on the side of the Republic in July 1936 might have saved liberalism and forestalled Russian, Italian and German gains. The March 1938 proposal of French intervention in Catalonia might have saved Czechoslovakia and the Russian alliance and overturned Hitler. Yet that same action might have provoked civil war in France and caused the loss of Britain as an ally.

It was these twin fears that dominated French thinking and paralysed French action.

In any case, from 1936 to 1939, the effect of foreign intervention on the course of the Spanish Civil War, and the effect of the Spanish Civil War on the course of the relations among the European Great Powers were both important aspects of the thirty-year crisis involving two World Wars. The Spanish episode cuts across and highlights the problems of nationalism, democracy, fascism, capitalism, communism and Great-Power rivalry in our times.

SUGGESTIONS FOR FURTHER READING

This chapter has been written almost entirely from primary sources, some of which are listed below in notes. Statistics for the German and Italian intervention are relatively accurate, because official primary sources are available. French and Russian statistics are approximations and subject to revision.

Documentary Collections and Memoirs

Indispensable for the German side are *Documents on German Foreign Policy 1918–1945*, series D, vol. iii (1950). Most revealing for the Italian side are works written by Mussolini's foreign minister, Count Galeazzo Ciano, *The Ciano Diaries, 1939–1943* (1946); *Ciano's Diplomatic Papers* (1948); and *Ciano's Hidden Diary, 1937–1938* (1953).

For the Soviet intervention, see *The Communist International: 1929–1943*, ed. Jane Degras, vol. iii (1965); and *Soviet Documents on Foreign Policy, 1933–1941*, ed. Jane Degras, vol. iii (1953). Reflecting Stalin's official line on the origins of the Popular Front is a book by the head of the Comintern, Georgi Dimitroff, *The United Front: The Struggle against Fascism and War* (1938). Louis Fischer, *Men and Politics* (1941), is the memoir of an American left-wing journalist close to the Comintern, who served in both Spain and the U.S.S.R. The only semi-official Russian accounts in English are by the Russian ambassador with the Non-Intervention Committee, Ivan Maisky, *Who Helped Hitler?* (1964) and *Spanish Notebooks* (1966). Walter Krivitsky, *In Stalin's Service* (1939), and Alexander Orlov, 'How Stalin Relieved Spain of $600,000,000', in *Readers Digest* (Nov 1966), are the memoirs of two N.K.V.D. officials involved in Spain who defected.

For the apologia of one of the chief British actors in the Spanish Civil War, see Anthony Eden, *Facing the Dictators* (1962). A semi-official biography of Neville Chamberlain is Keith Feiling's *The Life of Neville Chamberlain* (1947). Thomas Jones, *A Diary with Letters, 1931–1950* (1954), gives a revealing account of Baldwin and to a lesser extent of Chamberlain.

Secondary Accounts

Burnett Bolloten, *The Grand Camouflage: The Communist Conspiracy in the Spanish Civil War* (1961), sympathises with the anarchists; the best account, it goes down to May 1937. *Communism and the Spanish Civil War* by David T.

Cattell (1955), has a full bibliography; his interpretation is marred by the acceptance of Soviet statements at face value. His *Soviet Diplomacy and the Spanish Civil War* (1957) chronicles the official role of the U.S.S.R., but this book is less valuable. Patricia van der Esch, *Prelude to War: The International Repercussions of the Spanish Civil War* (1951), is somewhat out of date now, since it has been superseded by Puzzo and newly available documents. A sequel to his memoirs of 1941 is Louis Fischer's *Russia's Road from Peace to War: Soviet Foreign Relations 1917–1941* (1969). Noteworthy in his single summary chapter on the Spanish Civil War is the paragraph dismissing Soviet historiography on the subject. Nathanael Greene, *Crisis and Decline: The French Socialist Party in the Popular Front Era* (1969), shows how the Spanish issue divided the French socialist party. It is the best short account of the decisive French discussions on Spain in July and August 1936, but is biased in favour of Blum. Glen T. Harper, *German Economic Policy in Spain during the Spanish Civil War 1936–1939* (1967), is a scholarly analysis of German documents showing the economic penetration of Spain by the Germans during the Civil War. A more comprehensive account showing the political, ideological and military aspects of the German role as well as the economic one will soon be published by this author. Stanley Payne, *The Spanish Revolution* (1970), concentrates on the Russian and communist roles. It is the most anti-revolutionary, yet anti-Russian account. David Wingeate Pike, *Conjecture, Propaganda, and Deceit and the Spanish Civil War . . .* (1968), is a mine of information on official French policy and the underground French intervention. Based mostly on the French press, it also includes a few reports from the French interior ministry archives. Dante A. Puzzo, *Spain and the Great Powers 1936–1941* (1962), has the viewpoint of a Popular Front liberal grieving the loss of the Spanish Republic. His belief that there were 12,000 Germans (actually less than 5000) in Spain by January 1937 is an example of how pro-republican passion has led him astray. His conclusion that Franco's Spain became an Axis satellite in 1939–41 is not sound. Hugh Thomas, *The Spanish Civil War* (1961), is the best single book on the entire Civil War. It gives a detailed chronological account integrated from many sources. *Survey of International Affairs 1936–1939*, ed. Arnold J. Toynbee and Veronica M. Boulter, 3 vols (1937–9, 1954), is encyclopedic, and a good summary based on the British press of the time.

NOTES

1. Arnold J. Toynbee, assisted by V. M. Boulter, *Survey of International Affairs 1937*, ii: *The International Repercussions of the War in Spain (1936–1937)* (London, 1938), pp. 170–1.
2. It is very difficult to get comprehensive figures on the amount and distribution of foreign investments in Spain. In 1927 total foreign investment in Spain was 1,277,137,000 pesetas, of which 34·5 per cent, or 459,609,100, was French: Lucien Graux, *L'Espagne économique: Rapport à Monsieur le Ministre du commerce et de l'industrie sur ma mission économique en Espagne 1929–1931* (Paris, 1932), p. 437.
In 1933 the total was 1,201,600,000 pesetas: U.S. Department of Commerce, 'Spain: General Economic Survey' (Washington, Jan 1935, mimeographed), p. 50.

Marcel Chaminade, 'Le Capital' (24 Mar 1939, microfilmed: German Foreign Ministry, 5206/E307854–56), claims that the French held 60 per cent of the total foreign investment, over three times more than Britain. This does not seem credible. Perhaps the discrepancy stems from the fact that the French held stocks in the British Rio Tinto company.

3. General Karl Schweikard, 'Zu dem Stand der Bearbeitung der Geschichte der Legion Condor' (MS., Berlin, *Luftwaffe*, 8 Mar 1940, pp. 1–26: found in military archives at Freiburg, Germany, Militärgeschichtliches Forschungsamt, MFA/II L234/75, vol. i).

4. Robert H. Whealey, 'Mussolini's Ideological Diplomacy: An Unpublished Document', in *Journal of Modern History*, xxxix (Dec 1967), 432–7.

5. Roberto Cantalupo, *Fu la Spagna* (Milan, 1948), p. 63; Luis Bolin, *Spain* (London, 1967), pp. 52–3, 167–90, 173; Robert A. Friedlander, 'The July 1936 Military Rebellion in Spain: Background and Beginnings' (MS. thesis, Northwestern University, June 1963), ff. 215–25, and 'Great Power Politics', in *Historian* (Nov 1965), 77–8.

6. On communist fronts, see Robert Carew-Hunt, 'Willi Muenzenberg', in *International Communism* (St Antony Papers, no. 9), pp. 72–87; Jorgen Schleimann, 'The Organizational Man: The Life and Work of Willi Münzenberg', in *Survey*, iv (April 1965), 64–91; Helmut Gruber, 'Willi Münzenberg: Propagandist For and Against the Comintern', in *International Review of Social History*, x, pt 2 (1965), 188–210; for fronts in Spain, German Ambassador Welczeck, Madrid, to foreign ministry, 22 July 1933 (German Foreign Ministry, L187/L05679–82); *The Times* (London), 12 July 1933, 13; Burnett Bolloten, *The Grand Camouflage* (New York, 1961), p. 115.

7. Joaquín Arrarás, *La Cruzada*, xxxviii (Madrid, 1940), 99; Hugh Thomas, *The Spanish Civil War* (London, 1961), pp. 214, 232, who cites Arrarás, *La Cruzada*, and an ex-French communist. Also two articles by Jean Creach, *Le Monde*, 20–21 Dec 1950. Sketchy accounts were published at the time in *Le Matin*, 6 Aug 1936, and *The New York Times* (Paris), 7 Aug 1936, 3:3, and ibid. 11 Aug, 2:4.

8. Memo by Canaris, 5 Aug 1936 (German Naval Documents, PG 80604).

9. Schweikard, op. cit. pp. 66–68.

10. Luis Bolin, *Spain*, pp. 52–3, 167–90, 173.

11. Schweikard, op. cit. p. 45.

12. Cmd Pistorius Report, June 1939 (German Naval Documents, PG 80769); memo, Duce's private secretary, n.n., 'Weapons for Spain', Rome [23 Sept 1936] (Duce Files, 1062/062961–65).

13. Pistorius Report.

14. Schweikard, op. cit. p. 153.

15. Unpublished interrogation of General Warlimont by the U.S. state department, 17 Sept 1945, 'Poole Mission'.

16. General Karl Schweikard to foreign ministry, 27 April 1939 (German Foreign Ministry, 4366/E082304–08).

17. Testimony of Léon Blum to French chamber of deputies, 23 July 1947: 'Rapport fait au nom du commission chargé d'enquêter sur les événements survenus en France de 1933 à 1945', *Session de 1947: Annexes*, i, 215–20.
Pertinax, *Gravediggers of France* (New York, 1944), is one of those who argue the importance of British pressure, p. 433. The best account of the French problem is Nathanael Greene, *Crisis and Decline: The French Socialist in the Popular Front Era* (Ithaca, N.Y., 1969), pp. 78–9.

18. Malraux, *Man's Hope* (New York, 1938), p. 96; Telegram from U.S. Navy U.S.S. *Quincy*, Spanish waters, to state department, rec. 14 Aug 1936,

SD 852.00/2589; (uncensored report, Madrid via Hendaye, 17 Aug) *The New York Times*, 18 Aug 1936, 2:2 and 26 Aug 1936, 3:3.

19. Pistorius Report, June 1939 (German Naval Documents, PG 80769). See *Forze Armarte*, June 1939, for the Italian figure.

20. (A. P. Hendaye, 23 July) *The New York Times*, 24 July 1936, 3:5; J. Flanner, *Men and Monuments* (New York, 1947), pp. 38–9, says Malraux left 20 July. Reports of arms purchases in France: German counsellor in Paris to foreign ministry, 1 Aug 1936 (German Foreign Ministry, 655/257371); in Belgium, Counsellor Brauer, Brussels, to Foreign Ministry, 2 Aug 1936 (655/257372–73).

21. The vessel left Odessa 18 or 19 September: Counsellor von Tippleskirch, Moscow, to foreign ministry, 28 Sept 1936, *Doc. Germ. For. Pol.* (D), iii, doc. 88; Counsellor Volckers, Alicante, to foreign ministry, 29 Sept 1936, ibid. doc. 89; José Martín-Blazques, *I Helped to Build an Army* (London, 1939), pp. 241–4; (Riga) *The Times* (London), 23 Sept, 11:7; D. C. Watt, 'Soviet Military Aid to the Spanish Republic in the Civil War 1936–1938', in *Slavonic and East European Review*, xxxviii (June 1960), 536–41, 538, n. 6. The Italian ambassador at the Non-Intervention Committee alleged that the first arms were landed on 18 September at Valencia: Corbin to Delbos, 10 Oct 1936, *Doc. dip. français* (2), iii, doc. 331.

Stanley Payne, *The Spanish Revolution* (1970), p. 264, cites some shaky evidence that Russian planes left Odessa as early as 23 July. Both Cattell, *Communism*, p. 74, and Bolloten, *The Grand Camouflage*, p. 94, think Soviet weapons did not arrive until October. Officially, the U.S.S.R. admits nothing before October. Both Krivitsky and Orlov stress the importance of the 13–14 September meeting with Stalin. At this same time the Republic decided to send its gold to Cartagena. Willard C. Frank, 'Sea Power, Politics, and the Onset of the Spanish War, 1936' (Ph.D. MS., University of Pittsburg, 1969), ff. 357–65, adds some additional evidence on both sides of this controversy.

22. Report of French military attaché, San Sebastían, to Paris, 6 Oct 1936, *Doc. dip. français* (2), iii, doc. 316.

23. The size of the international brigades is difficult to assess. The French observers in Valencia say that in early November there were 1200 and by the end of the month there were 7000. Military Attaché Lieutenant-Colonel Morel to minister of war, 12 Dec 1936, *Doc. dip. français* (2), iv, doc. 141. Yet on 7 January the consul reported 15,000 Frenchmen alone: ibid., doc. 259. The American consul in Barcelona reported on 31 December 1936 a total of 20,000, of which 8000 were French: *For. Rel. of U.S.*, *1937*, i, 239. General Jalander, for the League of Nations withdrawal commission, at the end of 1938 reported 12,700 withdrawn and 6500 still remaining: Vincent Brome, *The International Brigades* (1965), p. 266. British naval intelligence used the figure of 18,000 for the entire war: Naval Intelligence Handbook, *Spain and Portugal*, iii (March, 1944), 40.

24. Brome, op. cit. p. 301. In the Second World War twenty million Germans were mobilised, of whom three million were killed, mostly on the Russian front: *Germany Reports* (1955), pp. 134–6.

25. Memo [Count Luca Pietromarchi] Spanish office, ministry of foreign affairs, to Mussolini, 18 Jan 1937 (Duce Files, 1062/062976–78).

26. *Doc. Germ. For. Pol.* (D), iii, doc. 457.

27. Watt, in *Slavonic and East European Review*, xxxviii.

28. Gestapo report of an agent attending the I.F.T.U. conference sent to the German foreign ministry (microfilmed, German Foreign Ministry, 1568/379542–56).

29. Report by Ambassador Schulenburg, *Doc. Germ. For. Pol.* (D), iii, doc. 615.

30. Speech in Leningrad, Degras (ed.), *Sov. For. Pol.* iii, 282–94.

31. J. R. Hubbard, 'British Public Opinion and the Spanish Civil War, 1936–1939' (Ph.D. thesis, University of Texas, June 1950), f. 161; Bolin claims the republicans had 1800, op. cit. p. 354. Daladier told Chamberlain that the republicans had 800 Russian and French planes, 25 Sept 1938, *Doc. Brit. For. Pol.* (3), iii, doc. 1093.

32. The $600,000,000 to $700,000,000 in Spanish gold is the best-known fact about the Civil War. It is cited by everybody, Thomas, Jackson, Fischer, Payne, Bolloten, Cattell, Bolin, et al. The $85,000,000 was a Soviet figure published by *Istoria Majdunardyki Otnostanni S.S.R.* (1957), quoted by British communist Andrew Rothstein, *The Munich Conspiracy* (London, 1958), p. 33. For the German figure, see n. 16.

For the Italian figure, Riccardi to Ciano, 22 Nov 1939, *Doc. Dip. Italiani* (9), ii, doc. 295. This is the lowest figure. Yet to the Germans in informal talks, Mussolini and Ciano cited their costs as 14 billion lire: Mackensen to foreign ministry, 26 Aug 1939, *Doc. Germ. For. Pol.* (D), iii, doc. 320; Ciano conversation with Hitler, 28 Sept 1940, ibid., xi, doc. 124.

33. Bolin admits the nationalists had 1100, op. cit. p. 354. The *Legion Condor* had about 100.

12. Anarchist Agrarian Collectives in the Spanish Civil War

HUGH THOMAS

AT the beginning of the Spanish war in 1936, large sections of Spain fell under the control of a movement usually described as anarchist. The movement itself would refer to itself as federalist or syndicalist, and certainly the purist would say that the use of the word anarchist *tout court* is always wrong where Spain is concerned. In full civil war, a leading intellectual of the movement, Federica Montseny, remarked that her intellectual formation derived less from Bakunin than from the nineteenth-century federalist Pi y Margall. The facts are that there was a large general labour confederation, the C.N.T. (National Confederation of Labour), in which anarchist or federalist ideas prevailed, which was loosely organised and whose membership is difficult to estimate accurately: possibly there were 350,000 actual members, who could however count on the sympathy and, in times of crisis, the support of a million more. Springing out of the C.N.T. there had been formed nine years before a smaller group, the F.A.I., the Iberian Anarchist Federation, whose main purpose was to sharpen militancy among the C.N.T., to provide the C.N.T. with an elite leadership and in some respects to alter the actual goals of the C.N.T.'s activity: for instance, it was not till the F.A.I. succeeded in gaining effective leadership of the C.N.T. in the early thirties that the C.N.T.'s agrarian policy was changed from the idea of the distribution of the great estates to that of formation of collectives. The F.A.I.'s numbers before the Civil War were estimated by the C.N.T. historian Peirats at about 30,000.

In July 1936, after many false starts and warnings, the Spanish officers rose against the centre-left minority government. It was not a fascist rising, except in the sense that any explicitly anti-democrat activity can be described as fascist. The actual Spanish fascists, the Falange, knew what was planned, but, though their leadership had made an agreement of a kind with the officers, they had generally no hand in the plans. The government was not the main force which caused the rising in many places to fail. This was organised labour, that is, the activity of the C.N.T. and F.A.I. and also of the socialist General Union of Workers (U.G.T.). Immediately after the defeat of the officers (in over half Spain), these organisations, together with the local representatives of the political parties of the Popular Front, became the masters of society. To say that they were the government would be misleading since during the defeat of the officers the conventional expressions of the centralised state had in most places disappeared. The Civil Guard, the priest, the barracks and, in larger places, the café or club where the upper classes might have been expected to gather, existed no longer.

This situation found the anarchist movement (as I shall persist erroneously in calling it) in a considerable quandary. First, it had never been supposed by anarchists that their great opportunity would occur where they would be allied with other working-class movements and even political parties, even bourgeois political parties. Secondly, the anarchists had naturally not expected to gain power in the middle of what was (as was evident from early on) a real war. And thirdly, even without these confusing factors, the anarchist movement was not really united on aims at the time they had this chance to apply them. In May there had been a show of unity when a faction of the movement, the *treintistas* (in 1931 expelled for their criticism of the F.A.I.), had been received back into the fold. At Saragossa a long programme of action to be enacted after the revolution, prepared by Dr Isaac Puente (killed afterwards by the army in Logroño), had been adopted, making clear that collectivisation rather than distribution of land was the official C.N.T. plan. But how far was this everywhere accepted? Not, as will be seen, everywhere, even by anarchists themselves.

Meantime, even at the outbreak of the Civil War, a number of collectives had already been set up. One had even been formed in the suburbs of Madrid: on 9 May 1936 Salomon Vázquez and Provencio Roque formed a collective after four market gardeners had been sacked and after the land had been found neglected. The local syndicate agreed to hand over the land to the peasants, and twelve men set out, finding at the end of the day that wages could be raised from 6·25 to 8·25 pesetas a day. After three weeks there was a fund of 3500. At this point the revolution began. There were other collectives in Catalonia and Estremadura formed in the spring.

Quite quickly after the outbreak of war, the anarchist leadership made a general agreement to share power with their allies. According to the most reliable commentator, Abad de Santillán, this was done specifically so that while a seat on the governing committee would have to be given to the communists and socialists even where the anarchists were powerful, the anarchists would, as a *quid pro quo*, get a similar seat in places where their strength was less – such as in Castile. In the first few weeks, the anarchists and left-wing socialists made the political pace. However, the middle-class parties, the right-wing socialists and the communists, made themselves the champions of the revival of the state. The demands of war and incessant defeats in southern and western Spain led to the gradual victory of this point of view. The anarchist movement (though not all the rank and file, by any means) explicitly accepted this, however much it meant the abandonment of what Malraux referred to as *l'illusion lyrique*: in September and anarchists entered the Catalan government, in November they joined the central government. Though their four ministers resigned in May 1937, they continued to collaborate with the government, anarchists serving in official positions in administration till the end of the war. In April 1938 an anarchist, Segundo Blanco, from Asturias, returned to the cabinet and remained there till the end of the war.

The entry into the government posed a great revaluation of aims and motives for those anarchists involved, and it is clear they entered not simply to help the war effort but also to try and prevent the total destruction of the movement by the communists. In this they were fairly successful. A number of anarchist leaders continued in the reorganised Republican Army. At the end of the war, as events at the time of Colonel Casado's anti-communist *coup* were to show, a considerable number of the commands in the central and southern zones of Spain were held by anarchists. By and large, the demands of war forced the gradual abandonment of the large variety of anarchist types of control in industry. As early as 20 July 1936 the anarchist leader, García Oliver, nominated Eugenio Vallejo to start a munitions industry in Catalonia, and the necessity of collaboration with the state and political parties was implicit from the start. By the end of the first year of war, most large industries had had to accept a lesser or greater extent of state direction even if they continued to operate under nominally anarchist management.

On the land, there was never any real resolution of the tension between the revolution and the state. Most detailed observation of the collectives in the countryside and small towns of republican Spain is by anarchist writers. The most complete series of accounts of the life of the collectives appears in the anarchist press, and this is far from complete and not unprejudiced. Two anarchist writers, Peirats and Gaston Leval (a Frenchman who was incidentally one of the five men to represent the C.N.T. in Moscow in 1921 when they were discussing whether or not to join the Comintern), gathered information on the activities of a number of collectives, but the details they give only extend to an apparently arbitrarily chosen selection of about eighty collectives out of what appear to be about 1500 in all. Much of even their information comes from newspapers at the time. Some writers went to a number of collectives at the time, but most were either (like Alardo Prats and Agustin Souchy) committed in favour of them or (like Borkenau and Kaminski) visited them in the early months, before they had had a chance to show how they would work after the exultant enthusiasm for the revolution in the early days had passed away. All the famous descriptive books on the anarchist collectives seem in fact to have been published in 1937, usually recounting events in 1936 – the exception being Alardo Prats (whose book appeared in 1938).

In the winter of 1936–7 there were well over 1000 agricultural collectives in republican Spain. They were agricultural in the sense that the work they carried on was mainly concerned with the land, but they were concentrated on the towns, small or big, which serve in most of Spain as the homes of agricultural workers and their families. Many of these collectives ran primitive forms of industry like wine and olive presses or flour mills, but their main activity was the land. In Aragon there were 450 collective towns, comprising about 433,000 persons, about 75 per cent of the population in republican hands.[1] The average Aragonese collective therefore consisted of about 960 members. 350 of these were totally collectivised towns, in the 100 others there were free or *individualista* elements. In Levante there were about 340 collectives, of which most were mixed.[2] In the centre and in the area of Andalusia still part of the Republic, there may have been 250 more, and in Catalonia another 200.[3] Possibly a majority of persons even in areas where there were collectives remained outside collective control.

The size of the collectives varied greatly. That at Tomelloso (Ciudad Real) had 5000 members; that at Villas Viejas (Albacete) consisted simply of two farms taken over by about twenty families (92 persons) who worked there. The national average was probably smaller than the Aragonese one of 960.

The majority of collectives were organised by an alliance of C.N.T. and U.G.T. Whatever differences continued on a national level between their leaders, at many small places local relations continued good throughout the war.[4] The first stage towards the formation of a collective was usually the constitution by the local C.N.T. and U.G.T. of a united union. A council of administration (*consejo de administración*) would be constituted. It was customarily composed of a president, secretary, vice-secretary and treasurer, together with a number of other *vocales* or *delegados* responsible for specific questions such as statistics, cattle, food, the olive crop and so on. There would also be various technical advisers who were not part of the *consejo*. Schoolmasters were often found as accountants.[5] Usually the collective as such would be formed after the *consejo*, and very often this would not be for several months after the beginning of the war: many collectives seem only to have been formally constituted in the winter of 1936 or early 1937. None of the members of these governing bodies of the collective were professional administrators; they had to find time for civic responsibilities after their own work for the day was over. (Work was compulsory, over the age of fifteen as a rule.) To avoid suspicion that personal advantage could be served through membership of the *consejo*, in some places the *consejo de administración* got less pay that other workers.[6]

At the heart of each collective there existed a shadowy organ described as the 'general assembly'. Possibly the word 'organ' is over-sophisticated, since the general assembly seems to have been in fact simply the gathering on the main square of the town of all the members of the collective who wanted to (it is not clear if every member of the collective was sometimes included, even women and at any rate working children, or whether, as is more likely, only workers were expected to attend). At any rate, there are instances of the general assembly electing the *consejo de administración*.[7] The collective of Cervera del Maestre (Castellón) was clearly set up by decision of an 'open assembly' in the main square. In some places the general assembly was probably an active body where the entire population was able, at least for a time, to guide the policy of the collective. At Ademuz (a dramatically beautiful town of Moorish origin in the extreme north of the province of Valencia), for instance, the general assembly met every Saturday to discuss 'future orientations'.[8] In Masroig the assembly had the power to expel *malas colectivistas*, and also to decide what should be imported and what should not.[9] In the collectives at San Mateo (Castellón) and Serós (Huesca) it was provided that the general assembly could expel members for 'immorality' – though apparently this power was never used, nor is it obvious what 'immorality' meant in these communities.[10] No account seems to have been made of a meeting of a general assembly.

It appears that in practice nearly everywhere power remained in the hands of the *consejo de administración* and that the members of this body never felt it necessary to have their mandate renewed. This was an obvious threat of petty dictatorship, though it was one which rarely became patent: the most outrageous case appears to have been in the collective at the Pyrenean frontier town of Puigcerdá, where the anarchist mayor, Antonio Martín, used the collective as a centre of smuggling, false passport manufacture and bribed escapes.

Although the collectives were supposed to function separately, almost as if they were little sovereign city-states of an imagined medieval Utopia, they were in fact linked, as Dr Isaac Puente had provided in his blueprint adopted at the Saragossa conference, with the provincial and the regional organisation of collectives. The administrative *delegado* of each collective was supposed to tell the 'comrade accountant' of the region of the balance of imports and exports into the collective and hand over any surplus to the *caja de compensación* of the region, to help towards the general economic equilibrium of the area. The *caja de compensación* was expected to help collectives which could not cover needs and costs with their own production. In many cases money was given over to collectives, though there is no national estimate of this aid: it was a gift and not a loan. It was natural with this system that rich collectives would tend to consume more than they absolutely needed, rather than hand over their profit for the benefit of others, and several collectives were reproached in anarchist newspapers for this.

The persons who formed the collectives were usually previously landless labourers, apart from a small number of professional men such as barbers, vets, doctors and so forth. But there were many exceptions: in Alcázar de Cervantes, the president of the collective was a farmer, Vidal Cruz, who brought with him six *fanegas* of his own land, together with three others which he had rented.[11] He was reported 'very satisfied with the economic and social rhythm of his new life'.[12] In Miralcampo (Guadalajara), a collective formed on land taken over from the old monarchist politician, the count of Romanones, two members of the five-man *consejo* had been, in the past, Romanones's overseer and agent.

How far private or tenant farmers were forced into membership of the collectives is hard to judge. In the early days it was often hard for a private farmer, if he held out, to market his goods without selling to the collective. Tenant farmers and peasant proprietors were usually denied the use of the collective shops. Thus a number of anti-collectivists probably joined collectives either for fear of being forced in any way or because the economic conditions of life outside were intolerable. Other people left, the bakers of Calaceite (near Tortosa) simply abandoning their shops; no replacements seem to have been found for a long time, if ever.[13] After a while, the championship of the small farmer by the communists, and to a lesser extent by the right-wing socialists and the government parties, gave new heart to independent agriculture: small farmers began even to be able to compete with collectives, except in Aragon, where the collectivist hold was very strong (until August 1937). In some places, after a while, separate facilities were provided for *colectivistas* and *individualistas*; at Calanda the German anarchist, Agustín Souchy, noted two cafés, one for the private farmers, one for members of the collective.[14] It was usually provided that people could withdraw from the collective to the value of the goods and machinery they brought with them, but if they did this after having been members for a year, there would be a deduction in the compensation they could take out. In some places too it became possible for a *colectivista* to keep a limited quantity of livestock in his backyard: at Piedras Henares (Guadalajara) this was allowed because of the remoteness of the town and its bad weather in winter; members of the collective there could keep eighteen chickens and three goats.

The anarchists themselves, in their examples of a selected number of collectives, admit several defections: in Iniesta (Cuenca), for instance, the *individualistas* appear to have been very strong, not communists but anarchists interested not in communal farming but in the *reparto*, redistribution of land. After the large landowners' properties, 13,913 hectares (about 33,000 acres), had been made the basis of the collective, the *individualistas* insisted on the *reparto* and succeeded in getting, by agreement, three-fifths of this land, together with half some of the stock and farm implements, three-fifths of others. Eighty families remained in the collective afterwards, and evidently they prospered, borrowing 13,000 pesetas from regional headquarters, so that 200 families were members of the collective at the end of 1937.[15] In Peñalba (Huesca) the outcome was a good deal less satisfactory. To begin with, in August 1936, the whole population of 1500 became part of the collective. But evidently this was not popular, almost certainly because one of the collective's chief tasks was to feed the Durruti column then quartered near by. As a result, the majority of the population, when they had gathered sufficient courage, or perhaps when they realised that they would have communist backing, announced their intention to resume independence and reclaim their property. A commission was entrusted to supervise the act of demolition, and apparently did so satisfactorily. 500 persons were left to carry on the collective. Even so, there are further mentions of *malas colectivistas* who, when everything was provided free, tried to accumulate goods and then either sell them or let them go bad.[16]

The economic life of different collectives is difficult to disentangle. Figures exist for total production in the republican zone of Spain in respect of some commodities. The ministry of agriculture[17] gave overall figures for the increase in the production of wheat: production in Catalonia and Levante went down in the years 1936–7, but up in Aragon and Castile. The overall increase amounted to 609,000 metric quintals, an increase of about 6 per cent. However, Aragon and Castile were in 1937 the main centres of collectives, and Catalonia and Levante the main centres of peasant proprietors; Castile, the main wheat-growing zone, grew 5·2 million quintals of wheat in 1936 and 6 million in 1937 – an increase of 850,000 quintals, or 17 per cent. The fact that the area where there were collectives showed an increase was naturally seized upon by the anarchists: 'Peasants of Castile,' wrote N. González in *Campo Libre* of October 9, 'here you have conclusive proof that the agrarian collective is not a folly; it is a system which . . . leads to maximum production! This, dear comrades, is the road to follow.'

The fact that the figures indicate a drop in production in Catalonia and Levante suggests to some extent their veracity, since they would hardly have been actually invented or twisted by a ministry of agriculture dominated by a communist minister and communist officials, with greater communist party strength in those areas than in Castile or Aragon. But a large number of peasant proprietors continued in the areas where there were collectives and it is of course possible that they played a part in the increased wheat production. Nor is it clear on what basis the 1935–6 figures were constituted. Though overall Spanish wheat production had gone down in the years before the war, they reached their lowest level ever in 1936, and might have been expected to increase in 1937 anyway, with a better harvest. Finally, even if it were proved that the collectives did show an increase in their first year, it is of course impossible to judge the superiority or otherwise of any system of agriculture simply on the strength of a single year. It is obvious that there were places where the collectives did introduce striking agricultural reforms, however: there is often mention of deep tilling with tractors (Montblanc), of modern chicken farms (Amposta), of irrigation (Monzón, Huesca).

In a limited number of collectives, some accounts for production are available (and, in even fewer cases, for the general financial structure). Production figures exist for Miralcampo (Guadalajara province). Of this collective (the one where Count Romanones's staff stayed on), we hear that 'during the period of effervescence, not to say madness, which dominated many places in Spain at the beginning – those days during which everything was out of control and when thrift, as a result, was not the outstanding characteristic – our comrades kept all the cattle on the farm, while in other places, such as in Santos de la Humosa, the communists sacrificed even the heifers about to calve'.[18]

Production figures for Miralcampo are as follows: wheat, in 1935–6, 3000 *fanegas*,[19] in 1936–7 7000; barley, 500 *fanegas* in 1935–6, rising to 2000 in 1936–7; wine moved up, in the same years, from 3000 *arrobas*[20] to 'over 4500'. Melons rose in value from 196,000 pesetas' worth to 300,000. These increases were explained as being due to an important piece of irrigation, achieved by diverting a stretch of the river Henares. Taken at face value, the increase seems considerable: an increase of 130 per cent in wheat, of 200 per cent in barley, of 50 per cent in wine. Now probably there was a genuine increase, though whether it was quite this much is doubtful. But it is not clear if, even given the continuing presence of Count Romanones's staff, the pre-revolutionary figures were the accurate ones. Is it not more likely that they were in fact the figures kept for the purpose of tax, while the real ones might have been closer to those achieved by the collective? This seems a matter which will never really be known, and it is an uncertainty which hangs over most of the collectives in Spain in the Civil War.

The most complete general account of a collective's finances is that of the 300-family collective of Almagro, in the province of Ciudad Real, a town with a population of 8592 in 1930. Assuming that the average size of the family was five, which is possibly a little high, it would appear that about one-sixth of the municipality was enrolled in the collective. (There was, however, an anomaly in that in the town there also existed an anarchist flour mill, run collectively but not as a part of the town collective.) Almagro is known for its mule fairs and its lace. Its wine is reportedly delicious. The accounts consist of an estimation of the value of the livestock and farm machinery and tools in 1937 as opposed to 1936, an inventory of goods held by the collective in 1936–7 in comparison with 1935–6 and a statement of incomings and outgoings into the town during the first year of the life of the collective. The town was, we hear, notable for being free of 'disorderly communists' and for good

I

relations between the parties. The old municipal council survived in a kind of supervisory role, the C.N.T. and F.A.I. having 6 seats out of 15 – the others being presumably 6 for the U.G.T. and 3 divided among the republican parties.

The figures are not really conclusive, though they suggest that the value of the stock of the collective rose in the year October 1936– October 1937 by about 17 per cent from just under 300,000 pesetas to just over 355,000. In each of the main items considered there was a small increase varying from a 5 per cent increase in the value of the farm machinery available to one of 26 per cent in the value of the mules retained in stock. Unfortunately nothing appears to be known of the numbers of animals held by the Almagro collective in 1937 as opposed to 1936, though this is the sort of information quite often known in respect of other collectives. And of course the figures do not take into account any variation in the value of money between 1936 and 1937. In fact, the size of the stock and its real value probably stayed the same in the course of this year: the 17 per cent increase in the alleged value of the stock is probably a rough indication of the fall in the local buying power of the republican peseta between these two years. Both in 1936 and 1937 by far the biggest single investment in the collective was farm machinery, though its percentage of the total was slightly less in 1937 (40 per cent of the whole as opposed to 45 per cent).

The figures for Almagro refer to products, not, unfortunately, to production. Thus it is only possible to compare the quantity of goods in store owned by the collective when it was founded with that existing a year later. But this is not without interest. There was 75 per cent more barley in 1937 than in 1936, 500 per cent more wine, 200 per cent more olive oil, 80 per cent more rye, 400 per cent more peas, 300 per cent more chick-peas, about 90 per cent more beans of varying sorts. At the same time, there was 50 per cent less wheat, no maize at all, and 60 per cent less vetch in 1937 than in 1936. The total value of the products possessed by the collective was about 50 per cent higher than in 1936. Meat, milk, eggs, clothing do not figure at all in the list. Overall, the collective estimated that it was worth 116,129 pesetas more in 1937 than in 1936, a sum equivalent to about £3000 by the rather misleading 1936 rate of exchange, a nominal increase per head, therefore, among the 300 families, of about £10.

The collective also gave figures for its 'exports' and 'imports' and, however anarchist the delegate for accounts was, he evidently had a nice sense of classical economics: imports were 376,000 pesetas, exports

371,000: a trade gap of a little over 4000 pesetas.

How far were these figures accurate and how far can they be regarded as representative? The figures were purportedly given to an anonymous anarchist reporter by the officials of the collective. His article appeared in Madrid, without much prominence and at a time when the war was mainly concentrated in a different zone. The anarchist collectives in Aragon had been repressed by the communists, but communist activity was not specially strong in the region of Almagro. The likelihood that someone solemnly sat down and worked out a series of bogus figures for Almagro seems remote. The probability is that this was a fairly accurate picture of the economy in the Almagro collective in the first year of the Civil War.

The facts that statistics were not generally published in the anarchist papers, and that these were, would suggest that they were generally more favourable than usual.[21] It would certainly seem obvious that Almagro was better off than most places. The reporter who visited it commented rather sharply that the collective ought to try and save, 'not for itself, but for others in the region less prosperous'. 'The collective of Almagro has almost forgotten,' says the reporter, 'that it is part of a federation.' The comrades who formed part of the administrative council in Almagro were too proud. On the other hand – and this was something which apparently by late 1937 could be said of few leaders in collectives – none of them smoked or drank.

Some figures are also given of the consumption of the collective. In the year 1 September 1936–31 August 1937, the 300 families used 3000 *arrobas* of olive oil, 30,000 kilogrammes of potatoes, 110,000 pesetas' worth of bread and 7000 *arrobas* of wine. The average family in the Almagro collective thus drank just under 750 pints of wine a year, 320 pints of olive oil and ate 3000 kilogrammes of potatoes and 300–350 pesetas' worth of bread. The bread, potatoes and olive oil were apparently distributed free to the families of the collective, as in many, though not all, collectives, and wine was also distributed free to workers during the day. A consumption of wine of just under two pints per day per family would seem rather low (if it was free), since many families had more than one worker.

Almagro was obviously a fairly well-off collective. The fact of its prosperity illustrates the chief weakness of the whole system of collectives: that the poverty or wealth of the town at the beginning determined the poverty or wealth later: nowhere is this shown more than in the enormous variation of wages in the collectives for which data are available. In the first few weeks of the war, money was abolished altogether in many places, but after a few months it reappeared either as cash or in the form of *vales* or *bonos*, which were, in fact, simply credit notes for getting goods in the collective. Real money replaced *vales* or *bonos* as the war went on – in some places, as at Montblanc (Tarragona), on the firm demand of the *colectivistas*.[22]

The wages paid, either as local or as real money, varied inside the collectives according to needs. Thus almost everywhere there was a separate scale for a working husband and his wife, with a bonus for each working son, a different bonus for each minor, a different bonus again for invalids living with the family, a separate wage altogether for bachelors, for widows and for retired couples. There were also a number of additional payments in different places specifically provided for, that is, quite apart from what might be got by good luck or personal arrangement. But this seems exceptional. In the Madrid region, collectives were paid very highly (higher than anywhere else) and were also given a ration of greens per day, valued at 2 pesetas (in a 270-strong collective just by Madrid) and at 3 pesetas (at Villaverde). The highest wage seems in fact to have been in these two collectives: 12 pesetas per day per working couple, with (most unusually) another 12 per working son; at the Madrid collective, another rate quoted is 10·20 pesetas per day for workers between 16 and 18, and 7·20 for workers between 14 and 16. At Villaverde, there is no quotation for minors, but there was one for widows and retired couples – the same one, inequitable surely (though there is no discussion of the reasons for the quotation), of 7·20 pesetas.[23]

Against these high rates of pay in Madrid, the lowest appears to be that at Iniesta (Cuenca province), where the wage was only 4 pesetas per working couple, i.e. only 25 per cent of the highest wage in the prosperous collective at Villaverde. In Iniesta the bonus for a working son was 1 peseta, and 50 centimos for minors. Now of course Iniesta is poor and remote, in comparison with Villaverde, though presumably real living costs in the latter were higher, being near Madrid, than elsewhere, despite control of prices. The variation in the wages in the collectives does not, as might be thought, derive from the fact that in the low-wage areas essential goods were distributed free and in the high-wage areas not: in Iniesta, food (wine, oil, meat, farm produce) was *sold* in the collective, at a price admittedly a little lower than the official rate. Significantly, it was at Iniesta that the *colectivistas* insisted on the redistribution of three-fifths of the land. The wage rate before the revolution was 5·50 pesetas (higher than the wage ultimately paid to a married couple without children after the formation of the collective).[24] In fact, wages simply had to vary according to the wealth of the collective itself. Any national wage, even guaranteed by, for instance, the regional peasants' committees, would have meant an acceptance of the idea of national organisation – a matter so foreign to anarchist doctrine that it does not seem even to have been discussed, at a time when, after all, anarchism was under such heavy fire from its enemies. There does not seem to have been adequate machinery for the treasury of a collective to be emptied at the end of the year, and so quite large surpluses were piled up unused. In at least one collective – Villaverde – 50 per cent of the profits were divided up among the 400 families, the other 50 per cent being divided up between 'general expenses', widows and hospitals.[25]

The average payment in all the collectives is not possible to estimate accurately for lack of data. A rough estimate would seem to place the average at something close to 7 pesetas a day, or 42 pesetas a week. This would compare with the 10–12 pesetas a day received by militiamen and ordinary soldiers at the front, and the 12 pesetas a day which seems to have been the average wage in factories. The most elaborate variation of wage in a single collective seems to have been that at Dosbarrios, a collective with 610 members out of a total population of about 1000, owning about 17,000 acres, in the province of Toledo. Bachelors got 32 pesetas a week. Childless couples got 45. Couples with children under age got 45, plus 1 peseta a day for each child, i.e. presumably seven days a week, not simply the six working days. Couples with working children got 45 pesetas plus 15 pesetas a week for each producer. Couples who had to keep elderly invalids got 45 pesetas plus 12 per invalid. Widows without sons got the same as bachelors (32 pesetas) if they worked, and if they did not they got 25 pesetas. Widows with sons who did not work got the normal widow's wage, plus 1 peseta a day, and widows with working sons got the widow's wage plus 15 pesetas per sons – though, if there was only one working son, the widow and the son would get 45 pesetas, the same, that is, as a childless couple.[26]

In some places wages would be further supplemented by the provision of a communal restaurant where bachelors could eat free or passers-by for the cost of a peseta.[27] Barbers were sometimes free, as at Calanda.[28] Extra money was made available if visits to other places were necessary – to a family in another town, or to a doctor; applications for this extra expense had to pass through the appropriate *delegado*. But of course there was 'no money for vice'.[29] When a collective member

wanted to marry he might be given a week's holiday, furniture and a
house – at least this occurred in Graus.[30] A bride might get a trousseau.[31]
There are many different provisions where wine is concerned. At
Alcázar de Cervantes, wine was free during harvest time, afterwards the
ration was a free litre a day (though this privilege was sometimes
withdrawn).[32] As has been seen, wine was always free at Almagro; in
Castro del Río, there was no wine; at Mebrilla, the *colectivistas* got 3 free
litres a week, at Calanda, 3 quarts a week.

Life in collectives had of course changed, but not perhaps out of all
recognition from that existing before the revolution. Hours of work
were usually the same in the country – almost always from sunrise to
sunset, though in some collectives an eight- or seven-hour day was
agreed. Festivals were generally ignored, except for those new ones of the
revolutionary tradition such as 1 May, the anniversary of the death of
Durruti, or the start of the war. A six-day week was normal. The
absence of young men at the front – 300 or so out of a town of 10,000, as
at Amposta – obviously made some difference. Another difference was
the presence of refugees from other parts of Spain who had fled in the
wake of advancing nationalist armies, from Estremadura or Andalusia.
In a town such as Villajoysa (Alicante), the refugees had increased the
population of the town from one of 9000 to one of 14,000. Schools had
undoubtedly multiplied, and the thirst for education by both young and
adults was at least partially satisfied, in converted convents or palaces,
by new schoolmasters, themselves finding learning difficult. The school-
leaving age was raised, at Amposta, to 15.[33] At Calanda, advanced pupils
were sent at the collective's expense to the *liceo* at Caspe.[34] Hospitals
and health services generally were improved – we hear of the doctor at
Villaverde having given 200 vaccinations and 400 other injections in
six months in a 400-strong collective.[35] For the vast majority of workers,
the death, absence or, in some instances, retirement of the old master
class, of the priest, of the church, of the whole complicated apparatus of
traditional Catholic living, and of all the things that went with it (such as
the subordination of women) was enough to sustain a persistent exhilara-
tion, making up for shortages and inconveniences caused by war, even
for the triumph of the communists in the machinery of the state.
Traditional life in Spain had been, in so many instances, in the small
towns of Castile or Aragon, extraordinarily limited. Now the windows
at least seemed open; the conquest of power by the workers had created
problems, but at least some of the obstinate tedium of the old life had
vanished in a wealth of slogans, encouragements to harder work,

revolutionary songs, old songs rewritten with modern words and wireless broadcasts. It is clear that in many places 'the poor lived as in a dream', as Prats put in when describing Graus.

From the government's point of view, the immense disadvantage of collectives was that they did not pay taxes; and though they 'judged it a sacred duty to take food directly to the front',[36] this arrived at irregular intervals, so that it could not be counted upon, and was therefore sometimes wasted. Also the industrial cities needed food as well as the front, and here the duty seems to have been regarded as less sacred. Further, despite the presence of U.G.T. representatives in most councils of administration, the collectives could not be counted on to carry out government directives. This was partly a question of oranisation. The collectives were organised locally, with responsibility for all activities resting with the council of administration. It was therefore difficult for the ministries of agriculture or industry even to communicate with local agricultural or industrial officials without going first to the collective's nominal leadership – much less give them orders. By December 1936 the chief officials of the ministry of agriculture from the minister downwards were communists.[37] But this communist control over yet another department of state did not bring victory in agriculture. On the contrary, the collectives persisted in their separate ways, and not even the communist military occupation of Aragon in August 1937 was enough to ruin the collectives there completely. The main change in the course of the first year of war was the removal of the judiciary powers assumed by collectives in the first few weeks; under the anarchist but conformist minister of justice, García Oliver, this removed the trappings of total sovereignty from the collectives, even though the state-backed revolutionary tribunals in the different towns seem often to have been composed of the same persons as would have been the case before.

The fate of collectives if the country had been at peace is impossible to speculate upon. For the very existence of the war and of the other revolutionary parties – perplexing and frustrating though both these seemed to the anarchists – may have been responsible for some of the success the collectives had. The war sustained anarchist discipline and the sense of communal service. At the same time, the government's and the communists' backing of the small farmer and *individualista* meant that all such people were certain of an ally in need: the local village *consejo de administración* could thus not go too far in bullying individuals to make them join or conform. The communist minister of agriculture made many speeches promising the *individualista* that his interests would be served by the communist party and the message seems certainly to have gone home: 30·7 per cent of communist party members in republican Spain were peasant proprietors in February 1937. The Peasant Federation of small farmers, organised by the ministry and communist-led, became the bulwark of defence against the collectivists.

It is possible to draw a few conclusions. First, the data are not available to prove whether or not the collectives were an economic success, if this is measured in terms of production, though the absence of overall planning possibilities makes it very difficult to see how national production could have been increased over a long term.

Secondly, even if total figures were to become available for every collective, no moral could be drawn about the merits or demerits of the collectives as agricultural experiments. War conditions are unlike those of peace. Communist pressure on the collectives may have given them the necessary urge to survive, otherwise they might have disintegrated. Anyway a period of a year or two is not enough to judge an agricultural system.

Thirdly, the success or failure of the collective depended economically over-greatly on the situation before: it was thus possible for Amposta to build a 200,000-peseta chicken farm, but this would not have been possible in places where that sort of money was not available – even allowing for gifts from regional headquarters. Thus, in respect of redistribution of wealth, anarchist collectives were hardly much improvement over capitalism. No effective way of limiting consumption in richer collectives was devised to help poorer ones.

Fourthly, the independence of the collectives probably was a handicap to the Republic, measured simply in terms of economics. It was not possible to impose, for instance, a national production plan. On the other hand, the fact that the collectives survived at all, in such adverse circumstances, testifies to the strength of the hold they must have had on their members. Their morale must have been high, and certainly in a civil war morale of the rearguard is important. Anyway, the Republic was chiefly handicapped not because of lack of food or lack of agricultural planning, but because of lack of weapons.

Fifthly, whatever the economics of the collectives, there is a good deal of evidence for thinking that they were a considerable social success. The painstaking apportionment of wages according to needs in Dosbarrios is immensely sympathetic; and of course the payment to widows, the maintenance of orphans, the care of invalids, was a genuine breakthrough into a new world. From the accounts of most of the collectives, even if they are written by anarchist sympathisers, there does radiate a considerable spirit of generous co-operation without many complaints at breach of privacy and at local tyrannies, though, as at Puigcerdá, there were certainly some. On the other hand, the possibility of leaving the collective and being politically protected by the communists if one did, may have been an essential factor in this. It is not clear how a large-scale rural or small-town community of such collectives could work alongside a differently organised urban society, and the survival of such communities would not seem likely in the long term, though in ideal circumstances they might have lasted during a few years while primitive misery was being overcome.

NOTES

1. Prats, *Vanguardia y Retaguardia de Aragón*, p. 81.
2. The Regional Congress of Farm Workers of Levante in November 1937 gave this figure (J. Peirats, *La CNT en la revolución española* (Toulouse, 1951), i, 340).
3. These figures are a guess based on the number of towns, since no proper estimate for this figure has been found.
4. There were some places (e.g. Los Hinojosos) which had, however, two collectives, one C.N.T., one U.G.T. Almagro had two C.N.T. collectives, though one was industrial.
5. Peirats, op. cit. i, 309.
6. *Campo Libre*, 11 Sept 1937. Members of the Tomelloso *consejo* got 11 pesetas less per week than ordinary workers – i.e. 28 pesetas instead of 39 for a childless couple, a drop of 25 per cent.
7. For example at Granadella in the province of Lérida and at Alcázar de Cervantes – the old Alcázar San Juan. *Campo Libre*, 29 Jan 1938.
8. Peirats, op. cit. i, 336.
9. Ibid. i, 308.
10. Ibid. i, 334–5. Whether general assemblies could sack *consejos* if necessary is also uncertain; some collective managements in industries were apparently elected annually, but I have not found reference to a similar or indeed any other period where agriculture is concerned.
11. A *fanega* is a piece of land large enough to sow a bushel and a half of wheat: usually about an acre and a half.
12. *Campo Libre*, 29 Jan 1938.
13. Souchy, *Entre los Campesinos de Aragón*, p. 85. At least the bakers had not been replaced when Souchy visited Calaceite. One of the difficulties of studying the collectives is that people who visited them often did not say when they went and often there is no evidence as to whether the practices they described continued for long.
14. Ibid. p. 45. Peirats also describes Calanda (op. cit. i, 324).
15. *Campo Libre*, 18 Dec 1937.
16. Peirats, op. cit. i, 321–2.

17. *Economía Política*, no. 60, series C, no. 33, reprinted in *Campo Libre*, 9 Oct 1937.

18. *Campo Libre*, 30 July 1937. Livestock is almost always slaughtered for food in the first stages of revolutions. Almost the only other collective where production figures can be compared between 1936 and 1937 is the tiny one at Villas Viejas (*Campo Libre*, 25 July 1937).

19. A *fanega*, when used as a dry weight measure, is about a bushel and a half.

20. An *arroba* is 32 pints, or 4 gallons.

21. These are the only detailed accounts given by Peirats in his survey of some forty collectives.

22. Peirats, op. cit. i, 311.

23. *Campo Libre*, 20 Nov 1937 and 4 Dec 1938.

24. Ibid. 18 Dec 1937.

25. Ibid. 20 Nov 1937.

26. Ibid. 29 Jan 1938.

27. This was at Seros (Peirats, op. cit. i, 307).

28. Souchy, loc. cit.

29. Kaminski, *Ceux de Barcelone* (Paris, 1937), p. 122.

30. Prats, quoted Peirats, op. cit. i, 318.

31. Ibid. i, 321.

32. *Campo Libre*, 29 Jan 1938.

33. Peirats, op. cit. i, 305–6.

34. Ibid.

35. *Campo Libre*, 20 Nov 1937.

36. Peirats, op. cit. i, 320 (here speaking of Alcolea de Cinca, in Aragon).

37. The then communist, Castro Delgado (*Hombres made in Moscú*, pp. 379–82), says his three priorities on taking over the Agrarian Reform Institute were to destroy the agrarian reform teams staffed by socialists; to force employers to accept that the rhythm of war was different from that of peace; and to enrol as many people as possible into the communist party.

This essay is a modified form of the study first published in *A Century of Conflict, 1850–1950: essays presented to A. J. P. Taylor*, ed. M. Gilbert (London, 1966).

Notes on Contributors

EDWARD MALEFAKIS is Assistant Professor of History at Northwestern University. He is the author of *Agrarian Reform and Peasant Revolution in Spain: Origins of the Civil War* (New Haven, Conn., 1970). He is at present working on the history of Spanish Socialism.

RICHARD ROBINSON is Lecturer in Modern History, University of Birmingham, and author of *The Origins of Franco's Spain* (London, 1970) and 'Calvo Sotelo's Bloque Nacional and its Manifesto' in the *University of Birmingham Historical Journal*, vol. x, no. 2 (1966).

STANLEY PAYNE is Professor of History at the University of Wisconsin. His works include *Falange* (Stanford, 1961), *Politics and the Military in Modern Spain* (Stanford, 1967), *Franco's Spain* (New York, 1967) and *The Spanish Revolution* (New York, 1970).

BURNETT BOLLOTEN was United Press correspondent during the Civil War and is the author of *The Grand Camouflage*.

RAMÓN SALAS LARRAZÁBAL is a Colonel in the Spanish Air Force. He served in the Spanish Civil War under General Yagüe, and has for fifteen years worked in the archives of the Servicio Historico Militar. He will shortly publish his larger work on the Popular Army of the Spanish Republic.

RICARDO DE LA CIERVA Y DE HOCES is Professor of the History of Ideas at the University of Madrid and Director of the Centre of the Contemporary History of Spain. He is author of a bibliography on the Civil War, and the first volume of his *Historia de la Guerra Civil Española* appeared in 1969.

ROBERT WHEALEY is Assistant Professor of History at Ohio University and is engaged on the diplomacy of the Spanish Civil War. He has published works on the ideological diplomacy of Mussolini.

HUGH THOMAS is Professor of History at the University of Reading and author of the standard work on the Spanish Civil War published in 1961.

Index

Volkman, General, 205
Voluntary Army, 164, 165, 167

Warlimont, General Walter, 217
Waugh, Evelyn, 124
Whealey, Robert H.: 'Foreign Intervention in the Spanish Civil War', 213–38
Workers' Alliance (1934), 10, 36

Yagüe, General Juan, 181, 208
Youth movements, 12–13
Yuste, General Gil, 191

Zalka, Maté (Lukacs), commander of 12th International Brigade, 176
Zugazagoitia, Julián, 150, 154: minister of the interior, 149